2018-2019
AT A GLANCE

Essential Tables for Financial Remedies

FLBA

FAMILY LAW BAR ASSOCIATION

At A Glance

First edition published 1992, reprinted 1992
Subsequent editions 1993 and annually thereafter
Twenty-seventh edition published 2018

A CIP catalogue record for this book is available from the
British Library

ISBN (print) 978 1 85959 679 1
ISBN (ebook) 978 1 85959 6 807

**Further copies of this publication
and future editions
may be ordered from**

**Suite 19A
Queensway Business Park
Dunlop Way
Scunthorpe
DN16 3RN**

**www.classlegal.com
info@classlegal.com**

**Telephone: 01652 652222
DX: 29825 Ashby**

Produced for The FLBA by
Class Legal
Suite 19A, Queensway Business Park
Dunlop Way, Scunthorpe
DN16 3RN

Cover design by Wendy Bann
Typeset by Stephen Theaker
Printed and bound by
CPI Group (UK) Ltd
Croydon CR0 4YY

Acknowledgements

The Family Law Bar Association thanks those who have agreed to the inclusion of their material:

Bank of England	LexisNexis
Church of England	LifeAssureOnline.co.uk
Economist Intelligence Unit	Lloyds Banking Group plc
Financial Times Business Centre	Nationwide House Price Index
Independent Schools Council	Office for National Statistics

**The Family Law Bar Association thanks the Editors
for the production of this volume:**

Sir Peter Singer   **Mr Justice Mostyn**

Lewis Marks QC   **Gavin Smith**

Individual thanks for very considerable assistance are due to David Salter and Simon James (Tables 21 and 22), Adrian Gallop (Table 10), Laura Poots (Tables 11 and 14 to 16) and Philippa Johnson (Table 23).

The Family Law Bar Association publishes *At A Glance* annually, incorporating fresh and updated material. The Editorial Committee would welcome suggestions, whether for the improvement of existing or for the addition of further Tables.

Although care has been taken to ensure the reliability of the contents of this volume neither the members of the Editorial Committee nor The Family Law Bar Association nor any of its officers or members warrant their accuracy.

Sir Peter Singer (PS), Sir Nicholas Mostyn (NM), Lewis Marks QC (LM) and Gavin Smith (GS) have in accordance with the Copyright, Designs and Patents Act 1988 asserted their rights in the Tables specified, which may not be reproduced without their permission: PS/NM 4; PS/NM/LM 9, 17 and 18; PS/LM 8, 10 and 13; PS/GS 20; PS 11, 12, 14, 15, 16 and 27; NM 5; NM/GS 19, 22 and Leading Cases; LM 7 (SDLT and ATED) and 24; GS 6, Leading Citations and Note on EU Maintenance Regulation.

Sir James Munby

On 27 July 2018, on attaining his 70th birthday, Sir James Munby will be forced into retirement. The valedictions, both in and out of Court 33, will chart his extraordinary and varied career across many fields but perhaps none will focus specifically on his contribution to ancillary relief law, both substantive and procedural. Therefore your editors have decided to eschew the usual Preface and to pen this appreciation of that contribution.

From his Chambers at 1 New Square, Chancery practitioner James Munby did not often venture forth into the main stream of ancillary relief work, but his advocacy in **Dart v Dart** (1996) can now in retrospect be recognised as truly prophetic. Mr Dart was worth, it will be recalled, £400M. James Munby QC argued that the then governing Court of Appeal decisions of **Wachtel** and **Preston** could be reconciled by awarding Mrs Dart the sum of £100M, being a figure that lay between the strict bounds of the needs result dictated by **Preston** and the full half which **Wachtel** postulated as fair in the absence of any accompanying maintenance award. This suggestion of £100M was, it has to be said, witheringly dismissed by Lord Justice Thorpe as 'hopeless'. Yet only four years later the tectonic plates shifted in **White**, and now an award of £100M for Mrs Dart looks perfectly feasible, even allowing for the fact that Mr Dart's fortune had largely been generated by his father.

In his last year at the Bar he appeared in the House of Lords for the husband in the asset-lite, but heavily influential, case of **Piglowska** (1999) which prompted Lord Hoffmann famously to define the limit of the remit of the appellate court's role when reviewing a trial court's exercise of its discretion.

Mr Justice Munby was appointed as a High Court judge in 2000. He was appointed Chairman of the Law Commission in 2009 (for a three-year term) and was promoted to the Court of Appeal in that same year. In 2013 he was appointed President of the Family Division in the melancholy wake of Sir Nicholas Wall's retirement through ill-health.

As a puisne judge he delivered some important ancillary relief judgments. Early in his judicial career he issued a seminal decision about *ex parte* freezing injunctions: **Re W (Ex Parte Orders)** (2000). In 2001 in **X v X (Y and Z intervening)** he enforced an *Edgar* agreement where the consequential consent order had been rejected by the district judge on the ground that the wife did not have the ostensible means to pay the agreed provision to the husband. In the short marriage case of **B v B** (2002) he gave an important judgment on the aptness of *Mesher* orders. In **Al-Khatib v Masry** (2002) he gave guidance as to what inferences could properly be drawn from a respondent's wholesale non-disclosure and refusal to engage. He delivered a defining decision about the treatment of inherited property in **P v P** (2004)). In **L v L** (2006) he made clear his preference for judicial watchdogs, who should be neither bloodhound nor ferret. He issued a ringing denunciation against the scourge of legal costs, even appending an extract from chapter 65 of Bleak House to his judgment in **KSO v MJO** (2008). In **Re N** (2009) he considered whether provision under Schedule 1 could extend beyond the conclusion of tertiary education, referring to 'the increasing modern phenomenon of adult children who refuse to fly the parental nest, what have been called KIPPERS (kids in parents' pockets eroding retirement savings)'. In **H v H** (2010) he, perhaps controversially, declined to disturb a unilateral allocation of assets by the husband in favour of the wife after the separation and during the proceedings.

In **Richardson** (2011), following his promotion to the Court of Appeal, he gave a key judgment on setting aside a judgment on the ground of mistake. In **Traversa v Freddi** (2011) he spelled out the applicable principles when, after foreign divorce, a respondent seeks to set aside a grant of leave under Part III of the MFPA 1984.

As President these past five years his contribution to the jurisprudence of ancillary relief has been more executive than judicial but some important judgments have issued nonetheless. Thus in **S v S** (2014) approval was given to the 'show cause' process where an arbitration award has been made but not implemented, and in his 2015 Practice Guidance he underscored judicial encouragement of arbitration as a N-CDR technique. In **CS v ACS** (2015) he declared *ultra vires* a provision of PD 30A which purported to require a challenge to a consent order to be made by way of appeal.

But the jurisprudential contribution for which we suggest he will be principally remembered in this field has been to emphasise in judgment after judgment that the Family Division 'is not some legal Alsatia where the common law and equity do not apply' (as he put it in **Richardson** (2011)). In this his views can again be seen as prophetic, for a similar observation was made by Lord Sumption in **Prest v Petrodel Resources Ltd** (2013): 'courts exercising family jurisdiction do not occupy a desert island in which general legal concepts are suspended or mean something different'. Thus, in **C v C** (2006) when counsel for the wife, seeking to freeze an Anstalt, baldly asserted that 'nothing has been put forward which would rebut the wife's assumption that the Anstalt is the alter ego of the husband' she fetched the withering response:

> 'That is the world of Humpty Dumpty, and even this Division does not go that far. It is for plaintiffs to establish their case, or at least to put forward a prima facie case. We do not work on a system by and large

> where the plaintiff simply asserts and says "well, unless and until the defendant produces evidence to disprove our bald assertion, our bald assertion holds the field".'

Similarly in **A v A (St George Trustees Ltd, interveners)** (2007), where it was suggested that certain trusts were shams or should otherwise be treated as the husband's property, he scathingly observed that:

> 'There is not one law of "sham" in the Chancery Division and another law of "sham" in the Family Division. There is only one law of "sham", to be applied equally in all three Divisions of the High Court, just as there is but one set of principles, again equally applicable in all three Divisions, determining whether or not it is appropriate to "pierce the corporate veil".'

Still in 2007, in conjoined ancillary relief and bankruptcy cases in **Whig** he repeated what had become a refrain, stating that 'a creditor is not to be prejudiced because a wife's application to annul the bankruptcy order on which he depends is heard by a Family Division judge any more than a wife is to be prejudiced because her application is heard by a Chancery judge'. In that case he drew upon sound historical support by reminding all of the famous dictum of Vaisey J in **In re Hastings (No 3)** (1959) that since the Judicature Acts there has been only the one court – the High Court of Justice – and all the judges of that court are simply judges of the High Court.

On that latter point he returned to the charge in **Ben Hashem v Al Shayif** (2008), a characteristically encyclopaedic judgment, and laid down the relevant principles in play where it is sought, in any court and in any proceedings, to penetrate incorporation's veil, adding for good measure definitive observations upon the principles to be applied where an application is made to vary a nuptial settlement. The formulation he unveiled on the former topic were largely upheld by the Supreme Court in **Prest** (notwithstanding that, as Lord Sumption wearily explained, everybody had in fact historically misunderstood everything).

In **Imerman v Tchenguiz** (2010) he contributed in the Court of Appeal to (and one suspects largely wrote) the monumental judgment which effectively proscribed the use in an ancillary relief case of so-called *Hildebrand* documents. Again, that judgment emphasised that there was not one rule for family cases and another rule for everyone else.

Most recently the President has returned to the theme in the case of **Kerman v Akhmedova** (2018) where a solicitor sought to challenge a witness summons issued against him during the trial but returnable after the principal judgment had been handed down. It was suggested that the Family Division had adopted different trial and post-trial procedures to those permitted by other divisions of the High Court. In what may prove to be his final ancillary relief judgment he held:

> 'It is time to give this canard its final quietus. Let it be said and understood, once and for all: the legal principles – whether principles of the common law or principles of equity – which have to be applied in the Family Division (and, for that matter, also, of course, in the Family Court) are precisely the same as in the Chancery Division, the Queen's Bench Division and the County Court.'

As President, Sir James has overseen the arrival of the FPR and the unrolling of the single national family court. It is fair to say that most of his initiatives and guidance have related to the non-financial aspects of family work, but in 2013 he appointed a small drafting group to produce a comprehensive set of orders the use of which would in due course become virtually mandatory throughout the family court and the Family Division. And then in 2014 he set up the Financial Remedies Working Group (FRWG) which in its interim report of 31 July 2014 recommended the formal adoption of standard orders for financial remedy cases. The FRWG reiterated this recommendation in its final report of 15 December 2014. In his Practice Guidance of 30 November 2017, the President promulgated the suite of Standard Financial and Enforcement Orders which are now generally to be used.

In his 18th View from the President's Chambers issued on 23 January 2018 he described ancillary relief as 'the Cinderella of family justice' which was in need of efficiency and specialisation measures. He announced the creation of a national system of Financial Remedies Courts, within the single family court, staffed by a cadre of specialist judges. This vision is to be initially piloted in the West Midlands. When (for we should not admit even of the possibility that there may be any 'if' about it) this comes to fruition it will complete the work begun by Mr Justice Thorpe in 1992, which culminated in the national roll-out of the (then) new procedure in 2000.

Thus viewed in its entirety the work of Sir James Munby in the field of ancillary relief has been extensive and significant. In his time and under his suzerainty it has been 'all change' both substantively and procedurally. His contributions as the engine driver of that change have been pivotal. His mantra that ancillary relief law is part of and not separate from the general law has been timely and important, keeps us on track and needs always to be held firmly in mind. His will be a hard act to follow.

Winds of Change

As his Presidential term of office draws to a close Sir James Munby has turned his attention to what he has described as the 'Cinderella of family justice', namely the procedural aspects of financial remedy law. Precisely the same description was used by Mr Justice Thorpe in his campaign from 1994 to reform ancillary relief procedure which led to the promulgation of the pilot scheme in 1996 and the national roll-out in 2000. The central features of the reforms (standardised disclosure by Form E, rigorous case management, the FDR) are now deeply embedded in the collective consciousness.

Over the last 18 years that scheme has worked well generally but is now in need of specialisation and efficiency measures, to provide for greater consistency in the delivery of substantive justice and improvements in procedural justice. Calls for the introduction of a national network of specialist financial remedy courts have been strongly supported by the President – see *Note by the President* [2016] Fam Law 1340 and *17th View from the President's Chambers: divorce and money – where are we and where are we going?*[1]

On 1 December 2017 the President announced in his circular of that date[2] that the Financial Remedies Court (FRC) project would be piloted in in February 2018 in London, the West Midlands and South-East Wales. The project would have a lead national judge (Mostyn J) and a deputy (HHJ Hess). Each area would have a hub with a lead local judge. The new court, which would be part of the national single family court, would be de-linked from the divorce centres processing petitions.

On 23 January 2018 the President in his *18th View: The on-going process of reform – Financial Remedies Courts*[3] took the project a stage further. He announced that after Easter 2018 the pilot areas would be expanded to cover the remainder of the Midland Circuit, the North-Eastern Circuit and at least parts of the South-Eastern Circuit. He stated:

> 'My core ambition for financial remedy work is to improve significantly both the application of procedural justice and the delivery of substantive justice.'

The View envisaged that a new, much more detailed, Form A should be used, as well as a revised Form E as proposed by the FRWG in its interim report of July 2014.[4] Unfortunately PD 36 authorisation for the use of these new Forms was not in place when the first pilot commenced. Pending such authorisation, therefore, the applicant must on issue of a Form A at the pilot hub also file a completed allocation memorandum to enable a judicial gatekeeper as the first step after issue to allocate the case to the right judge at the right level at the right place.

Since the View was issued the President has decided to commence the pilot exercise in the West Midlands alone with Birmingham as the hub, for which purpose HHJ Rowland has been appointed as the lead judge. At the time of publication this will be the only operational pilot zone. Others are expected to follow after Easter.

It should be noted that in the new FRCs first instance work will be undertaken by the full range of judges, i.e. circuit judges, district judges, recorders and deputy district judges.

In the 18th View the President stated that the introduction of standard forms of order is an important component of the reforms associated with the introduction of the FRC. To that end he on 30 November 2017 issued his *Practice Guidance: Standard financial and enforcement orders* [2018] Fam Law 89, to which were attached the standard financial and enforcement orders.[5] These were reissued on 22 January 2018 to correct a trivial error affecting a few forms. They have been published by Class Publishing in the *Standard Family Orders Handbook: Volume 1 – Financial and Enforcement*.[6]

These standard orders must now be used in all courts, and not merely in the FRCs in the pilot zones.

Finally, on 28 February 2018 the President issued his Guidance: *Jurisdiction of the family court: Allocation of cases within the family court to High Court judge level and transfer of cases from the family court to the High Court*.[7]

In it he stated:

> 'It is very important for the family court, which has now been in existence for nearly four years, to gain the respect it deserves as the sole, specialist, court to deal with virtually all family litigation. Except as specified in the Schedule to this Guidance, cases should only need to be heard in the High Court in very limited and exceptional circumstances.'

So far as financial remedy cases are concerned this Guidance confirms the requirement of FPR 5.4 that they must all be issued in the family court, even if technically the High Court has jurisdiction (for example under Part III of the 1984 Act). This includes variation cases where the original order was made in the High Court.

Within the family court the Guidance confirms the criteria for allocation to High Court judge level as stated in the Efficiency Statement dated 1 February 2016 (p. 72 *post*). Subject to allocation under those criteria, an application for a freezing order, or for permission under Part III of the 1984 Act, should be determined by a district judge, or at circuit judge level if efficient deployment of local resources so requires.

The Guidance reminds all that the effect of FPR 29.17 is that only a puisne judge of the High Court (or a judge of yet higher rank) may transfer a case substantively to the High Court. It points out that in any event it is 'virtually impossible to conceive of a divorce or financial remedy case which needs to be transferred from the family court to the High Court'.

---

[1] www.judiciary.gov.uk/wp-content/uploads/2014/08/view-from-presidents-chamber-17-may-2017.pdf

[2] www.judiciary.gov.uk/announcements/president-of-the-family-division-circular-financial-remedies-courts-2/

[3] www.judiciary.gov.uk/wp-content/uploads/2014/08/view-from-the-president-of-family-division-20180123.pdf

[4] www.judiciary.gov.uk/wp-content/uploads/2014/08/report-of-the-financial-remedies-working-grp-annex1.pdf

[5] www.judiciary.gov.uk/publications/practice-guidance-standard-financial-and-enforcement-orders/

[6] Available interactively at www.familyorders.co.uk

[7] www.judiciary.gov.uk/publications/presidents-guidance-jurisdiction-of-the-family-court/

Essential Tables

Table 1 Retail Prices Index

	1979	1980	1981	1982	1983	1984	1985	1986	1987	1988
Jan	52.52	62.18	70.29	78.73	82.61	86.84	91.20	96.25	100.0	103.3
Feb	52.95	63.07	70.93	78.76	82.97	87.20	91.94	96.60	100.4	103.7
Mar	53.38	63.93	71.99	79.44	83.12	87.48	92.80	96.73	100.6	104.1
Apr	54.30	66.11	74.07	81.04	84.28	88.64	94.78	97.67	101.8	105.8
May	54.73	66.72	74.55	81.62	84.64	88.97	95.21	97.85	101.9	106.2
Jun	55.67	67.35	74.98	81.85	84.84	89.20	95.41	97.79	101.9	106.6
Jul	58.07	67.91	75.31	81.88	85.30	89.10	95.23	97.52	101.8	106.7
Aug	58.53	68.06	75.87	81.90	85.68	89.94	95.49	97.82	102.1	107.9
Sep	59.11	68.49	76.30	81.85	86.06	90.11	95.44	98.30	102.4	108.4
Oct	59.72	68.92	76.98	82.26	86.36	90.67	95.59	98.45	102.9	109.5
Nov	60.25	69.48	77.79	82.66	86.67	90.95	95.92	99.29	103.4	110.0
Dec	60.68	69.86	78.28	82.51	86.89	90.87	96.05	99.62	103.3	110.3

	1989	1990	1991	1992	1993	1994	1995	1996	1997	1998
Jan	111.0	119.5	130.2	135.6	137.9	141.3	146.0	150.2	154.4	159.5
Feb	111.8	120.2	130.9	136.3	138.8	142.1	146.9	150.9	155.0	160.3
Mar	112.3	121.4	131.4	136.7	139.3	142.5	147.5	151.5	155.4	160.8
Apr	114.3	125.1	133.1	138.8	140.6	144.2	149.0	152.6	156.3	162.6
May	115.0	126.2	133.5	139.3	141.1	144.7	149.6	152.9	156.9	163.5
Jun	115.4	126.7	134.1	139.3	141.1	144.7	149.8	153.0	157.5	163.4
Jul	115.5	126.8	133.8	138.8	140.7	144.0	149.1	152.4	157.5	163.0
Aug	115.8	128.1	134.1	138.9	141.3	144.7	149.9	153.1	158.5	163.7
Sep	116.6	129.3	134.6	139.4	141.9	145.0	150.5	153.8	159.3	164.4
Oct	117.5	130.3	135.1	139.9	141.8	145.2	149.8	153.8	159.5	164.5
Nov	118.5	130.0	135.6	139.7	141.6	145.3	149.8	153.9	159.6	164.4
Dec	118.8	129.9	135.7	139.2	141.9	146.0	150.7	154.4	160.0	164.4

	1999	2000	2001	2002	2003	2004	2005	2006	2007	2008
Jan	163.4	166.6	171.1	173.3	178.4	183.1	188.9	193.4	201.6	209.8
Feb	163.7	167.5	172.0	173.8	179.3	183.8	189.6	194.2	203.1	211.4
Mar	164.1	168.4	172.2	174.5	179.9	184.6	190.5	195.0	204.4	212.1
Apr	165.2	170.1	173.1	175.7	181.2	185.7	191.6	196.5	205.4	214.0
May	165.6	170.7	174.2	176.2	181.5	186.5	192.0	197.7	206.2	215.1
Jun	165.6	171.1	174.4	176.2	181.3	186.8	192.2	198.5	207.3	216.8
Jul	165.1	170.5	173.3	175.9	181.3	186.8	192.2	198.5	206.1	216.5
Aug	165.5	170.5	174.0	176.4	181.6	187.4	192.6	199.2	207.3	217.2
Sep	166.2	171.7	174.6	177.6	182.5	188.1	193.1	200.1	208.0	218.4
Oct	166.5	171.6	174.3	177.9	182.6	188.6	193.3	200.4	208.9	217.7
Nov	166.7	172.1	173.6	178.2	182.7	189.0	193.6	201.1	209.7	216.0
Dec	167.3	172.2	173.4	178.5	183.5	189.9	194.1	202.7	210.9	212.9

	2009	2010	2011	2012	2013	2014	2015	2016	2017	2018
Jan	210.1	217.9	229.0	238.0	245.8	252.6	255.4	258.8	265.5	276.0
Feb	211.4	219.2	231.3	239.9	247.6	254.2	256.7	260.0	268.4	
Mar	211.3	220.7	232.5	240.8	248.7	254.8	257.1	261.1	269.3	
Apr	211.5	222.8	234.4	242.5	249.5	255.7	258.0	261.4	270.6	
May	212.8	223.6	235.2	242.4	250.0	255.9	258.5	262.1	271.7	
Jun	213.4	224.1	235.2	241.8	249.7	256.3	258.9	263.1	272.3	
Jul	213.4	223.6	234.7	242.1	249.7	256.0	258.6	263.4	272.9	
Aug	214.4	224.5	236.1	243.0	251.0	257.0	259.8	264.4	274.7	
Sep	215.3	225.3	237.9	244.2	251.9	257.6	259.6	264.9	275.1	
Oct	216.0	225.8	238.0	245.6	251.9	257.7	259.5	264.8	275.3	
Nov	216.6	226.8	238.5	245.6	252.1	257.1	259.8	265.5	275.8	
Dec	218.0	228.4	239.4	246.8	253.4	257.5	260.6	267.1	278.1	

These 'all items index' figures derive from the Office for National Statistics (ONS) (© Crown Copyright 2018). Later figures obtainable from www.ons.gov.uk/economy/inflationandpriceindices/timeseries/chaw/mm23, ONS' recorded message service on ☎ 0800 0113703 or its enquiry service on ☎ 01633 456900, or by emailing cpi@ons.gsi.gov.uk. More detailed information may be obtained at www.ons.gov.uk/economy/inflationandpriceindices.

For full RPI analysis, data back to 1950 (and comparable data for Consumer Prices Index) see @eGlance.

How to calculate the effect of inflation from one month to any subsequent month*

The formula is **X** x **A** ÷ **B**

Where   **X** is the figure to be inflated
       A is the RPI for the later month
       B is the RPI for the earlier month

*if you don't already have **@eGlance** which with ease does this and so much more

Table 2 Interest Base Rates

Base rate change dates

Date	New rate (%)	Date	New rate (%)	Date	New rate (%)
1983		6 June	8.25	11 December	6.25
12 January	11.00	7 June	8.50	**1999**	
15 March	10.50	22 June	9.00	8 January	6.00
15 April	10.00	29 June	9.50	5 February	5.50
15 June	9.50	5 July	10.00	8 April	5.25
4 October	9.00	19 July	10.50	10 June	5.00
1984		8 August	10.75	8 September	5.25
7 March	8.875	9 August	11.00	4 November	5.50
15 March	8.625	25 August	11.50	**2000**	
10 May	9.125	26 August	12.00	13 January	5.75
27 June	9.25	25 November	13.00	10 February	6.00
9 July	10.00	**1989**		**2001**	
11 July	11.00	24 May	14.00	8 February	5.75
12 July	12.00	5 October	15.00	5 April	5.50
9 August	11.50	**1990**		10 May	5.25
10 August	11.00	8 October	14.00	2 August	5.00
20 August	10.50	**1991**		18 September	4.75
7 November	10.00	13 February	13.50	4 October	4.50
20 November	9.875	27 February	13.00	8 November	4.00
23 November	9.625	25 March	12.50	**2003**	
1985		12 April	12.00	6 February	3.75
11 January	10.50	24 May	11.50	10 July	3.50
14 January	12.00	12 July	11.00	6 November	3.75
28 January	14.00	4 September	10.50	**2004**	
20 March	13.75	**1992**		5 February	4.00
21 March	13.50	5 May	10.00	6 May	4.25
29 March	13.25	16 September	12.00	10 June	4.50
2 April	13.125	17 September	10.00	5 August	4.75
12 April	12.875	22 September	9.00	**2005**	
19 April	12.675	16 October	8.00	4 August	4.50
12 June	12.50	13 November	7.00	**2006**	
7 July	12.25	**1993**		3 August	4.75
16 July	12.00	26 January	6.00	9 November	5.00
29 July	11.75	23 November	5.50	**2007**	
30 July	11.50	**1994**		11 January	5.25
1986		8 February	5.25	10 May	5.50
9 January	12.50	12 September	5.75	5 July	5.75
19 March	11.50	7 December	6.25	6 December	5.50
8 April	11.25	**1995**		**2008**	
9 April	11.00	2 February	6.75	7 February	5.25
24 April	10.50	13 December	6.50	10 April	5.00
27 May	10.00	**1996**		8 October	4.50
14 October	11.00	18 January	6.25	6 November	3.00
1987		8 March	6.00	4 December	2.00
10 March	10.50	6 June	5.75	**2009**	
19 March	10.00	30 October	6.00	8 January	1.50
29 April	9.50	**1997**		5 February	1.00
11 May	9.00	7 May	6.25	5 March	0.50
7 August	10.00	9 June	6.50	**2016**	
26 October	9.50	11 July	6.75	4 August	0.25
5 November	9.00	8 August	7.00	**2017**	
4 December	8.50	7 November	7.25	1 November	0.50
1988		**1998**		**2018**	
2 February	9.00	5 June	7.50		
17 March	8.50	9 October	7.25		
11 April	8.00	6 November	6.75		
18 May	7.50				
3 June	8.00				

The software program @eGlance enables you for any period from April 1904 to date (and indeed into the future) instantaneously to compute the interest upon your selected principal sum, and then to save and print a fully itemised report.

The program can perform these tasks not only for any base rate (simple or compound, and including '± x%' variants) but also authoritatively to provide judgment debt or legal aid charge interest calculations.

Table 3 Financial Times Indexes

Level of the FTSE 100 Index at month-end

Year	Jan	Feb	Mar	Apr	May	Jun	Jul	Aug	Sep	Oct	Nov	Dec
02	5,164.78	5,100.96	5,271.76	5,165.58	5,085.07	4,656.36	4,246.21	4,227.28	3,721.75	4,039.66	4,169.41	3,950.36
03	3,567.41	3,655.58	3,613.28	3,925.97	4,048.14	4,031.17	4,157.02	4,161.06	4,091.31	4,287.59	4,342.60	4,476.87
04	4,390.68	4,492.21	4,385.67	4,489.70	4,430.70	4,464.10	4,413.10	4,459.30	4,570.80	4,624.20	4,703.20	4,814.30
05	4,852.30	4,968.50	4,894.40	4,801.70	4,964.00	5,113.20	5,282.30	5,296.90	5,477.70	5,317.30	5,423.20	5,722.60
06	5,760.30	5,791.50	5,964.60	6,023.10	5,723.80	5,833.40	5,928.30	5,906.10	5,960.80	6,129.20	6,048.80	6,152.40
07	6,203.10	6,171.50	6,308.00	6,449.20	6,621.40	6,607.90	6,360.10	6,303.30	6,466.80	6,721.60	6,432.50	6,456.90
08	5,879.80	5,884.30	5,702.10	6,087.30	6,053.50	5,625.90	5,411.90	5,636.60	4,902.50	4,337.30	4,288.00	4,434.20
09	4,149.60	3,830.10	3,926.10	4,243.70	4,417.90	4,249.20	4,608.40	4,908.90	5,133.90	5,044.50	5,190.70	5,412.90
10	5,188.50	5,354.50	5,679.60	5,533.30	5,188.40	4,916.90	5,258.00	5,225.20	5,548.60	5,675.20	5,528.30	5,899.90
11	5,862.90	5,994.00	5,908.80	6,069.90	5,990.00	5,945.70	5,815.20	5,394.50	5,128.50	5,544.20	5,505.40	5,572.30
12	5,681.60	5,871.50	5,768.50	5,737.80	5,320.90	5,571.10	5,635.30	5,711.50	5,742.10	5,782.70	5,866.80	5,897.80
13	6,276.90	6,360.80	6,411.70	6,430.10	6,583.10	6,215.50	6,621.10	6,412.90	6,462.20	6,731.40	6,650.60	6,749.10
14	6,510.40	6,809.70	6,598.40	6,780.00	6,844.50	6,743.90	6,730.10	6,819.80	6,622.70	6,546.50	6,722.60	6,566.10
15	6,749.40	6,946.70	6,773.00	6,960.60	6,984.40	6,521.00	6,696.30	6,247.90	6,061.60	6,361.10	6,356.10	6,242.30
16	6,083.80	6,096.10	6,174.90	6,241.90	6,165.80	6,504.33	6,721.06	6,781.51	6,899.33	6,954.22	6,783.79	7,142.83
17	7,099.15	7,263.40	7,322.90	7,203.94	7,519.95	7,312.72	7,372.00	7,430.60	7,372.80	7,493.10	7,326.67	7,687.77
18	7,533.55	7,231.91										

Published daily, this Index reflects the value of the 100 most highly capitalised blue chip UK companies.

Level of the All Share Index at month-end

Year	Jan	Feb	Mar	Apr	May	Jun	Jul	Aug	Sep	Oct	Nov	Dec
02	2,496.02	2,466.98	2,557.40	2,512.04	2,475.57	2,263.11	2,050.81	2,046.21	1,801.48	1,938.71	2,002.97	1,893.73
03	1,722.28	1,759.08	1,735.72	1,891.50	1,968.83	1,971.26	2,045.82	2,064.74	2,027.72	2,125.37	2,146.72	2,207.38
04	2,187.10	2,243.41	2,196.97	2,237.30	2,201.80	2,228.70	2,192.22	2,214.19	2,271.67	2,297.66	2,345.21	2,410.75
05	2,441.22	2,495.46	2,457.73	2,397.05	2,483.35	2,560.17	2,644.75	2,659.21	2,745.79	2,664.40	2,741.05	2,847.02
06	2,928.56	2,956.12	3,047.96	3,074.26	2,916.85	2,967.58	3,004.28	3,007.51	3,050.44	3,140.47	3,119.85	3,178.59
07	3,211.84	3,198.28	3,283.21	3,355.60	3,438.70	3,404.14	3,289.12	3,260.48	3,316.89	3,454.12	3,280.87	3,286.67
08	3,000.10	3,013.02	2,927.05	3,095.68	3,082.26	2,855.69	2,749.21	2,868.69	2,483.67	2,183.69	2,133.99	2,209.29
09	2,078.92	1,929.75	1,984.17	2,173.06	2,252.64	2,172.08	2,353.47	2,520.66	2,634.79	2,584.59	2,648.43	2,760.80
10	2,660.49	2,736.80	2,910.19	2,863.35	2,673.17	2,543.47	2,715.36	2,696.72	2,867.58	2,936.15	2,861.61	3,062.85
11	3,044.27	3,106.58	3,067.73	3,155.03	3,121.07	3,096.72	3,026.02	2,800.51	2,654.38	2,860.86	2,835.84	2,857.88
12	2,932.91	3,043.91	3,002.78	2,984.67	2,760.62	2,891.45	2,927.27	2,972.63	2,998.86	3,024.40	3,065.30	3,093.41
13	3,287.38	3,349.39	3,380.64	3,390.18	3,473.82	3,289.71	3,509.94	3,410.43	3,443.85	3,585.32	3,548.45	3,609.63
14	3,496.51	3,666.66	3,555.59	3,619.83	3,655.01	3,600.19	3,585.62	3,639.54	3,533.93	3,503.46	3,458.54	3,532.74
15	3,621.81	3,687.08	3,663.58	3,760.06	3,770.75	3,570.58	3,652.79	3,434.66	3,335.92	3,484.60	3,492.13	3,348.10
16	3,335.90	3,345.84	3,395.19	3,421.70	3,429.77	3,515.45	3,653.83	3,697.19	3,755.34	3,768.14	3,692.40	3,873.22
17	3,864.48	3,953.42	3,990.00	3,962.49	4,116.08	4,002.18	4,046.20	4,072.98	4,049.89	4,117.69	4,033.84	4,221.82
18	4,137.66	3,981.61										

Published daily, this Index represents an aggregation of the FTSE 100, 250 and SmallCap indexes.

Equivalent data and comparison calculators for these FTSE and also the Dax, Dow Jones, Hang Seng and Nasdaq Indexes are available within @eGlance

Stamp duty at 0.5% (rounded up to the next £5) is payable on share purchases which exceed £1,000.

Table 4 Child Support

The 2008 Regime

The 2008 Regime has now been in full force since 26 November 2013 and there have been no reports of significant operational problems nor of complaints about the re-imposition of fees which took effect on 30 June 2014.

By s. 2 of the Child Maintenance and Other Payments Act 2008 (in force since 24 July 2008) the main objective imposed on the Secretary of State (**SoS**) is 'to maximise the number of those children who live apart from one or both of their parents for whom effective maintenance arrangements are in place'. The subsidiary objectives are (1) 'to encourage and support the making and keeping by parents of appropriate voluntary maintenance arrangements for their children' and (2) 'to support the making of applications for child support maintenance under the Child Support Act 1991 and to secure compliance when appropriate with parental obligations under that Act'.

In early 2010 the government established the **Child Maintenance Options** service to provide free, impartial information and support to help people make informed decisions about the type of maintenance arrangement that best suits their circumstances. Since November 2013 a 'mandatory gateway conversation' with the service must take place before a claim may be made. The service is delivered by phone, via a website (www.cmoptions.org), and for those in most need of more personalised help through a 'face-to-face service'. The helpline is ☎ 0800 988 0988. 'Clients' are now 'supported to make choices', either to negotiate private arrangements or to continue with their current arrangements. A standard form has been promulgated (www.cmoptions.org/en/pdfs/refresh/family-based-arrangement -form-aug-2015.pdf) for private agreements the final words of which state *'This is not a legal document but signing this agreement is a clear statement of our commitment to our children.'* This is inaccurate, as in fact the agreement will be legally binding as a maintenance agreement under s. 9(1) and (2) of the 1991 Act, and its existence will entitle the court to make an order in its terms under s. 4(10) which will have the effect of preventing any further child support calculation for 12 months.

Key features of the 2008 Regime:

* The upper age limit is now 20.
* The former rule under s. 6 of the 1991 Act has been abrogated, which required benefit claimants to make an application for child support, as also has the consequential power to make a Reduced Benefit Direction under s. 46 in relation to parents who failed to cooperate.
* Strong encouragement for parents to make consensual arrangements – see 2008 Act, s.2(2)(a).
* The basis for assessment is gross, not net, income. For calculation purposes the gross income returned to HMRC for the most recent tax year will generally be used, but relievable pension contributions will be deducted.
* Rates:
  (a) A nil rate for non-resident parents (**NRPs**) who fall into certain categories, such as students in full-time education or where NRP's income is less than £5 p.w.
  (b) For all other NRPs the minimum weekly payment is £7 and the absolute maximum is £482.
  (c) A £7 p.w. flat rate applies for gross incomes of less than £100 p.w, or where certain prescribed benefits are received by NRP or (in some instances) their partner.
  (d) A 'reduced rate' is prescribed in the Child Support and Claims and Payments (Miscellaneous Amendments and Change to the Minimum Amount of Liability) Regulations 2013 (SI 2013 No. 1654) for gross incomes between £100 and £200 p.w.
  (e) For gross incomes of £200 to £800 p.w., basic rates of 12% (1 child), 16% (2 children) and 19% (3 or more children) are applied.
  (f) For gross incomes over £800 p.w. the basic rates are 9% (1 child), 12% (2 children) and 15% (3 or more).
  (g) For the purpose of benefit calculations any maintenance paid is disregarded.
* Reduced liability in cases of shared or split care (see *below*).
* Where NRP cares for other children in a new family a reduction to gross weekly income is applied of 11% (1 child in new family), 14% (2 children) and 16% (3 or more).
* SoS may make liability orders.
* Strong enforcement procedures are available to SoS, including surrender of passports and curfew orders.
* Not notifying changed address is an offence: 2008 Act, s. 36.
* Anti-avoidance similar to s. 37 MCA 1973 applies: 2008 Act, s. 24.

NRP's liability may be reduced by the rules on **apportionment** and **shared care**. For worked examples of each see page 7.

For **apportionment** the rule is that if NRP is liable for more than one qualifying child, in respect of whom there is more than one parent-with-care (**PWC**), then the child support (**CS**) payable is to be divided by the number of qualifying children, and shared rateably among the PWCs according to the number of qualifying children each PWC has.

For **shared care** the rule is that where a qualifying child's care is shared so that from time to time NRP cares for the child overnight, the CS otherwise due to PWC is decreased by reference to the number of nights in a prescribed 12 month period that child stays with NRP. If PWC cares for more than one qualifying child of NRP, and shares care with NRP, then the applicable decrease is the sum of the appropriate fractions in the Table *below* divided by the number of such qualifying children.

If the applicable fraction is one-half in relation to any qualifying child, the total amount payable to the person with care decreases by a further £7 p.w. for each such child. Any such reduction cannot reduce the amount payable below £7 p.w. (although that will be apportioned between different PWCs where appropriate).

Nights p.a. with NRP	Fraction to subtract
<52	Nil
52-103	1/7 (14.29%)
104-155	2/7 (28.57%)
156-174	3/7 (42.86%)
175+	1/2 (50%) and deduct further £7 p.w. per child

In **JH v Secretary of State for Work and Pensions and LH** [2016] UKUT 440 (AAC) the Upper Tribunal held that it was an error of law for the FTT to determine into which band the case fell by reference to the terms of the Family Court child arrangements order. Rather, the calculation should be done strictly by reference to the number of nights actually spent with the NRP in the 12 month period prior to the relevant date.

The ordinary rules are subject to modification if the case falls within one of the prescribed **Special Cases**. The most prominent are:

Table 4 Child Support

- where a local authority in part provides a child's care NRP's liability is reduced as in **shared care**
- if NRP is subject to a court order for maintenance of other children, CS is reduced by apportionment
- where a child attends boarding school or is a hospital in-patient, PWC is deemed to be the person providing such care notwithstanding child's absence.

Calculated CS liabilities are subject to 2 classes of **variation**:

- **Special expenses** are confined to contact costs, the costs of illness or disability of another relevant child, the cost of discharging certain debts incurred when the parties were together as a couple, and the maintenance (as opposed to the educational) element of boarding school fees. Such expenses are deducted from NRP's net weekly income.
- **Additional income** cases comprise three categories: (1) where NRP's income is not taken into account or (2) has been diverted or (3) where NRP has unearned income.

The **income not taken into account** variation category applies where NRP's income would ordinarily be disregarded because it includes prescribed benefits or because NRP would otherwise fall outside the Act altogether (for example because he is a student), but where it is established that he has net weekly income in excess of £100. In such a case the whole of such income (not merely the excess over £100) is taken into account if the application for variation is successful.

The **diverted income** variation category applies where SoS is satisfied that NRP is diverting his income whether earned or unearned. NRP must have the ability to control his income and SoS must be satisfied that he has unreasonably reduced his income by diverting it to other destinations in order to reduce his liability to pay maintenance. The purpose of any diversion of income must be shown to be avoidance of CS. In such a case the whole of the diverted income is taken into account for the purposes of the calculation. In **EH v Sec of State for Work & Pensions** [2015] UKUT 621 (AAC) the Upper Tribunal held that repayments of a director's loan could constitute diverted income: the cases on the subject were analysed.

The **unearned income** variation category is for rental, savings, and miscellaneous income defined in Part 5 of the Income Tax (Trading and Other Income) Act 2005: this can be invoked only to the extent such income exceeds £2,500 gross p.a.

SoS must be satisfied that it is **just and equitable** to do so before directing a variation. See **RC v C-MEC** [2009] UKUT 62 (AAC) for an exposition of the applicable principles.

The 2008 regime abolished the **assets** ground of variation. In **Green v Adams (No. 1)** [2017] EWFC 24 at [22] and **Green v Adams (No.2)** [2017] EWFC 52 at [23 to 25] Mostyn J bemoaned its disappearance and urged the Government to consider its reinstatement. In that case NRP had assets in excess of £5M yet was required to pay the minimum amount of £7 p.w.

GW v RW [2003] 2 FLR 108 at [74] suggested that in circumstances where a court makes a child maintenance order the appropriate starting point should almost invariably be the amount arrived at by application of CS rules. In **Re TW & TM (Minors)** [2015] EWHC 3054 (Fam), [2016] 2 FLR 1386 at [7 to 9] it was held that the same principle should apply in cases governed by the 2008 Regime, commenting 'consistency of approach is obviously desirable in order to satisfy the need for the law, particularly in these days when so many people are unrepresented, to be predictable and accessible. Arbitrariness is to be avoided wherever possible'.

In **R (Kehoe) v Secretary of State for Work and Pensions** [2006] 1 AC 42, [2005] 3 WLR 252, the House of Lords decided that a PWC has no right to play any part in the enforcement processes of the CSA, and that they do not engage her rights under Art 6(1) of the European Convention on Human Rights. Her only remedy would be to take judicial review proceedings if the CSA's refusal to enforce a claim arose from an error of law (such as misunderstanding the extent of its statutory powers).

In **Gray v Secretary of State for Work and Pensions & Anor** [2012] EWCA Civ 1412 the CA decided that SoS is not bound to accept a liable parent's gross income is as stated in the information provided to HMRC; SoS is entitled to make his own findings of fact as to the parent's actual income.

In **Dickson v Rennie** [2014] EWHC 4306 (Fam) Holman J held that a top-up could only be sought from the court under s. 8(6)(b) of the 1991 Act where SoS has actually made a maximum calculation. The court is not entitled to make a finding for the purposes of the top-up jurisdiction that SoS should have made a maximum calculation where he had in fact not done so.

In **AB v CD (Jurisdiction: Global Maintenance Orders)** [2017] EWHC 3164 (Fam) Roberts J at [48] to [49] rejected a challenge to a 'Segal' global maintenance order. Provided that there is a substantial ingredient of spousal support, such orders are a legitimate means of meeting the needs of the children.

Facing is a Table of 2008 Regime calculations

Caveat: *This text is a basic survey of the 2008 Regime and is not comprehensive. Notwithstanding the asserted transparency and simplicity of the 2008 Regime calculations may still be highly complex, both legally and algebraically. Reference must needs be made to the Child Support Act 1991 as amended and to the numerous applicable Regulations.*

The 1991 and 2000 Regimes

As there are many unclosed cases under these regimes reference should be made to the 2014-15 edition of *At A Glance* for details and Tables, or to the current release of *@eGlance* where calculators remain available.

The DWP in December 2014 announced a closure programme for different categories of these cases, envisaging that the process would be complete by September 2017. In October 2017 the target closure date was put back to 31 December 2018.

The December 2017 publication *Child Support Agency Case Closure Statistics* reported that the case closure process had started in 98% of cases with a CSA liability; 87% of cases 'proactively selected' had completed case closure; and 670,300 cases had had their CSA liability ended. Where liability ended via case closure 21% of cases had now applied to the CMS; and the overall CSA caseload was reduced from 1.53M to 906,000 since the closure process began.

These rosy statistics do not tell the full story. The CSA *Quarterly Summary of Statistics for Great Britain* (data to September 2017) states that as at that date maintenance was still being paid to 86,400 children under these old schemes. Under these schemes £3.075B of arrears remained outstanding, a reduction of a mere £774M since December 2013. It is obvious that vast sums of arrears will never be recovered.

@eGlance *has Child Support calculators for all three Regimes.*

Table 4 Child Support

Weekly maintenance calculations (2008 Regime)

Qualifying children → Gross weekly income of paying parent ↓	None 1	None 2	None 3+	One other 1	One other 2	One other 3+	Two other 1	Two other 2	Two other 3+	Three (or more) other 1	Three (or more) other 2	Three (or more) other 3+	
<100	7	7	7	7	7	7	7	7	7	7	7	7	Min.
100	7	7	7	7	7	7	7	7	7	7	7	7	
120	10	12	13	10	11	12	10	11	12	9	11	12	
140	14	17	19	13	15	18	12	15	17	12	15	17	
160	17	22	26	15	20	23	15	19	22	14	18	21	
180	21	27	32	18	24	28	18	23	27	17	22	26	
199	24	32	38	21	28	33	20	27	32	19	26	31	
200	24	32	38	21	28	34	21	28	33	20	27	32	
210	25	34	40	22	30	36	22	29	34	21	28	34	
225	27	36	43	24	32	38	23	31	37	23	30	36	
300	36	48	57	32	43	51	31	41	49	30	40	48	
350	42	56	67	37	50	59	36	48	57	35	47	56	
400	48	64	76	43	57	68	41	55	65	40	54	64	
450	54	72	86	48	64	76	46	62	74	45	60	72	
500	60	80	95	53	71	85	52	69	82	50	67	80	
550	66	88	105	59	78	93	57	76	90	55	74	88	
600	72	96	114	64	85	101	62	83	98	60	81	96	
650	78	104	124	69	93	110	67	89	106	66	87	104	
700	84	112	133	75	100	118	72	96	114	71	94	112	
750	90	120	143	80	107	127	77	103	123	76	101	120	
800	96	128	152	85	114	135	83	110	131	81	108	128	
850	101	134	160	91	121	144	88	117	139	86	114	136	
900	105	140	167	96	128	152	93	124	147	91	121	144	
950	110	146	175	100	133	159	98	130	155	96	128	152	
1,000	114	152	182	104	139	166	101	135	161	100	133	158	
1,100	123	164	197	112	149	179	109	146	174	107	143	171	
1,200	132	176	212	120	160	192	117	156	187	115	153	183	
1,300	141	188	227	128	171	206	125	166	200	122	163	196	
1,400	150	200	242	136	182	219	132	176	213	130	173	208	
1,500	159	212	257	144	192	232	140	187	226	137	183	221	
1,600	168	224	272	152	203	246	148	197	238	145	193	234	
1,700	177	236	287	160	214	259	156	207	251	153	203	246	
1,800	186	248	302	168	224	272	163	218	264	160	213	259	
1,900	195	260	317	176	235	286	171	228	277	168	224	271	
2,000	204	272	332	184	246	299	179	238	290	175	234	284	
2,100	213	284	347	192	256	312	187	249	303	183	244	297	
2,200	222	296	362	200	267	326	194	259	316	190	254	309	
2,300	231	308	377	208	278	339	202	269	329	198	264	322	
2,400	240	320	392	216	288	352	210	280	342	205	274	334	
2,500	249	332	407	224	299	366	218	290	355	213	284	347	
2,600	258	344	422	232	310	379	225	300	367	221	294	360	
2,700	267	356	437	240	320	392	233	311	380	228	304	372	
2,800	276	368	452	248	331	406	241	321	393	236	314	385	
2,900	285	380	467	256	342	419	248	331	406	243	324	397	
2,999	294	392	482	264	352	432	256	341	419	251	334	410	
>3,000	294	392	482	264	352	433	256	342	419	251	334	410	Max.

(Rows 100–199 form the **Reduced rate band**; rows 200–2,999 form the **Standard rate band**.)

Child Support Regime 2008 Examples (all amounts are £p.w.)

Apportionment: F has 4 children. Two live with M1, 1 lives with M2 and 1 lives with F and his new partner M3. There are thus 3 qualifying children. F's gross income is £450. The calculation is £76.10 (see Table). 2/3 is payable to M1 (£50.73) and 1/3 to M2 (£25.37).

Shared care (1): F has 3 children. 1 lives with him and M2 and 2 live with M1. There are thus 2 qualifying children. Those children spend every other weekend (Friday p.m. to Sunday p.m.) with him, and two weeks in the summer holidays. F's gross income is £1,500. The basic calculation would be £192.20 (see Table). However, this is reduced by 1/7 as the qualifying children spend about 62 nights p.a. with him, reducing the calculation to £164.74.

Shared care (2): as (1) *left*, save that now 1 of the qualifying children spends every Friday p.m. to Monday a.m. with F during term-time and three-quarters of the school holidays (say 9 weeks) – making a total of 177 nights, although the other child is still spending time with F in accordance with the regime *left* (i.e. 62 nights p.a.). The calculation is: a basic calculation of £192.20 – subject to a reduction of 1/2 for one child and a reduction of 1/7 for the other – which (added together and divided by two) gives a total reduction of 9/28 (32.14%) – which equals £130.42, less less a further £7 for the '50% child', resulting in a net total of £123.42.

Table 5 School Fees

Average termly fees as at January 2017

	Full boarding fee (£)	Day fee (boarding schools) (£)	Day fee (day schools) (£)	Day fee (average) (£)	Overall average fee (£)
Sixth-form	11,243	6,791	4,846	5,277	7,304
Senior	10,618	6,325	4,701	5,002	5,943
Junior	7,850	4,788	4,172	4,223	4,290
Overall	10,753	5,913	4,388	4,606	5,432
Increase in preceding 12 months	4.20%	3.90%	3.80%	3.60%	3.57%

The Table *above* is derived from data contained in the 2017 Independent Schools Council census.

That review, conducted annually, shows average termly fees for various types of independent school at the start of that year, together with the percentage increase over the previous year.

The overall average fee increase of **3.6%** for the year to January 2017 (a modest increase on the preceding year's 2.9% average increase) must be viewed in the context that the rate of inflation for calendar year 2016 (measured according to the Retail Prices Index figures for the months of December 2015 and December 2016: see **Table 1**) was **2.5%**.

Thus the real rate of increase in school fees over that year was **1%** ($1.036 \div 1.025 = 1.01$).

Annual RPI inflation over the ten years to 2016 averaged **2.8%**, while the average annual rate of increase in school fees over that period has been **3.54%**. It would therefore seem to be a reasonable hypothesis to project a **real rate of increase** in fees computed as **0.72% p.a.** ($1.0354 \div 1.028 = 1.0072$), so that the forecast is that in each successive year the cost of the relevant stage and form of private schooling would amount to 0.72% more in real terms than in the year before. This figure of 0.72% is only coincidentally identical to last year's.

The next Table shows the effect of this postulated real rate of increase of 0.72% on a fee-payer parent who has an initial net income of £100,000. This Table assumes that this net income increases annually with the same average annual rate of change as the Retail Prices Index has shown over the ten years to 2016 (2.8%); and that school fees will continue to increase annually at the average rate of increase over that same period (see *above*) of 3.54%.

The inflationary cost of school fees: an illustration

Year	Net income (£)	School fees (£)	% of income paid
1	100,000	10,000	10.00%
2	102,797	10,354	10.07%
3	105,673	10,721	10.15%
4	108,629	11,101	10.22%
5	111,668	11,494	10.29%
6	114,792	11,901	10.37%
7	118,003	12,323	10.44%
8	121,304	12,759	10.52%

The full Independent Schools Council review of its census is at www.isc.co.uk/media/4069/isc_census_2017_final.pdf.

It must be emphasised that the assumptions utilised will certainly prove unfounded as the future unfolds, and are intended, in the same way as **Duxbury Calculations**, as no more than a guide and an illustration.

Table 6   Tertiary Education Costs and Funding

This summary applies to students resident in England who commence full-time undergraduate courses at a UK university or higher education college on or after 1 August 2018. Different regimes apply to part-time courses and for students resident elsewhere in the United Kingdom. For the regimes applicable to students whose courses started before 1 August 2018 see the relevant edition of **At A Glance**.

Tuition fees and loans

The maximum annual tuition fee for 2018-19 remains at £9,250. Non-means-tested tuition fee loans are available from Student Finance England (**SFE**) to meet the entire cost. Payment is made direct to the university or college: 25% at the start of each of the first two terms and 50% at the start of the third.

Maintenance loans

Maintenance grants are not available for students starting in or after 2016-17. Under the current scheme of partially means-tested maintenance loans, maximum/minimum loan amounts for 2018-19 (up by 3.2% over 2017-18) are: £7,324/£3,224 (student at home); £8,700/£4,054 (student not at home, outside London); £11,354/£5,654 (student not at home, in London); £9,963/£4,816 (student on year abroad). Gross household income (**GHI**) up to £25,000 is ignored. Above that level the loan reduces by £1 for each: £8.10 up to £58,215 (student at home); £8.01 up to £62,215 (student not at home, outside London); £7.87 up to £69,860 (student not at home, in London); £7.93 up to £65,816 (student on year abroad).

Household income

Complex rules govern the assessment of GHI, which includes most forms of income received by the student apart from earned income, and parental income where the student is a dependant. Where parents are divorced or separated SFE takes into account the income of the parent (and of any new partner of that parent) on whom the student is financially dependent. Maintenance payments are not treated as income. The period of assessment is the tax year 2016-17. However, income can be assessed for the current tax year if anticipated to be 85% or less than in 2016-17. A student who elects not to be assessed is eligible for the minimum loan.

Maintenance loans based on a range of GHI are shown *below*.

GHI (£)	At home (£)	Not at home – out of London (£)	Not at home – London (£)
25,000 or less	7,324	8,700	11,354
30,000	6,707	8,076	10,719
35,000	6,090	7,452	10,084
40,000	5,473	6,828	9,449
45,000	4,855	6,204	8,813
50,000	4,238	5,579	8,178
55,000	3,621	4,955	7,543
58,215	3,224	4,553	7,134
60,000	3,224	4,331	6,907
62,215	3,224	4,054	6,625
65,000	3,224	4,054	6,272
69,860 or more	3,224	4,054	5,654

Higher rates are payable for students on benefits. Additional grants and allowances are available for disabled students, single parents and those with certain child care costs, and dependent adults.

Repayment of student loans

For courses commencing after 1 September 2012, student loans become repayable once the student is no longer studying and is earning more than £25,000 gross per annum. Annual repayment is at the rate of 9% of gross income over £25,000. Interest accrues from the date of drawdown at varying rates depending on income.

Other financial assistance

Other assistance may be available in the form of bursaries, grants and scholarships awarded by individual institutions. For more information on loans and grants see www.gov.uk/student-finance; www.studentfinancewales.co.uk; www.studentfinanceni.co.uk (Northern Ireland) and www.saas.gov.uk (Scotland).

Table 7 Housing Costs

Standardised indices showing change in property prices over 8 years since 2009

National index (all houses)

Year	Index	%	Average price	Year	Index	%	Average price
10	325.1	0.5	162,971	14	377.0	8.3	189,002
11	328.7	1.1	164,785	15	393.1	4.3	197,044
12	325.0	(1.1)	162,924	16	410.8	4.5	205,937
13	348.0	7.1	174,444	17	421.8	2.7	211,433

Regional indices (all houses)

Year	North		Yorks/Humb.		N. West		E. Midlands		W. Midlands		E. Anglia	
	Index	%	Index	%	Index	%	Index	%	Index	%	Index	%
10	255.7	0.6	269.5	(3.6)	265.4	(1.9)	306.1	1.7	279.3	0.6	327.0	3.4
11	253.3	(1.0)	273.9	1.6	262.1	(1.2)	308.0	0.6	280.2	0.3	331.8	1.5
12	250.1	(1.3)	266.9	(2.5)	257.9	(1.6)	305.4	(0.8)	278.0	(0.8)	325.4	(1.9)
13	254.8	1.9	286.6	7.4	270.8	5.0	324.1	6.1	295.3	6.2	349.6	7.4
14	265.9	4.4	290.9	1.5	281.0	3.8	343.5	6.0	315.3	6.8	383.8	9.8
15	271.8	2.2	292.1	0.4	282.7	0.6	356.0	3.6	320.3	1.6	392.3	2.2
16	272.0	0.1	303.7	4.0	293.1	3.7	373.5	4.9	333.3	4.1	431.8	10.1
17	272.6	0.2	309.1	1.8	304.8	4.0	390.8	4.7	350.7	5.2	441.8	2.3

Year	S. West		S. East		London		Wales		Scotland		N. Ireland	
	Index	%	Index	%	Index	%	Index	%	Index	%	Index	%
10	339.5	2.1	358.5	2.0	422.6	2.5	275.2	(1.9)	261.9	(2.1)	360.9	(9.5)
11	341.6	0.6	364.3	1.6	445.4	5.4	279.4	1.5	259.9	(0.8)	328.6	(8.9)
12	342.2	0.2	363.6	(0.2)	448.7	0.7	271.8	(2.7)	251.2	(3.3)	301.6	(8.2)
13	361.8	5.7	391.2	7.6	515.6	14.9	288.6	6.1	260.6	3.7	322.8	7.0
14	390.8	8.0	432.5	10.6	607.5	17.8	292.5	1.4	271.6	4.2	349.1	8.1
15	405.7	3.8	461.5	6.7	681.5	12.2	294.5	0.7	266.4	(1.9)	371.6	6.5
16	423.7	4.4	493.4	6.9	706.6	3.7	301.6	2.4	272.3	2.2	374.2	0.7
17	444.0	4.8	508.7	3.1	703.4	(0.5)	311.6	3.3	279.4	2.6	381.8	2.0

Incorporating data from the Nationwide House Price Index. The ± percentage change is from the preceding year.

The @eGlance House Price Index module accesses data for a greater range of indices (including the Savills Prime Central London Residential Capital Value Index) than can be included on this page, and can demonstrate index-based changes in value for given properties over any given period of time, including earlier years.

Council Tax Bands: for properties valued as at 1 April 1991 (England) and 1 April 2005 (Wales)

Council Tax band	Valuation bands (England)	Valuation bands (Wales)
A	Up to £40,000	Up to £44,000
B	£40,001 to £52,000	£44,001 to £65,000
C	£52,001 to £68,000	£65,001 to £91,000
D	£68,001 to £88,000	£91,001 to £123,000
E	£88,001 to £120,000	£123,001 to £162,000
F	£120,001 to £160,000	£162,001 to £223,000
G	£160,001 to £320,000	£223,001 to £324,000
H	Over £320,000	£324,001 to £424,000
I	–	Over £424,000

Table 7 Housing Costs

The annual cost of a repayment mortgage over various terms

Initial borrowing	Annual cost (monthly instalment x 12) over 25 year term, at interest rates of:										
	1.5%	2.0%	2.5%	3.0%	3.5%	4.0%	4.5%	5.0%	5.5%	6.0%	6.5%
30,000	1,440	1,526	1,615	1,707	1,802	1,900	2,001	2,105	2,211	2,319	2,431
40,000	1,920	2,034	2,153	2,276	2,403	2,534	2,668	2,806	2,948	3,093	3,241
50,000	2,400	2,543	2,692	2,845	3,004	3,167	3,335	3,508	3,684	3,866	4,051
60,000	2,880	3,052	3,230	3,414	3,604	3,800	4,002	4,209	4,421	4,639	4,861
70,000	3,360	3,560	3,768	3,983	4,205	4,434	4,669	4,911	5,158	5,412	5,672
80,000	3,839	4,069	4,307	4,552	4,806	5,067	5,336	5,612	5,895	6,185	6,482
90,000	4,319	4,578	4,845	5,121	5,407	5,701	6,003	6,314	6,632	6,958	7,292
100,000	4,799	5,086	5,383	5,691	6,007	6,334	6,670	7,015	7,369	7,732	8,103
150,000	7,199	7,629	8,075	8,536	9,011	9,501	10,005	10,523	11,054	11,597	12,154
200,000	9,598	10,173	10,767	11,381	12,015	12,668	13,340	14,030	14,738	15,463	16,205
250,000	11,998	12,716	13,458	14,226	15,019	15,835	16,675	17,538	18,423	19,329	20,256
300,000	14,398	15,259	16,150	17,072	18,022	19,002	20,010	21,045	22,107	23,195	24,307

Initial borrowing	Annual cost (monthly instalment x 12) over 20 year term, at interest rates of:										
	1.5%	2.0%	2.5%	3.0%	3.5%	4.0%	4.5%	5.0%	5.5%	6.0%	6.5%
30,000	1,737	1,821	1,908	1,997	2,088	2,181	2,277	2,376	2,476	2,579	2,684
40,000	2,316	2,428	2,544	2,662	2,784	2,909	3,037	3,168	3,302	3,439	3,579
50,000	2,895	3,035	3,179	3,328	3,480	3,636	3,796	3,960	4,127	4,299	4,473
60,000	3,474	3,642	3,815	3,993	4,176	4,363	4,555	4,752	4,953	5,158	5,368
70,000	4,053	4,249	4,451	4,659	4,872	5,090	5,314	5,544	5,778	6,018	6,263
80,000	4,632	4,857	5,087	5,324	5,568	5,817	6,073	6,336	6,604	6,878	7,158
90,000	5,211	5,464	5,723	5,990	6,264	6,545	6,833	7,128	7,429	7,737	8,052
100,000	5,791	6,071	6,359	6,655	6,960	7,272	7,592	7,920	8,255	8,597	8,947
150,000	8,686	9,106	9,538	9,983	10,439	10,908	11,388	11,879	12,382	12,896	13,420
200,000	11,581	12,141	12,718	13,310	13,919	14,544	15,184	15,839	16,509	17,194	17,894
250,000	14,476	15,177	15,897	16,638	17,399	18,179	18,979	19,799	20,637	21,493	22,367
300,000	17,372	18,212	19,077	19,965	20,879	21,815	22,775	23,758	24,764	25,791	26,841

Initial borrowing	Annual cost (monthly instalment x 12) over 15 year term, at interest rates of:										
	1.5%	2.0%	2.5%	3.0%	3.5%	4.0%	4.5%	5.0%	5.5%	6.0%	6.5%
30,000	2,235	2,317	2,400	2,486	2,574	2,663	2,754	2,847	2,942	3,038	3,136
40,000	2,980	3,089	3,201	3,315	3,431	3,551	3,672	3,796	3,922	4,050	4,181
50,000	3,724	3,861	4,001	4,143	4,289	4,438	4,590	4,745	4,902	5,063	5,227
60,000	4,469	4,633	4,801	4,972	5,147	5,326	5,508	5,694	5,883	6,076	6,272
70,000	5,214	5,406	5,601	5,801	6,005	6,213	6,426	6,643	6,864	7,088	7,317
80,000	5,959	6,178	6,401	6,630	6,863	7,101	7,344	7,592	7,844	8,101	8,363
90,000	6,704	6,950	7,201	7,458	7,721	7,989	8,262	8,541	8,825	9,114	9,408
100,000	7,449	7,722	8,001	8,287	8,579	8,876	9,180	9,489	9,805	10,126	10,453
150,000	11,173	11,583	12,002	12,430	12,868	13,314	13,770	14,234	14,708	15,189	15,680
200,000	14,898	15,444	16,003	16,574	17,157	17,753	18,360	18,979	19,610	20,253	20,907
250,000	18,622	19,305	20,004	20,717	21,447	22,191	22,950	23,724	24,513	25,316	26,133
300,000	22,347	23,166	24,004	24,861	25,736	26,629	27,540	28,469	29,415	30,379	31,360

These tables show the annual cost of various levels of borrowing over various terms, at the rates of interest shown. Instalments are paid from taxed income.

Use your @eGlance for infinitely bespoke quotes which you can save and print for negotiations or court

Table 7 Housing Costs

Stamp Duty and other tax on Residential Properties in 2018-19

Stamp Duty Land Tax (SDLT) is paid at progressive rates upon the segment of the purchase price within each band.

Band	Price	Band Rate
First £125,000	Under £125,000	0%*
Next £125,000	£125,001 to £250,000	2%
Next £675,000	£250,001 to £925,000	5%
Next £575,000	£925,001 to £1,500,000	10%
Thereafter	Over £1,500,000	12%
Enveloped properties (see *below*)	Over £500,000	15%
Second homes and buy-to-let (see *below*)	Over £40,000	Add 3%

* A first time buyer is exempt from SDLT on purchases up to £300,000, and for the first £300,000 of purchases up to £500,000.

The Table *below* shows SDLT as a percentage of price for purchases other than of second homes or buy-to-lets (see *below*). SDLT for other prices can be calculated by interpolation from examples *within the same Rate Band.*

Band (%)	Overall (%)	Price (£)	SDLT (£)	Band (%)	Overall (%)	Price (£)	SDLT (£)
	0.00	125,001	0		6.25	1,500,001	93,750
	0.33	150,000	500		7.07	1,750,000	123,750
2	0.57	175,000	1,000		7.69	2,000,000	153,750
	0.75	200,000	1,500		8.17	2,250,000	183,750
	0.89	225,000	2,000		8.55	2,500,000	213,750
	1.00	250,001	2,500		8.86	2,750,000	243,750
	1.67	300,000	5,000		9.13	3,000,000	273,750
	2.14	350,000	7,500		9.54	3,500,000	333,750
2	2.50	400,000	10,000	2	9.84	4,000,000	393,750
+	3.00	500,000	15,000	+	10.08	4,500,000	453,750
5	3.33	600,000	20,000	5	10.28	5,000,000	513,750
	3.57	700,000	25,000	+	10.43	5,500,000	573,750
	3.75	800,000	30,000	10	10.56	6,000,000	633,750
	3.89	900,000	35,000	+	10.67	6,500,000	693,750
	3.92	925,001	36,250	12	10.77	7,000,000	753,750
	4.08	950,000	38,750		10.85	7,500,000	813,750
2	4.38	1,000,000	43,750		10.92	8,000,000	873,750
+	4.89	1,100,000	53,750		10.99	8,500,000	933,750
5	5.11	1,150,000	58,750		11.04	9,000,000	993,750
+	5.31	1,200,000	63,750		11.09	9,500,000	1,053,750
10	5.67	1,300,000	73,750		11.14	10,000,000	1,113,750
	5.98	1,400,000	83,750		11.22	11,000,000	1,233,750
	6.25	1,500,000	93,750		11.28	12,000,000	1,353,750

Second homes and buy-to-let properties purchased for more than £40,000 attract an SDLT supplement of 3% chargeable on the whole price. Disposals of such properties in 2018-19 (even if the 'first home' is not in the UK) attract enhanced CGT rates: 18%/28% rather than 10%/20%.

Enveloped Properties are dwellings valued at over £500,000 (as at 1 April 2017 or date of acquisition, if later) owned by 'non-natural persons' where the purchaser is a company, a partnership of which at least one partner is a company, or a collective investment scheme: but not the trustee of a settlement. SDLT on them is 15% on the **entire purchase price**.

Such properties also attract an **Annual Tax on Enveloped Dwellings (ATED)**, which from 1 April 2018 is charged thus:

Property value	Annual chargeable amount for year from 1 April 2018
More than £500,000 but not more than £1 million	£3,600
More than £1 million but not more than £2 million	£7,250
More than £2 million but not more than £5 million	£24,250
More than £5 million but not more than £10 million	£56,550
More than £10 million but not more than £20 million	£113,400
More than £20 million	£226,950

CGT is payable at the rate of 28% on gains on disposal of Enveloped Dwellings subject to ATED.

Table 8 Company Cars

HMRC Car Benefit Charges 2018-19

Percentage of the list price to be taxed					
CO$_2$ g/km	**Taxable %**		**CO$_2$ g/km**	**Taxable %**	
	Petrol	**Diesel**		**Petrol**	**Diesel**
Up to 50	13	17	125 to 129	26	30
51 to 75	16	20	For every additional 5g/km band from '130 to 134' up to '155 to 159' add 1%, then:		
76 to 94	19	23			
95 to 99	20	24			
100 to 104	21	25	160 to 164	33	37
105 to 109	22	26	165 to 169	34	37
110 to 114	23	27	170 to 174	35	37
115 to 119	24	28	175 to 179	36	37
120 to 124	25	29	180 or more	37	37

The taxable benefit of a company car is based solely on the carbon dioxide each vehicle model produces, measured in grams per kilometre (the CO$_2$ g/km rating). Tax is levied on Car Benefit calculated by reference to the appropriate percentage (*above*) of the manufacturer's list price for the vehicle (whatever the actual price paid), plus the list price of options/extras. There is no maximum chargeable limit on the list price, but a capital contribution made to the purchase by an employee reduces the list price commensurately.

For 2018-19 the percentage benefit chargeable for vehicles producing up to 50 g/km is 13% for petrol, 17% for diesel engines (as diesel powered cars attract a 4% surcharge) and from 51 upwards as shown *above*. The maximum percentage is 37% (180 g/km and above for petrol vehicles; 160 g/km and above for diesel). Second and subsequent cars are taxed in an identical manner.

For cars registered on or after 1 March 2001 the CO$_2$ g/km rating is shown on the DVLA Registration Form V5.

Indicative CO2 g/km ratings for both old and new cars can be found at carfueldata.direct.gov.uk.

HMRC Fuel Benefit Charge 2018-19

The taxable benefit where an employer supplies fuel for private use (or allows reimbursement for fuel for private journeys) is based on the CO$_2$ g/km rating of the car used. To calculate the Fuel Benefit Charge the appropriate percentage (see Table *above*) is multiplied by a set figure (£23,400 for 2018-19). The minimum chargeable benefit for 2018-19 is £1,170 (5%), the maximum is £8,190 (35%). So where a diesel vehicle's CO$_2$ g/km rating is 102 and thus 25% applies, the taxable fuel benefit is £5,850 (25% x 23,400).

No charge arises if fuel is provided only for business or if the employee must pay for private fuel use.

HMRC Approved Mileage Allowance Payments (AMAPs) 2018-19

Vehicle	Pence per mile
Cars and vans	
up to 10,000 miles	45
above 10,000 miles	25
plus per passenger*	5
Motorcycles	24
Cycles	20

Mileage payments to employees using their own transport for business purposes attract no tax if within these authorised rates.

*When paid to driver for each fellow employee carried as passenger on shared business trip.

Table 9 Duxbury Calculations

Capitalising female and male lifetime net income needs to three significant figures (in £000s)

Age	£10,000		£15,000		£20,000		£25,000		£30,000		£40,000		£50,000		£60,000	
	F	M	F	M	F	M	F	M	F	M	F	M	F	M	F	M
40	178	178	289	287	400	396	511	505	623	615	862	849	1,112	1,093	1,365	1,341
41	172	171	282	280	392	388	502	496	613	604	849	836	1,097	1,078	1,347	1,323
42	168	168	277	275	387	382	496	489	605	597	839	825	1,084	1,064	1,332	1,306
43	165	164	273	270	381	376	489	483	598	589	829	814	1,071	1,050	1,316	1,290
44	161	160	268	264	375	368	482	472	590	576	818	795	1,057	1,025	1,300	1,258
45	157	156	263	259	369	362	475	464	582	567	807	783	1,043	1,010	1,283	1,240
46	153	152	258	253	363	355	468	457	573	559	795	771	1,029	994	1,265	1,222
47	148	147	252	248	356	348	460	449	564	549	783	758	1,014	978	1,248	1,202
48	144	143	247	242	350	341	453	440	555	540	771	745	999	962	1,229	1,183
49	139	138	241	236	343	334	444	432	546	530	758	732	983	945	1,210	1,162
50	135	133	235	230	335	326	436	423	536	520	745	718	967	928	1,191	1,141
51	130	128	229	224	328	319	427	414	526	509	732	704	950	910	1,170	1,120
52	124	123	222	217	320	311	418	404	516	498	718	689	933	891	1,150	1,098
53	119	118	216	210	312	302	409	394	505	487	704	674	915	872	1,128	1,075
54	114	112	209	203	304	293	399	384	494	475	689	659	896	853	1,107	1,051
55	108	107	202	196	295	284	389	373	483	462	674	643	878	833	1,084	1,027
56	102	101	194	188	286	275	378	362	471	450	659	626	858	812	1,061	1,002
57	96	94	186	180	277	265	368	351	458	437	643	610	838	790	1,037	976
58	83	82	172	166	261	249	350	333	439	417	622	587	812	763	1,007	945
59	77	75	164	157	251	239	338	321	426	402	605	569	791	741	981	917
60	70	68	155	148	241	228	326	308	412	388	587	550	769	717	955	889
61	62	60	146	138	230	216	313	294	397	372	569	530	747	693	928	860
62	55	53	136	129	218	204	300	280	382	356	550	510	724	668	900	830
63	47	46	127	121	207	197	287	273	366	349	531	503	700	662	872	825
64	34	33	112	106	190	180	268	254	346	327	506	478	672	633	839	790
65	52	21	128	92	204	164	280	235	356	306	510	452	670	602	832	754
66	51	20	124	89	198	158	272	227	345	296	495	437	650	581	807	728
67	49	46	121	113	192	179	264	246	335	313	480	447	629	585	780	725
68	48	44	117	108	186	173	255	237	324	301	463	430	607	562	753	697
69	46	43	113	104	179	166	246	227	313	289	447	412	585	539	725	667
70	44	43	108	104	173	166	237	227	301	289	430	412	562	539	697	667
71	44	41	108	100	173	159	237	217	301	276	430	394	562	515	697	637
72	43	39	104	95	166	151	227	207	289	263	412	376	539	490	667	606
73	41	37	100	90	159	143	217	197	276	250	394	356	515	464	637	573
74	39	35	95	85	151	135	207	186	263	236	376	336	490	438	606	540
75	37	35	90	85	143	135	197	186	250	236	356	336	464	438	573	540
76	35	33	85	80	135	127	186	174	236	221	336	316	438	410	540	506
77	35	30	85	74	135	118	186	162	236	206	336	294	438	382	540	471
78	33	28	80	69	127	109	174	150	221	191	316	272	410	353	506	435
79	30	28	74	69	118	109	162	150	206	191	294	272	382	353	471	435
80	28	26	69	63	109	100	150	137	191	175	272	249	353	323	435	398

Table 9 Duxbury Calculations

£75,000		£100,000		£125,000		£150,000		£175,000		£200,000		£250,000		£300,000		Age
F	M	F	M	F	M	F	M	F	M	F	M	F	M	F	M	
1,770	1,734	2,493	2,437	3,227	3,153	3,988	3,889	4,767	4,650	5,530	5,394	7,064	6,887	8,595	8,382	40
1,746	1,709	2,459	2,402	3,185	3,110	3,933	3,833	4,703	4,584	5,458	5,319	6,973	6,793	8,486	8,268	41
1,725	1,686	2,428	2,370	3,145	3,067	3,880	3,779	4,641	4,519	5,386	5,245	6,882	6,699	8,376	8,153	42
1,702	1,663	2,396	2,337	3,104	3,024	3,827	3,723	4,577	4,452	5,313	5,169	6,789	6,602	8,263	8,036	43
1,679	1,619	2,363	2,271	3,061	2,939	3,772	3,614	4,512	4,318	5,239	5,015	6,694	6,405	8,149	7,796	44
1,656	1,594	2,330	2,236	3,018	2,893	3,717	3,556	4,445	4,246	5,163	4,935	6,598	6,302	8,031	7,671	45
1,632	1,569	2,296	2,199	2,974	2,846	3,661	3,497	4,377	4,173	5,085	4,852	6,499	6,197	7,911	7,544	46
1,608	1,544	2,261	2,162	2,929	2,798	3,604	3,437	4,307	4,099	5,006	4,767	6,398	6,090	7,789	7,413	47
1,583	1,518	2,225	2,124	2,883	2,748	3,546	3,377	4,236	4,023	4,925	4,681	6,296	5,980	7,664	7,280	48
1,558	1,492	2,188	2,085	2,836	2,698	3,487	3,315	4,162	3,946	4,842	4,592	6,191	5,868	7,536	7,144	49
1,533	1,465	2,151	2,045	2,787	2,647	3,427	3,252	4,088	3,868	4,757	4,501	6,083	5,754	7,405	7,006	50
1,507	1,438	2,113	2,005	2,738	2,594	3,366	3,187	4,012	3,789	4,670	4,409	5,974	5,638	7,272	6,864	51
1,480	1,409	2,073	1,963	2,687	2,540	3,304	3,121	3,935	3,709	4,581	4,314	5,862	5,519	7,136	6,719	52
1,453	1,380	2,033	1,921	2,636	2,485	3,241	3,054	3,857	3,627	4,490	4,217	5,748	5,397	6,997	6,572	53
1,425	1,351	1,992	1,877	2,583	2,429	3,176	2,985	3,778	3,544	4,397	4,118	5,631	5,273	6,855	6,421	54
1,396	1,320	1,951	1,833	2,529	2,371	3,110	2,914	3,697	3,460	4,302	4,017	5,512	5,146	6,710	6,268	55
1,367	1,289	1,908	1,787	2,473	2,312	3,042	2,842	3,615	3,374	4,205	3,915	5,391	5,017	6,563	6,111	56
1,336	1,256	1,864	1,741	2,417	2,252	2,973	2,768	3,532	3,287	4,106	3,811	5,267	4,885	6,412	5,951	57
1,300	1,218	1,815	1,689	2,355	2,187	2,898	2,689	3,443	3,193	4,001	3,702	5,136	4,748	6,255	5,784	58
1,268	1,184	1,769	1,640	2,296	2,124	2,825	2,612	3,357	3,102	3,899	3,594	5,007	4,610	6,098	5,617	59
1,235	1,148	1,722	1,591	2,235	2,059	2,751	2,533	3,270	3,008	3,795	3,486	4,875	4,468	5,938	5,447	60
1,201	1,112	1,675	1,541	2,173	1,994	2,676	2,453	3,180	2,913	3,689	3,375	4,740	4,324	5,774	5,274	61
1,167	1,075	1,626	1,489	2,110	1,927	2,598	2,370	3,088	2,816	3,581	3,263	4,602	4,176	5,607	5,096	62
1,131	1,069	1,576	1,484	2,046	1,922	2,519	2,366	2,995	2,811	3,472	3,258	4,460	4,174	5,437	5,093	63
1,091	1,027	1,522	1,427	1,977	1,850	2,436	2,279	2,896	2,709	3,359	3,140	4,314	4,022	5,261	4,910	64
1,077	984	1,491	1,369	1,930	1,777	2,373	2,189	2,819	2,604	3,266	3,020	4,183	3,866	5,101	4,722	65
1,044	949	1,443	1,320	1,865	1,710	2,293	2,106	2,723	2,504	3,155	2,904	4,035	3,714	4,922	4,537	66
1,009	938	1,393	1,294	1,799	1,663	2,211	2,042	2,625	2,423	3,041	2,806	3,885	3,577	4,741	4,365	67
974	900	1,344	1,242	1,732	1,592	2,128	1,955	2,525	2,319	2,925	2,685	3,732	3,420	4,555	4,171	68
938	862	1,294	1,188	1,663	1,520	2,042	1,866	2,423	2,213	2,806	2,561	3,577	3,261	4,365	3,972	69
900	862	1,242	1,188	1,592	1,520	1,955	1,866	2,319	2,213	2,685	2,561	3,420	3,261	4,171	3,972	70
900	822	1,242	1,133	1,592	1,447	1,955	1,774	2,319	2,104	2,685	2,435	3,420	3,100	4,171	3,771	71
862	781	1,188	1,077	1,520	1,373	1,866	1,681	2,213	1,993	2,561	2,306	3,261	2,935	3,972	3,567	72
822	739	1,133	1,019	1,447	1,299	1,774	1,586	2,104	1,880	2,435	2,174	3,100	2,766	3,771	3,360	73
781	696	1,077	959	1,373	1,222	1,681	1,489	1,993	1,764	2,306	2,040	2,935	2,594	3,567	3,151	74
739	696	1,019	959	1,299	1,222	1,586	1,489	1,880	1,764	2,174	2,040	2,766	2,594	3,360	3,151	75
696	652	959	897	1,222	1,144	1,489	1,391	1,764	1,646	2,040	1,903	2,594	2,419	3,151	2,937	76
696	606	959	834	1,222	1,063	1,489	1,292	1,764	1,525	2,040	1,763	2,594	2,240	3,151	2,718	77
652	559	897	769	1,144	979	1,391	1,190	1,646	1,403	1,903	1,620	2,419	2,057	2,937	2,496	78
606	559	834	769	1,063	979	1,292	1,190	1,525	1,403	1,763	1,620	2,240	2,057	2,718	2,496	79
559	511	769	702	979	893	1,190	1,086	1,403	1,279	1,620	1,474	2,057	1,871	2,496	2,269	80

Table 9 Duxbury Calculations

Duxbury relies on an iterative computation, seeking the amount which if invested to achieve capital growth and income yield (both at assumed rates and after tax on the yield and realised gains) could theoretically be drawn down in equal inflation-proofed instalments over a period (usually the recipient's actuarial life expectancy) but would be completely exhausted at the end of the period. **The computation is not, and never has been, an attempt to identify the sum necessary to guarantee a particular level of expenditure**, and is better viewed as a guide to the net present value of a right to receive periodical payments at the target annual rate for the remainder of the payee's life.

The standard underlying 'assumptions' are (1) a uniform income yield of 3% p.a. (1.5% in the first year) (2) a uniform rate of capital growth of 3.75% p.a. (3) a uniform rate of inflation at 3% p.a. (4) a consistent regime of taxation – with bands/allowances increasing in line with inflation (5) a constant level of drawdown in real terms (6) a consistent rate of 'churn' (the realisation of capital gains other than to fund expenditure) and that the recipient will (7) survive for precisely the expected average of her (or his) contemporaries and (8) be or become entitled to a 'full' state pension (but see *below*) while (9) that pension will increase at the assumed rate of inflation and (10) the age from which the state pension is payable will not alter in the meantime. The assumptions are all necessarily simplifications which will not materialise: at best they are 'guesstimates', or approximations of what may be an average of events to happen over a future of something between about 15 and 50 years.

While there is scope for debate about the appropriate assumptions to use, it is clear that predictions about what may happen over the next 15 to 50 years cannot be overly reliant upon what has happened in the last 15 to 50 months, let alone the last 15 to 50 weeks. The past is an imperfect guide but it is, perhaps, the best so far available, and history tells us that average real returns of 3.75% p.a. are – over the long term – achievable even with a cautious investment strategy. Interest rates remain low, but stock market indices achieved new record levels in early 2018 (albeit they have fallen back somewhat from that peak), and over the longer term both capital growth and income yield from a balanced portfolio remain achievable. Inflation has been well below the assumed rate of 3% p.a. for some years but has recently crept back up towards, and even occasionally beyond, that level.

In **JL v SL (No.3)** [2015] EWHC 555 (Fam), Mostyn J reviewed the performance of the financial markets and concluded that on that basis the assumed real return of 3.75% 'is a very reasonable guess'.

The March 2017 reduction to -0.75% in the discount rate in the Ogden Tables applicable in personal injury cases largely reflects the much higher than general rate of inflation applicable to the medical and care costs components. For the reasons explained by Lady Hale in **Simon v Helmot** [2012] UKPC 5 where precisely the same issue arose, the position of a patient in need of enduring medical care and that of an ex-spouse seeking financial security are not the same.

The Duxbury calculation is now principally used (i) as a guide for capitalising an existing periodical payments order, or (ii) to assist quantification of a clean-break order in a non-sharing case, or (iii) as a cross-check on whether the application of the sharing principle is likely to meet the needs of the recipient, or (iv) in the context of 'maintenance' in an Inheritance Act claim, where income may be provided 'by way of a lump sum from which both income and capital can be drawn over the years', as in **Ilott v The Blue Cross** [2017] UKSC 17 at [15].

The assumptions must be such as strive to achieve fairness between the parties. A financial remedy award is a 'nil gain sum' – so any benefit to one party is necessarily a detriment to the other. Standardisation inevitably leads to anomalies and occasionally to unfair results in individual cases. A payee of a capitalised periodical payments order calculated on Duxbury assumptions is a net winner if she soon remarries or, more paradoxically, if she dies young. On the other hand, she will be a net loser if she lives singly for longer than her average contemporary. The likelihood of remarriage by the payee, or a payer's inability to continue to make periodical payments long into his old age, are factors which tend to favour the former over the latter. For a fuller discussion of these topics see *An Alternative View of Duxbury* [2010] Fam Law 614.

The arithmetic of the table is affected from year to year by changes in life expectancy data and tax rates. This year, for reasons explained in the commentary to Table 10, life expectancy assumptions at all ages have been reduced.

The overall assumptions remain favourable to recipients in that (i) no attempt to shelter income from tax, e.g. by the use of ISAs, is assumed and (ii) all income is assumed to be taxable at normal rates for savings, and not at the lower rates applicable to dividends (therefore ignoring the annual tax-free dividend allowance) although a balanced portfolio of any size would be likely to include a substantial element of equities and therefore some dividend income.

The Table shows approximate figures for recipients in the age range 40 to 80 but the usefulness of Duxbury calculations for recipients with a life expectancy of less than about 15 years (women over about 74 and men over about 72) is dubious. The likelihood is that recipients of that age will fall foul of the so-called 'Duxbury paradox' – that the longer the marriage the smaller the lump sum requirement. The proportionate margin of error in relation to life expectancy (in particular) is also extremely high, with some recipients likely to live more than twice as long as expected: not a fate which can afflict recipients at the outset aged 40, 50 or even 60 years. And the shorter the expectancy the less likely it is that average returns return to those historically achievable over longer terms.

Analysis of the vexed question of how the anticipated receipt of future pension income and/or lump sum receipt or capital release, whether from a pension sharing order or otherwise, is to be factored into a bespoke Duxbury calculation is beyond the scope of this narrative. Broadly the options are to include as taxable income the entire 'projected' future pension from the pension age, or to include the current CETV as an immediate accretion to the fund – albeit in practice not yet available, or to introduce separately the 'tax free' lump sum element and the projected reduced pension annuity from the pension date. None is entirely satisfactory, but any might constitute a justifiable basis on the facts of a particular case.

The introduction of the 'new state pension' (£8,546 p.a.) for those born after 6 April in 1951 (men) and 1953 (women), in place of the 'old' state pension (£6,549 p.a.) produces

Table 9 Duxbury Calculations

apparently anomalous Duxbury calculations at the cusp of those transitions. Thus, for example, in the table the figure for a woman requiring £10,000 p.a. aged 65 is £52,000, whereas for a woman aged 64 the figure is *lower* at £34,000. The effect is slightly ameliorated by the postponement of the attainment of pension age for younger people.

The assumption incorporated in this Table's computations that a Duxbury recipient qualifies for a 'full' state pension has a dramatic impact on the resulting figure. In broad terms it is always at least £40,000 to £50,000 (for the very youngest and the very oldest), compared to the figure if they have no such pension entitlement, but can be as much as £122,000 for a woman of 64 or a man of 65. The impact reduces marginally as the 'required income' increases. If the recipient will not be entitled to a full state pension a bespoke calculation should be undertaken, for example using *Capitalise*.

More refined calculations are available within *@eGlance* and yet more bespoke via *Capitalise*.

Table 10 Life Expectancy

10

Remaining life expectancy in years according to age and sex (for use in the year 2018)

Age	Men (ONS16M)							Women (ONS16F)						
	20	30	40	50	60	70	80	20	30	40	50	60	70	80
0	67.5	56.4	45.7	35.2	25.3	16.5	9.1	70.3	59.3	48.4	37.8	27.7	18.3	10.3
1	66.4	55.3	44.6	34.2	24.3	15.6	8.5	69.2	58.2	47.3	36.7	26.7	17.5	9.6
2	65.2	54.3	43.6	33.2	23.4	14.8	7.9	68.1	57.1	46.3	35.7	25.7	16.6	8.9
3	64.1	53.2	42.5	32.1	22.5	14.0	7.3	67.0	56.0	45.2	34.7	24.8	15.7	8.3
4	63.0	52.1	41.4	31.1	21.6	13.3	6.8	65.9	54.9	44.1	33.7	23.8	14.9	7.7
5	61.9	51.0	40.4	30.1	20.7	12.5	6.3	64.7	53.8	43.1	32.6	22.9	14.1	7.1
6	60.8	49.9	39.4	29.1	19.9	11.8	5.8	63.6	52.7	42.0	31.6	22.0	13.3	6.5
7	59.7	48.9	38.3	28.2	19.0	11.1	5.3	62.5	51.6	40.9	30.6	21.0	12.5	6.0
8	58.6	47.8	37.3	27.2	18.1	10.4	4.9	61.4	50.6	39.9	29.6	20.1	11.8	5.5
9	57.5	46.7	36.2	26.2	17.3	9.7	4.5	60.4	49.5	38.8	28.6	19.2	11.0	5.1

Life expectancy is the actuarial prediction of the period of time to elapse before 50% of the members of the particular cohorts, of men and of women (all sharing the same year of birth), will have died. It is based on collated data on ages at death and predictions of improvements as a consequence of medical as well as general health advances.

These expectancies are taken from ONS16, one of numerous available life tables in the UK, derived from the latest UK national population projections published in October 2017. These ONS16 tables relate to the age a man or woman attains in 2018, and have been adopted as the most appropriate basis for the **Duxbury Calculations**.

These figures are 'cohort life expectancies' and incorporate future mortality changes projected beyond 2018, as experience and life tables agreed, usually, that people live progressively longer. However, it has emerged that increases in life expectancy (i.e. decreases in mortality) have been less dramatic over the last few years than previously expected with the result that for some ages expectancy is now marginally lower than predicated in previously published tables. This does not mean that people are dying earlier than previous cohorts, merely that they are dying less later than previously expected.

Table 11 Income Tax

Tax treatment of 2018-19 income (net of the reliefs and allowances shown *opposite*)

In simplified terms, the various categories of income are taxed as follows:

Income other than from savings and dividends is taken as the first tranche of income.

Savings income is taxed as the next tranche, at basic and/or higher rate.

- However a starting **0% savings rate** applies to up to £5,000 of savings income, available only to individuals whose non-savings income does not exceed the personal allowance by more than £5,000, and reduced by the excess if less than £5,000.
- In addition, a zero-rate **personal savings allowance** is available, depending on the taxpayer's marginal tax rate: £1,000 if basic rate; £500 if higher rate. No allowance is given to those with income in the additional rate band.

Dividend income tax: regime change and comparative effect

For all individual taxpayers the **dividend allowance** now renders tax-free the first £2,000 of dividends received during 2018-19. Any dividends an individual receives which exceed the £2,000 allowance are taxed at banded dividend tax rates applied on the basis that the dividend income is treated as the top tranche of the total income.

The dividend rate bands are:

- 7.5% (the dividend ordinary rate) for any dividends falling to be taxed within the basic rate band
- 32.5% (the dividend upper rate) for any falling within the higher rate band
- 38.1% (the dividend additional rate) for any falling within the additional rate band

A taxpayer whose only income is derived from dividends now starts to pay tax on dividends received in excess of £13,850 (the personal allowance plus the dividend allowance).

Special rules, beyond the scope of this Table, apply to dividends from overseas companies.

For all individuals irrespective of age whose income exceeds £100,000 the personal allowance is reduced by £1 for every £2 of income over £100,000, and extinguished if income exceeds £123,700.

If a tax calculation is needed **where a spouse or civil partner was born before 6 April 1935**, see www.gov.uk/married-couples-allowance.

The marriage tax allowance enables up to £1,185 of unutilised personal allowance of one spouse or civil partner to be transferred to and thus to relieve the other from tax. For this allowance to be available to a couple the recipient must be a basic rate taxpayer, and both must have been born after 6 April 1935.

Restricted tax relief is available to the payer of **maintenance** who or whose former spouse was born before 6 April 1935, limited to a tax reduction of 10% of up to a maximum of £3,360 of qualifying payments falling due. No tax is payable on maintenance received.

Income within discretionary and accumulation trusts: The first £1,000 of income is taxed at basic rate or dividend ordinary rate. The excess is taxed at 45% on non-dividend income and at 38.1% on dividends. Beneficiaries who are not additional rate taxpayers may be entitled to a refund of part of the tax paid by the trustees when the income is distributed, but such intricacies are beyond the scope of this Table.

Working Tax and **Child Tax Credits** (and, where and when available, **Universal Credit**) and (for those over 60) **Pension Credit** are available to certain lower income families and lone parents, reducing as income rises: see Table 23, *post*, and *@eGlance*.

Impact of domicile status: Whereas a UK-resident individual is usually subject to income tax on worldwide income and gains as they arise, those who are not domiciled in the UK can choose to make use of the remittance basis (paying, in some cases, a charge to do so). Broadly, this allows them to be taxed on foreign source income and gains only if and to the extent such are remitted to the UK.

Domicile status is determined in accordance with the general law, but there are now two categories of

Table 11 Income Tax

individual who are to be treated as domiciled in the UK for tax purposes and therefore are not able to rely on the remittance basis:

- those born in the UK with a domicile of origin in the UK, while they are resident here
- those resident in the UK for at least 15 of the 20 prior tax years

The taxation rules in relation to non- and deemed domicile status are very complex and have CGT and IHT ramifications: specialist and case-specific advice are imperative.

	Tax year					
	18-19	*17-18*	*16-17*	*15-16*	*14-15*	*13-14*
Income Tax Rates						
20% on first taxable	34,500	33,500	32,000	31,785	31,865	32,010
40% higher rate on next	115,500	116,500	118,000	118,215	118,135	117,990
and 45% additional rate over	150,000	150,000	150,000	150,000	150,000	150,000
Income Tax Reliefs						
Personal allowance	11,850*	11,500*	11,000*	10,600*	10,000*	9,440*
Personal Savings Allowance						
(basic rate taxpayers)	1,000	1,000	1,000	—	—	—
(higher rate taxpayers)	500	500	500	—	—	—
Dividend allowance	2,000	5,000	5,000	—	—	—
Age allowances						
Born after 5 April 1938 but before 6 April 1948**	—	—	—	—	10,500*	10,000*
Born before 6 April 1938**	—	—	—	10,660*	10,660*	10,660*
Born before 6 April 1935: Married couple's allowance* **	8,695	8,445	8,355	8,355	8,165	7,915
income limit	28,900	28,000	27,700	27,700	27,000	26,100

*   These personal allowances are reduced (potentially unto extinction) by £1 for every £2 of income over £100,000.

**   These age-related allowances were reduced (as far as the basic personal allowance) by £1 for every £2 of income over the income limit.

*** For allowances thus marked the tax saving is restricted to 10%.

Table 12 National Insurance Contributions

Class 1 Earnings Limits and Thresholds, Class 2, 3 and 4 Limits, and State Pension Contributions

		2018-19	2017-18
Class 1	Lower earnings limit (LEL)	£116 p.w.	£113 p.w.
	Primary threshold (PT)	£162 p.w.	£157 p.w.
	Secondary threshold (ST)	£162 p.w.	£157 p.w.
	Upper earnings limit (UEL)	£892 p.w.	£866 p.w.
Class 2	Flat rate contribution	£2.95 p.w.	£2.85 p.w.
	Small profits threshold (SPT)	£6,205 p.a.	£6,025 p.a.
Class 3	Flat rate voluntary contribution	£14.65 p.w.	£14.25 p.w.
Class 4	Lower profits limit (LPL)	£8,424 p.a.	£8,164 p.a.
	Upper profits limit (UPL)	£46,350 p.a.	£45,000 p.a.
	Contribution rate		
	up to LPL	nil	nil
	LPL to UPL	9%	9%
	over UPL	2%	2%

Single Tier State Pension		
Primary contribution (employee)	On weekly earnings up to PT (£162)	nil
	then on weekly earnings up to UEL (£892)	12%
	and on any earnings above UEL	2%
Secondary contribution (employer)	On weekly earnings up to ST (£162)	nil
	then on any above that threshold, without limit	13.8%

Note

Since 6 April 2016 the basic State Pension and the State Second Pension provisions have been replaced by a new single-tier State Pension, and consequently the former ability to contract out of the State Second Pension with a Contracted-out Salary Related (COSR) pension scheme (also known as a 'defined benefit' (DB) scheme) then came to an end.

See Table 21 for more detail and a table of comparisons between the old and the new State Pensions.

No Class 1 contributions are payable by or for those whose earnings do not exceed PT (£162 p.w.).

The Class 1 reduced contribution rate for married women and widow optants is 5.85% of earnings from £162 p.w. up to £892 p.w., and 2% on any earnings which exceed that amount.

Class 2 NICs are paid at a weekly flat rate of £2.95 by all self-employed persons unless their profits are below SPT (£6,205 p.a.).

Class 3 NICs can be paid by contributors to make the year a qualifying year for basic State Pension, new State Pension and Bereavement Benefit purposes.

Table 13 Income Tax and National Insurance Marginal Deductions

Marginal rates of income tax are well known (0%, 20%, 40% and 45%) and in this Table are aggregated with National Insurance rates (12% above this year's primary threshold of £162 p.w., reducing to 2% on income over £46,350 p.a.) to arrive at overall marginal rates for income from employment.

The cumulative effect of these deductions and thus the overall percentage impact on gross income is opaque because of personal allowances, tax banding and the progressive withdrawal of personal allowances on income over £100,000.

The Table shows the overall deduction rate on selected earned incomes and the marginal rate of tax applied to the top tranche of a taxpayer's gross income from employment.

Overall deduction rate (%)	Gross income (£)	Applicable marginal rate (%)	Composition
10.00	15,368	32	Basic rate (20%) + NI (12%)
12.50	17,338		
15.00	19,887		
17.50	23,317		
20.00	28,175		
22.50	35,588		
24.71	46,351	42	Basic rate ceiling / Higher rate commences
25.00	47,133		Higher rate (40%) + NI (2%)
27.50	55,259		
30.00	66,771		
30.55	70,000		
31.98	80,000		
32.50	84,343		
33.10	90,000		
33.99	100,001	62	Begin withdrawal of personal allowance
35.00	103,750		Higher rate (40%) + NI (2%) + withdrawal of personal allowance
37.50	114,337		
39.35	123,701	42	Personal allowance exhausted
39.48	130,000		
39.66	140,000		
39.82	150,001	47	Higher rate ceiling / Additional rate commences
40.00	153,894		Additional rate (45%) + NI (2%)
42.50	239,390		
43.00	269,314		
43.50	307,788		
44.00	359,085		
44.50	430,903		
45.00	538,628		
45.50	718,172		
46.00	1,077,258		
46.25	1,436,343		
46.50	2,154,505		

This Table utilises 2018-19 income tax and national insurance contribution rates.

No account is taken in these examples of any savings or dividend income.

See Tables 11 for **Income Tax**, 12 for **National Insurance Contributions**, and 17 for **Gross Salary and Net Income**.

Table 14 Capital Gains Tax

Capital Gains Tax for disposals (actual or notional) during 2018-19

Basis and rate of tax

Gains (the excess of disposal proceeds over *base cost*, which includes acquisition and disposal costs and enhancement expenditure) which surpass any available *annual exempt allowance* (AEA) are taxable.

- The rate is **10%** where total taxable gains **and** income in aggregate do not exceed the upper limit of the income tax basic rate band (£34,500 for 2018-19), and **20%** for any part of a gain above that limit.
- On any part of a disposal of residential property (including property bought to let) that does not qualify for *private residence relief* (see *below*), the rates are instead **18%** below and **28%** above that same limit.
- In calculating total taxable gains and income for this purpose all allowable deductions (including losses, and the income tax personal allowance) and the AEA (see *below*) are taken into account.
- Individual taxpayers when calculating CGT can apply losses and the AEA to reduce their chargeable gain in the way most advantageous to them, although this is subject to some restrictions. So the AEA and losses may be applied to gains which would otherwise attract tax at 28% or 20%.
- For trustees and personal representatives of deceased persons, the rate is 20% (or 28% for residential property) regardless of their total income and gains (unless Entrepreneurs' Relief *below* applies).

The annual exempt allowance (AEA). For 2018-19 the first £11,700 of gains made by individuals is exempt from tax. For estates the same exemption applies in the tax year of death and for the next two years. The exemption for trustees is normally half that applicable to individuals.

The base cost of any asset acquired before 31 March 1982 is its market value on that date.

Capital losses are set against current year gains or, so far as losses exceed gains, future gains.

Fungible assets (intangible assets of the same type, such as shares of the same class in a company) acquired in separate transactions at varying base costs, are pooled and treated as a single asset. Where part-disposal of the holding is made, the base cost of the part sold is the average of the aggregate base cost of all acquisitions.

Private residence relief

Any gain on the disposal of the former matrimonial home (if the spouses' principal private residence) will usually be relieved from tax, though relief may be restricted or unavailable in some cases such as where:

- the couple has more than one residence
- they did not elect the property as their principal private residence throughout their period of ownership
- the property has been let
- they have not lived in it throughout the period of their ownership
- one or both of the spouses was not resident for tax purposes in the UK throughout the period of ownership.

Disposals between spouses

Disposals between spouses in tax years up to and including the year of separation are treated as made at an amount which produces neither a gain nor a loss.

Entrepreneurs' Relief

Broadly, individuals and trustees who dispose of all or part of a business or asset used in a business may qualify for relief which has the effect of reducing the tax rate to 10% on gains up to a *lifetime* limit of £10M per individual. The same relief applies also to disposals of shares where the owner holds at least 5% of the ordinary shares in a trading company and is a director or employee. This relief will in due course also be available to long-term external investors to whom shares have been issued on or after 17 March 2016: to qualify such shares must be in an unlisted trading company, and be held for at least a 3-year period subsequent to 6 April 2016. *These rules are complex: specialist advice must be sought where applicable.*

Enveloped Dwellings liable to ATED are liable to CGT at the rate of 28% on any gain on disposal (see Table 7 at page 12).

Capital gains by companies

These are calculated after applying indexation relief throughout the ownership period. The gains less allowable capital losses are added to the profit for corporation tax and taxed at the company's corporation tax rate. There is no annual exemption. A capital loss that cannot be offset against gains is carried forward. *Company taxation generally is a complex area outside the scope of this Table.*

The information in this Table is necessarily summarised in condensed form: specialist taxation advice should always be sought in all but the most straightforward situations.

Calculators for CGT liabilities arising (actually or notionally) during 2018-19 will be found in @eGlance

Table 15 Inheritance Tax

Inheritance Tax rates for chargeable transfers during the year commencing 6 April 2018

	Nil rate band (NRB)	Excess over £325,000
On death	First £325,000	Chargeable at 40%
Lifetime transfers (other than PETs)	First £325,000	Chargeable at 20%

Transfer of NRB may be available on the death of a surviving spouse. This applies whenever the first spouse died. Where one spouse or civil partner dies with a chargeable estate of less than the NRB applicable at the date of the first death, the unused *proportion* of the NRB at that date is transferred to the surviving spouse. On the death of the surviving spouse, that *proportion* is applied to the NRB in force in the year of the second death, and is available in addition to the surviving spouse's own NRB.

Reasons why the chargeable estate of the first to die may be less than the NRB include where he or she leaves all or part of their estate to the surviving spouse or civil partner as such legacy is exempt, or is subject to legacies and/or lifetime gifts (*below*) within the NRB.

Lower rate: A reduced rate of 36% applies on death where 10% or more of the value of the estate (above the NRB) is donated to charity. The legislation is complex: expert advice should be sought.

From 6 April 2017 an additional NRB (initially £100,000 for 2017-18; £125,000 for 2018-19) applies when a residence passes on death to a direct descendant. The additional NRB is tapered (potentially to extinction) where the estate exceeds £2M. This additional NRB may also be available where the deceased has down-sized or sold a residence after 8 July 2015. This relief to any extent unused is transferable to a surviving spouse or civil partner. Expert advice should be sought.

For individuals, **unlimited exemption** applies to gifts in life or on death to –

- a UK domiciled spouse or civil partner (or, if that person elects to be treated as UK domiciled, to either)
- UK registered charities
- qualifying political parties

and to regular lifetime gifts out of income.

There are also **exemptions** for –

- lifetime gifts of £3,000 per fiscal year in total (plus any unused balance from the previous year)
- small gifts of up to £250 per fiscal year per donee
- lifetime gifts in consideration of marriage or registration of a civil partnership up to:
  - £5,000 by each parent of either party
  - £2,500 by a grandparent or other direct linear ancestor of either party
  - £2,500 from one party to the other
  - £1,000 by any other donee.

The following paragraphs apply to transactions after 22 March 2006.

Lifetime gifts to individuals constitute **potentially exempt transfers (PETs)**. PETs are not subject to inheritance tax at the date of gift, but if the donor dies within seven years thereafter are taxable at death rates.

The rate progressively reduces by 20% upon the donor surviving to the third and each subsequent anniversary of the gift, and thus after seven years the liability is extinguished. Successive lifetime chargeable transfers within seven years are cumulated, as are PETs which have become chargeable transfers on death.

Lifetime gifts not ranking as PETs (such as gifts to most trusts) are immediately chargeable at the lifetime rates pertaining at the date of the gift. This liability is revised to death rates if the donor dies within seven years, with progressive reduction as for PETs.

For **trusts**, except for certain trusts for minors and where there was an existing life tenant at 21 March 2006, a charge to tax potentially arises:

- where assets cease to be held on trust
- up to a maximum of 6% every ten years from the date on which the trust was set up.

The effect of these rules is ameliorated for certain trusts for minors and disabled beneficiaries, but the rules and calculations are complex and beyond this note's scope. Specialist advice should be sought in this area.

Caveats: The taxation principles outlined deal only with UK domiciled individuals.

Other reliefs apply to certain transfers of business and agricultural property and of shares in specific types of company.

Professional advice should invariably be sought as this is only a simplified and condensed summary

Table 16   Taxing Times

Income tax and capital gains tax

Under the self-assessment regime tax is to be paid on and returns filed by the following dates:

Due date	Requirement	Assessment year
31 July 2018	Second payment on account	2017-18
31 October 2018	Last filing date for paper return	2017-18
31 January 2019	Balance of income tax	2017-18
	Capital gains tax	2017-18
	Last filing date for online return	2017-18
	First payment on account	2018-19
31 July 2019	Second payment on account	2018-19
31 January 2020	Balance of income tax	2018-19
	Capital gains tax	2018-19
	First payment on account	2019-20

Each payment on account is 50% of the preceding year's total net income tax bill, unless the taxpayer applies and HMRC agree that the payment be reduced. If the reduced amount proves insufficient to cover one half of the year's liability, interest will be charged on the balance of the original on account amount from each due date until the balance is paid. Penalties (see *below*) may also arise.

The onus is on the taxpayer to pay the correct tax due, whether or not he has an up-to-date statement and payslip from HMRC and irrespective of the amount of tax shown on any payslip.

Interest
Interest is chargeable on tax, national insurance contributions and penalties paid after the date on which they were due to be paid. At the time of writing the rate is 3% per annum.

Penalties: Late and Incorrect Returns (in relation to 2010-11 and subsequent years)
Penalties (cumulative) for *failure to file a tax return on time* without reasonable excuse:
- up to 3 months late: £100
- up to 6 months late: a daily penalty of £10 for 90 days
- up to 12 months late: higher of £300 or 5% of tax established as due on the return when filed (even if already paid on account)
- over 12 months late: a further penalty of the higher of £300 or 5% of tax due (established as *above*) or up to 100% if information which would enable HMRC to assess the tax due is deliberately withheld (but up to 200% if relating to offshore matters).

Further penalties are payable *in the event of an incorrect return*. A tariff applies: between nil and 30% of extra tax due if the error was as a result of a lack of reasonable care; between 20% and 70% if deliberate; or between 30% and 100% if deliberate and concealed. These penalties can rise to 200% for offshore matters.

Penalties will be towards the lower end of the tariff ranges shown if the taxpayer admits the mistake to HMRC unprompted, and also if assistance is given in determining the extra tax due.

Penalties: Late Payment (in relation to 2010-11 and subsequent years)
Penalties (cumulative) for *late payment of tax due* without reasonable excuse:
- after 30 days: 5% of tax due
- after 6 months: additional 5% of tax due
- after 12 months: additional 5% of tax due.

No penalties will be levied where HMRC has agreed that payment may be deferred for a period.

Interest on tax overpaid
'Repayment supplement' is payable on tax repayments, including:
- repayments of interim payments and other tax paid directly, from the date paid until the repayment date
- repayments of tax deducted at source, from 31 January following the year of assessment until the repayment date.

At the time of writing the rate is 0.5% per annum.

Table 16 Taxing Times

Inheritance tax

On chargeable lifetime transfers

Between 2 October and 5 April	Six months after the end of the month in which the chargeable transfer is made
Between 6 April and 1 October	On 30 April in the following year.

On death

Six months after the end of the month in which death occurred (save where payment by instalments is available, see *below*).

Where the IHT account is delivered before six months after the end of the month in which the death occurs, tax must be paid on delivery of the account.

Tax arising in cases where lifetime transfers become chargeable on the death — Six months after the end of the month in which the death occurred (save where payment by instalments is available, see *below*).

Tax arising on the transfer on death of *inter alia* land and buildings, certain shares and businesses may be paid by ten equal yearly instalments.

Interest

Interest is chargeable with effect from the due date on late paid inheritance tax.

At the time of writing the rate is 3% per annum.

Penalties

HMRC are empowered to charge penalties:

- for failure to submit timely inheritance tax accounts without reasonable excuse

- for inaccurate accounts.

Legislation provides for penalties for late payment but no announcement has yet been made of anticipated commencement dates.

Corporation tax

Under self-assessment a company's corporation tax is due nine months after the end of the accounting period. Large companies (broadly companies whose profit exceeds £1.5M) are required to pay corporation tax in quarterly instalments commencing six months and 13 days from the start of the accounting period. Such arrangements (including the interest provisions) are beyond the scope of this Table.

Interest

Corporation tax paid late is subject to an interest charge, at the time of writing of 3% per annum.

Overpayments of corporation tax

These attract interest ('repayment supplement') of 0.5% per annum at the time of writing.

Value added tax

Return and payment 1 month from quarter end (plus 7 days if paid online); or, if an annual accounting scheme, by 2 months after annual accounting date (plus interim payments meanwhile).

Stamp duty land tax

Payable 30 days from completion.

Sanctions arise on default.

Table 17 Gross Salary and Net Income

Net income derived from gross annual salary for 2018-19

A	B	C	D
Gross salary (£ per annum)	**Net income (£ per annum)**	**Gross salary (£ per annum)**	**Net income (£ per annum)**
Up to 8,424	Same as gross	20,000	16,501
9,000	8,931	25,000	19,781
10,000	9,811	27,500	21,421
11,000	10,691	30,000	23,061
12,000	11,541	32,500	24,701
13,000	12,221	35,000	26,341
14,000	12,901	37,500	27,981
15,000	13,581	40,000	29,621
16,000	14,261	45,000	32,901
17,000	14,941	50,000	36,113
18,000	15,621	55,000	38,923
19,000	16,301	60,000	41,733
20,000	16,981	65,000	44,543
21,000	17,661	70,000	47,353
22,000	18,341	80,000	52,973
23,000	19,021	90,000	58,593
24,000	19,701	100,000	64,213
25,000	20,381	125,000	74,013
26,000	21,061	150,000	87,573
27,000	21,741	175,000	100,635
28,000	22,421	200,000	113,473
29,000	23,101	250,000	139,148
30,000	23,781	300,000	164,823
35,000	27,181	350,000*	190,773*
40,000	30,581	400,000*	217,273*
50,000	37,013	500,000*	270,273*

The assumptions

Columns **A** & **B**: assume no pension contributions.

Columns **C** & **D**: assume 3% contributory pension (but for the asterisked entries contributions are capped at £10,000 as gross salary exceeds £333,333, as explained in Table 21, **Pension Overview**).

For individualised calculations which allow for non-salary income (including savings, dividends and from self-employment), pension contributions and capital gains use @eGlance's calculator

Table 18 Grossed-up Net Maintenance

The gross-income equivalent of maintenance, and some comparable salaries: 2018-19 tax rates

Maint. (£)	Gross (£)	Comparable gross salaries
10,000	10,575	
12,000	13,139	Army (new entrant) £14,931, NHS Care Support Worker (B) £15,404
14,000	16,188	
14,456	16,286	National Living Wage (over 25s £7.83 p.h. x 40 hrs x 52 weeks) £16,286
16,000	19,236	Army Private (B) £18,488, Nurse (new-qualified) £22,128, Teacher (new-qualified, B) £22,467
18,000	22,285	Junior Hospital Doctor (B) £22,862, Minimum stipend (CofE) £23,800
20,000	25,334	Lance Corporal (B) £25,524, Registered nurse (T) £28,747
22,500	29,145	NHS Registrar (B) £30,302
25,000	32,956	Sergeant (B) £33,490, Archdeacon £34,700, Bishop (B) £35,500, Senior Nurse (T) £35,577
27,500	36,767	Teacher (Advanced Skills, B) £38,984, Captain (B) £40,025
30,000	40,578	Bishop (T) £43,510, Head Teacher (B) £44,102
32,500	44,389	NHS Registrar (T) £47,647
35,000	48,020	Matron (T) £48,514, Major (B) £50,417
37,500	52,469	
40,000	56,917	Teacher (Advanced Skills, T) £59,264
42,500	61,365	Bishop of London £62,970, Civil Service Band 1 (B) £65,650
45,000	65,814	Archbishop of York £68,700
47,500	70,262	Lieutenant Colonel (B) £70,760
50,000	74,711	NHS Consultant (B) £76,001, MP £76,011
52,500	79,159	Archbishop of Canterbury £80,160
55,000	83,607	Salaried GP (T) £84,453, Colonel (B) £85,726, Civil Service Band 2 (B) £87,870
57,500	88,056	
60,000	92,504	
62,500	96,953	
65,000	101,401	Brigadier (B) £102,158, District Judge £104,990, Junior Gov't Minister £105,073, Civil Service Band 3 (B) £107,060
67,500	107,303	Head Teacher (T) £108,283, Major General (B) £113,810
70,000	114,096	Minister of State £115,093, District Judge (CFC) £116,826
72,500	120,889	Civil Service Band 1 (T) £123,736, Major General (T) £125,384
75,000	127,629	
77,500	132,077	Lieutenant General (B) £132,420, Circuit Judge £134,841
80,000	136,525	
82,500	140,974	
85,000	145,422	Senior Circuit Judge £145,614, Permanent Secretary (B) £147,848
87,500	149,871	Prime Minister £151,451
90,000	154,319	
92,500	159,157	Lieutenant General (T) £160,518
95,000	164,026	
97,500	168,894	Civil Service Band 2 (T) £170,688, General (B) £173,715
100,000	173,763	NHS Consultant (T) £179,019, High Court Judge £181,566
105,000	183,500	
110,000	193,237	General (T) £194,630
115,000	202,974	Lord Justice of Appeal £206,742
120,000	212,711	Supreme Ct Justice & Fam Div President £217,409, Civil Service Band 3 (T) £218,585
125,000	222,449	Master of the Rolls £225,091
130,000	232,186	Chief of Defence Staff (B) £250,270
140,000	251,660	Lord Chief Justice £252,079, Chief of Defence Staff (T) £265,589
150,000	271,134	Permanent Secretary (T) £288,468

In calculating the grossed-up equivalent salary 3% pension contributions have been assumed.

Most salaries effective April 2017 (the latest figures available when we went to press: updated 2018-19 figures will be in *@eGlance v2019.2*).

All categories are subject to varying terms and conditions, and some benefit (more or less) from expenses. (B) and (T) indicate bottom/top of range/seniority for rank/post.

Table 19 Financial Remedy Procedure

*Table A sets out procedural steps for all applications for a financial remedy (FPR 2.3: see page 62) currently issued in the Family Court **save for** (a) the applications to which Chapter 5 applies (**Table B** below); (b) pension sharing orders (see Table 22); and (c) pension attachment orders (see **@eGlance**).*

Table B sets out the shorter Chapter 5 procedure (see Financial Remedy Rules at page 67) for variation applications generally and applications under: CA 1989 Sch 1; DPMCA 1978 (and corresponding proceedings under CPA 2004); art 56 of the EU Maintenance Regulation; and art 10 of the 2007 Hague Convention (in the latter two cases following transmission of the application via the Central Authority: see MS v PS (Case C-283/16), [2017] 1 FLR 1163, CJEU, AB v JJB (EU Maintenance Regulation: modification application procedure) [2015] EWHC 192 (Fam), [2015] 2 FLR 1143). The Chapter 5 procedure applies to all such applications unless the Court directs that the standard Chapter 4 procedure be followed.

***Venue, allocation and transfer**: see the President's Guidance: Jurisdiction of the Family Court etc. (28 February 2018), summarised in **Winds of Change** at page vi. By virtue of para 18 of this Guidance a financial remedy application ancillary to divorce, dissolution etc. must be issued in the Family Court (FC) even where the High Court (HC) also has jurisdiction. In the currently piloted Financial Remedies Courts Form A must be issued at the local hub. Applications must otherwise be issued in the divorce centre (with the sole exception that it is permissible to file a Form A at the CFC, notwithstanding that the petition has been issued at a (non-pilot) divorce centre, on completion of a certificate of financial complexity: see para 9.10 of the **@eGlance** Commentary). There is no such restriction on the issue of a Form A seeking other forms of financial remedy. Judicial allocation within the FC is regulated by the Family Court (Composition and Distribution of Business) Rules 2014 (in **@eGlance**). For the procedure and guidance where parties seek allocation to a HC Judge see page 74. Proceedings may be transferred between HC and FC, but FC may transfer its own proceedings to HC only if PD 29C applies or the transfer is ordered by the President, or a Court of Appeal or HC judge (rule 29.17(3), as to which see page 71).*

*Before any financial remedy application (a) the MIAMs requirement applies and (b) the Court expects compliance with the **Pre-application Protocol (Annex to PD 9A)** (see **@eGlance**). The overriding objective (rules 1.1 to 1.4) applies to every stage of financial remedy proceedings.*

*Note that the **Bundles Practice Direction** (PD 27A: see page 75) applies to **all** hearings in the FC, whatever the length of time estimate. Urgent applications are only excepted to the extent that compliance with the Direction is impossible.*

Table A: standard financial remedy procedure

Phase 1: To end of First Appointment ('FA')

	Step	Party	Timing	FPR rule or PD
1	Filing of application including, where it relates to land, details of any mortgagee	Either		PD 9A para 1.3
	Unless the application is by consent, it must contain or be accompanied by a MIAM form			3.6 to 3.8 and PD 3A paras 11, 13 and 14
	(Form A – financial orders)		In an application for a matrimonial / civil partnership order or at any time after such an application has been made	9.4(a) and (b)
	(Form A1 etc – other financial remedies)		At any time	PD 5A para 3.1
2	In the Family Court, allocation to the appropriate level of judge	Court		FC(CDB) Rules 2014, rule 15 and Sch 1 and rule 20 and the Self-Certification Guidance of 1 February 2016: see page 74
	Where there has been allocation without a hearing, a party may request the Court to reconsider allocation at a hearing	Either	At the hearing at which the applicant party first has notice of allocation or in writing no later than 2 days before the first hearing after receiving notice of allocation	29.19
3	Fixing of First Appointment **12 to 16 weeks** ahead (**Form C**)	Court	When Form A is issued	9.12(1)(a)
	NB: No cancellation of date without permission			9.12(3)
4	Service of copy of applications in Form A / A1 etc and C	Court OR	Within **4 days** after Form A / A1 etc filed	9.12(1)(b)
		Applicant	Within 4 days of receipt of Form A / A1 etc and C from the Court	9.12(2)(c)(i)

Table 19 Financial Remedy Procedure

	Step	Party	Timing	FPR rule or PD
5	Filing of certificate where service effected by Applicant	Applicant	At or before the First Appointment	9.12(2)(c)(ii)
6	Filing and **simultaneous exchange** of **Form E / E1 as applicable** completed and verified by a statement of truth by each party*, and attaching • the documents **required** by the Form • any other documents **necessary** to explain or clarify the information • pension information provided under 9.30 or 9.37(2), (4), or (5) (but no other documents). The **required** documents are • property valuations obtained in last 6 months • most recent mortgage statements • last 12 months' bank statements • latest statement or dividend counterfoil for stocks, shares and similar investments • surrender valuations of insurance policies • last 2 years' business accounts • any available documentation on the basis of which the value of a business is estimated • CE of pension arrangements (in the case of the additional state pension, valuation of rights) / PPF entitlement valuation • last 3 payslips and most recent P60 and P11D • (self employed / partnership) last tax assessment or accountant's letter in default • (self employed / partnership) where next 12 months' estimated income differs significantly from last 12 months', management accounts for period since last accounts	Both	At least **35 days** before FA	9.14(1) 9.14(2)(b)(i) and (ii) 9.14(2)(b)(iii) and (iv) See schedule of documents to accompany Form E
	Bundle of exhibits to Form E must comply with PD 22A (and note in particular paras 11.3 and 13.1)	Both		PD 9A para 5.1
	* Note different provision for art 56, EUMR and art 10, Hague Convention cases			9.14(2ZA) and (2A)
7	Service of documents required by but unavoidably not attached to Form E (with explanation)	Either	At earliest opportunity	9.14(3)
	But **NO general disclosure or inspection before FA**	Neither		9.14(4)
8	Filing and service of • Concise statement of issues • Chronology • Questionnaire, **referable to the statement of issues**, seeking further information and documents, or a statement that none are required • Notice **(Form G)** stating whether that party will be able to proceed to FDR at the FA	Both Both Both Both	At least **14 days** before FA	9.14(5)
	Confirmation of service of persons referred to in rule 9.13(1) to (3)	Applicant		9.14(6)
	Parties should also if possible with a view to identifying and narrowing the issues exchange and file a **case summary, agreed schedule of assets and proposed directions** including name of any proposed expert (subject to requirements of Part 25)			PD 9A paras 4.1 and 4.2
9	Produce first costs estimate **(Form H)**	Both	At FA	9.27(1) & PD 9A paras 3.1 to 3.2
	Information in Form H must be as full and accurate as possible and set out clearly sums already paid			PD 9A para 3.2
	If a party intends to seek a summary assessment of costs, produce a Woolf costs schedule following **N260** as closely as possible		24 hours before FA	PD 28A para 4.5; CPR PD 44, para 9.5(3) and (4)(b)

19

Table 19 Financial Remedy Procedure

	Step	Party	Timing	FPR rule or PD
10	**THE FIRST APPOINTMENT** **Objective:** to define issues and save costs	Both parties to attend personally unless otherwise directed Court	On date fixed 12 to 16 weeks after filing of Form A (Step 3)	9.15(1) 9.15(8)
	Directions as to: • Answering questions and producing documents, and any further **necessary** documentation, **to be verified by a statement of truth**			9.15(2) PD 9A para 5.2
	• Valuations (joint if appropriate)			9.15(3)
	• Obtaining and exchanging expert evidence			
	• Evidence to be adduced by each party			
	• Further chronologies, schedules			
	Consideration may need to be given to possible joinder of a party/parties			9.26B
	Court must direct FDR unless First Appointment effective as FDR or for exceptional reasons FDR is inappropriate.		Date for FDR on **Form D**	9.15(4)
	If FDR is inappropriate the Court must direct one or more of:			9.15(5)
	• Hearing for further directions			
	• Hearing for interim order			
	• Final hearing (and at which judicial level)			
	• Adjournment for ADR, if appropriate			3.3
	The Court *may* in addition / alternative:			9.15(7)
	• Make interim order, if such application listed for consideration			
	• Having regard to Forms G (see Step 8), treat appointment or part of it as FDR			
	• Direct party with pension rights to file and serve Pension Inquiry Form (Form P) / Pension Protection Fund Inquiry Form (Form PPF)			
	Costs: In considering whether to make a costs order under rule 28.3(6) the Court must have particular regard to the extent to which each party has complied with the requirement to send documents with Form E, and to any breach of the pre-action protocol or PD 9A	Court		9.15(6) & 28.3(5) PD 9A paras 3.3 and 3.4

Phase 2: To end of Financial Dispute Resolution Appointment ('FDR')

	Step	Party	Timing	FPR rule or PD
11	**Comply with all directions made at FA**	Both	As per directions order	
	Any further production of documents only with Court permission	Both	Between the FA and FDR	9.16(1)
12	**Application for / giving of further directions OR application for / directing FDR**	Both / Court	By application at any stage	9.16(2)
13	Where FDR has been ordered:			
	Notice to Court of all offers, proposals and responses, including without prejudice offers (but excluding offers made during non-court dispute resolution)	Applicant	At least **7 days** before FDR	9.17(3) PD 9A para 6.4
	Produce second costs estimate in Form H	Both	At FDR	9.27(1) & PD 9A para 3.1 to 3.2
	Information in Form H must be as full and accurate as possible and set out clearly sums already paid			PD 9A para 3.2

Table 19 Financial Remedy Procedure

	Step	Party	Timing	FPR rule or PD
14	**THE FDR APPOINTMENT** For practical advice on the FDR see the *Financial Dispute Resolution Appointments: Best Practice Guidance* produced by the Family Justice Council in December 2012 (available online and in *@eGlance*) **Objective:** 'parties must use best endeavours to reach agreement' **Ground rules:** • 'A meeting held for the purposes of discussion and negotiation': see *Rose v Rose* [2002] 1 FLR 978 • Parties must approach the occasion openly and without reserve and non-disclosure of the content of the meeting is vital • The Court will expect the parties to make offers and proposals and consider those received • Conducted by a judge who will not have anything else to do with the case save as set out *below* • Legal representatives will be expected to have full knowledge of the case • Offer details lodged are not to be kept on Court file after FDR **DJ *may* then only** (*Myerson* [2009] 1 FLR 826) • Adjourn from time to time • Make appropriate consent order • Give further directions / fix final hearing Note: Where FDR has failed in a substantial case narrative affidavits of the financial history should be ordered: *W v W* [2000] Fam Law 473 per Wilson J **Costs:** The Court may make an order for costs where it is appropriate because of the conduct of a party in relation to the proceedings (see Step 20 for the matters to which the Court must have regard) and having regard to any breach of the pre-action protocol or PD 9A	Both parties to attend personally unless otherwise ordered: 9.17(10)	On date fixed at FA (Step 10)	9.17(6) 9.17(1) and PD 9A para 6.1 PD 9A para 6.2 PD 9A para 6.3 9.17(2) PD 9A para 6.5 9.17(5) 9.17(7) 9.17(8) 9.17(9) 28.3(6), PD 28A paras 4.3 and 4.4 and PD 9A paras 3.3 and 3.4
15	**Application for interim order** • The Part 18 procedure applies to an application for an interim order, which should be made in form D11 • Where the Applicant applies before filing of Form E, the written evidence must explain why the application is necessary and give up to date information about his means • Unless he has filed Form E, the Respondent must file and serve a statement of means at least 7 days before the hearing • A party may at any stage apply **without notice** for interim orders apart from maintenance or variation orders • Rule 28.3 (costs) only applies to interim variation applications • Specific rules apply to applications for legal services payment orders	Either Either	At any time Service at least 14 days before hearing	9.7(2); 18.8(1)(b) 9.7(3) 9.7(4) 9.7(5) 28.3(4)(b) and PD 28A paras 4.1; 4.2 PD 9A paras 12.1 and 12.2

Table 19 Financial Remedy Procedure

Phase 3: To final hearing

	Step	Party	Timing	FPR rule or PD
16	**Directions orders made at FDR to be complied with appropriately**	Both	As per directions order	
17	**Further directions / FDR**	Either party may apply or Court may direct	Any time	9.16(2)
18	**Statement of open proposals, setting out concise details, including the amounts involved** Unless Court otherwise directs, file with Court and serve on other party	Applicant	Not less than **14 days** before final hearing	9.28(1)
		Respondent	Not more than **7 days** after receipt of Applicant's statement	9.28(2)
19	**THE FINAL HEARING**		On date fixed at First Appointment (Step 10) or at FDR (Step 14) or otherwise	
	Unless Court otherwise directs, file and serve a statement of costs in Form H1 Information in Form H1 must be as full and accurate as possible and set out clearly sums already paid	Both	Not less than 14 days before final hearing	9.27(2) PD 9A para 3.2
20	**Costs after judgment** • Only open offers to settle are admissible at the final hearing • The general rule is that the Court will not make an order requiring one party to pay the costs of another; but the Court may make such an order where it considers it appropriate to do so because of the conduct of a party in relation to the proceedings • For the financial remedies to which the general rule applies see 28.3(4)(b) and PD 28A paras 4.1 and 4.2 • In deciding what order if any to make under 28.3(6) the Court must have regard to: – failure to comply with the rules, an order or relevant practice direction – any open offer to settle – whether it was reasonable for a party to raise, pursue or contest a particular allegation or issue – the manner in which a party has pursued or responded to the application or a particular allegation or issue – any other aspect of a party's conduct in relation to the proceedings which the Court considers relevant – the financial effect on the parties of any costs order CPR 44.2(1), (4) and (5) are disapplied CPR 44.2(6) to (8) and 44.12 are applied			PD 28A para 4.3 28.3(5) and PD 9A para 3.3 28.3(6) and PD 28A paras 4.3 and 4.4 28.3(7) 28.3(2) 28.3(3)

Table 19 Financial Remedy Procedure

Table B: abridged procedure for variation applications and applications under: DPMCA 1978/Sch 6, CPA 2004; Sch 1, CA 1989; art 56, EU Maintenance Regulation and art 10, 2007 Hague Convention

	Step	Party	Timing	FPR rule or PD
1	On issue of application Court fixes **first hearing date**	Court	Not less than 4 weeks and not more than 8 weeks after filing	9.18(1)(a)
	Unless the application is by consent, it must contain or be accompanied by a MIAM form			3.6 to 3.8 and PD 3A paras 11, 13 and 14
2	Unless Applicant wishes to serve application, Court will • Serve application on Respondent • Give notice of first hearing to both parties • Send blank financial statement to both parties (unless application made under art 56 of Maintenance Regulation or Art 10 of 2007 Hague Convention using prescribed forms)	Court	Within 4 days of filing of application	9.18(1)(b) 9.18(4)
3	If Applicant wishes to serve application and so notifies Court on filing • Court will return application and notice of first hearing date • Applicant must serve both on Respondent • Applicant must serve blank financial statement • File certificate of service	Applicant	 Within 4 days of receipt from Court At or before first hearing	9.18(2) 9.18(2)(b) 9.18(2)(c)
4	NB no cancellation of dates except with Court's permission: on cancellation new date must be fixed	Court		9.18(3)
5	If the Applicant wishes to seek direction that Chapter 4 procedure applies (as to which see **Table A** *above*) application must state reasons *'Examples of cases in which it may be appropriate to make such a request include an application under Schedule 1 to the 1989 Act in which there are contested issues about the settlement of property, or a variation application in which a capital payment or pension sharing order is proposed.'*	Applicant		9.18A(1) and (2) PD 9A para 1.2(b)
6	Court will determine application under Step 5 without notice and before first hearing and so inform parties and of any consequential directions	Court	Before first hearing	9.18A(3)
7	Simultaneous exchange and filing of financial statements (E1 / E2 in domestic cases) To be verified by statement of truth (save where application made under art 56 of Maintenance Regulation or Art 10 of 2007 Hague Convention using prescribed forms, in which case Court may direct verification)	Both	Not more than 14 days after issue of application	9.19(1) 9.19(2)(a) 9.19(2A)
8	Financial statements to contain only required documents and those necessary to explain or clarify information	Either		9.19(2)(b)
9	Service and filing (with explanation of failure to send with financial statement) of documents required by but unavoidably not attached to financial statement	Either	At earliest opportunity	9.19(3)
10	No disclosure or inspection between filing and first hearing except copies sent with financial statement or subsequently under Step 9	Both		9.19(4)
11	Unless able to determine application, Court may direct further evidence and set date for directions hearing / appointment / final hearing	Court		9.20

Table 20 The IFLA Arbitration Scheme

This arbitration procedure for financial dispute resolution was launched by the Institute of Family Law Arbitrators (**IFLA**, www.ifla.org.uk) in February 2012. Its stakeholders are Resolution, the FLBA and the Chartered Institute of Arbitrators (**CIArb**). The Scheme is governed by the Arbitration Act 1996 (**AA96**) and IFLA's Financial Arbitration Scheme Rules (**the Rules**: currently the 2016 (5th edition) Rules). IFLA on its website lists details of the **Panel of arbitrators**: experienced family law practitioners accredited by IFLA who have been trained by CIArb. Accredited arbitrators are awarded Membership of CIArb and are subject to its code and disciplinary procedures. A parallel IFLA Scheme for the resolution of private law children disputes was launched on 18 July 2016.

By art 2.1 of the Rules, the Scheme may be adopted for financial and property disputes arising from: marriage and its breakdown (including financial provision on divorce, judicial separation or nullity); civil partnership and its breakdown; co-habitation and its ending; parenting or sharing parental responsibility; and provision for dependants from a deceased's estate. The Scheme covers, but is not limited to, claims under the following statutes: MWPA 1882, s. 17; MCA 1973, Pt II; I(PFD)A 1975; MFPA 1984, Pt III (financial relief after overseas divorce); CA 1989, Sch 1; TLATA 1996; CPA 2004 Sch 5, or Sch 7, Part 1, para 2 (financial relief after overseas dissolution) (art 2.2).

The Scheme cannot be used to resolve questions directly concerning: the liberty of individuals; the status either of individuals or of their relationship; bankruptcy or insolvency; or any person or organisation not a party to the arbitration (art 2.3).

In their Form ARB1FS (Arbitration agreement), which they must submit to IFLA, parties may agree upon a particular Panel arbitrator, whom they may approach direct; or agree a shortlist, the 'at random' nomination of any one of whom by IFLA they would accept; or invite IFLA to offer the appointment to a Panel arbitrator whom it considers appropriate. IFLA will offer the appointment to the agreed arbitrator or (where IFLA is invited to select) to the arbitrator so nominated. If the appointment is not accepted by their first choice of arbitrator the parties may, if they agree, make a second or subsequent choice. Otherwise, it will be offered to another Panel member chosen by IFLA. For the detail of the procedure see art 4 of the Rules.

By their Form ARB1FS the parties agree to be bound by the arbitrator's written decision (the award), subject to (a) any right of appeal or other available challenge; (b) (insofar as the subject matter of the award requires it to be embodied in a court order) any changes which the court making that order may require; and (c) (in the case of an award of continuing payments) any future award or order varying the award (para 6.4 and art 13.3). They also agree that during the arbitration they will not apply to court save in connection with the arbitration or to seek relief that is not available in the arbitration (para 6.2); and, if and so far as the subject matter of the award makes it necessary, to apply to an appropriate court for an order in the same or similar terms as the award or the relevant part of the award (para 6.5 and art 13.4).

Disputes under the Scheme are arbitrated in accordance with the mandatory and non-mandatory provisions of AA96 as applied by the Rules, and subject to any modifying agreement of the parties (art 1.3). However, the parties may not agree to exclude, replace or modify the art 3 imperative that the substance of the dispute be arbitrated only in accordance with the law of England and Wales (art 1.3(c)). Thus the parties are able to shape their own process (with the agreement of the arbitrator once the arbitration commences (art 1.4)), subject always to the mandatory provisions of AA96 and art 3 of the Rules. Party autonomy is enshrined in the s. 1(b) of AA96 provision that 'the parties should be free to agree how their disputes are resolved, subject only to such safeguards as are necessary in the public interest'.

The arbitrator will generally give procedural directions at the outset of the arbitration, and as necessary during its course. The procedure adopted will depend on the nature of the issues in dispute and will range from determination on paper alone to full hearing with oral evidence, fashioned to meet the needs, means and particular characteristics of the case.

The award will be in writing and, unless the parties agree otherwise or the award is by consent, must contain sufficient reasons to show how and why the arbitrator has reached the decisions it contains (art 13.2).

While there are presumptions (unless the parties agree otherwise) that there will be no order for costs *inter partes* and that the parties will be liable for the arbitrator's fees in equal shares (art 14.4), the arbitrator has discretion to impose costs orders on the basis of conduct (art 14.5).

How the award is implemented will depend on the nature of the dispute. In financial remedy cases parties will in general apply to the court for an order confirming the terms of the award. Firm guidance supportive of the binding effect of an IFLA arbitration agreement and award was given by Munby P in *S v S* [2014] EWHC 7 (Fam), [2014] 1 FLR 1257, the import of which is that, while the jurisdiction of the court may not be ousted, it is only in rare circumstances that the court will decline to uphold the award. Express approval was given for 'fast tracking' consent orders based on arbitral awards as in the case of collaborative agreements (*S v P (settlement by collaborative process)* [2008] 2 FLR 2040).

Where, on the other hand, the court does not have a supervisory role (as for instance where the dispute involves a property claim between an unmarried couple) the award may be enforced, with leave of the court, as though it were a court judgment or order (AA96, s. 66(1)).

Table 20 The IFLA Arbitration Scheme

There are limited rights of challenge under the Act, and appeal on a point of law only (unless excluded by agreement): AA96, ss. 67 to 71. These remedies, and the court's jurisdiction to decline to uphold an award because of a *Barder* event or mistake, were comprehensively reviewed in *DB v DLJ* [2016] EWHC 324 (Fam), [2016] 2 FLR 1308.

In November 2015 the President issued Practice Guidance dealing with the interface between the arbitration process and the courts. In November 2017 he approved a number of arbitration-specific standard orders.

For more detail about the Scheme visit FamilyArbitrator.com where many up-to-date materials are also available for general use.

The text of AA 1996, the Rules, a word-processable Form ARB1FS, as well as the President's Practice Guidance and the suite of arbitration-specific orders, are all available in the arbitration module of @*eGlance*.

Key procedural provisions of the IFLA Scheme (based on the 2016 edition of the Rules)

	Step	IFLA Rules / AA96 section
1	Parties check that the dispute falls within the **scope** of the Scheme.	Art 2
2	Parties sign Form ARB1FS (application for family arbitration, available in @*eGlance* and at FamilyArbitrator.com) seeking EITHER the appointment of an arbitrator ('A') whom they may jointly approach direct OR that IFLA select at random one from a shortlist submitted by the parties OR that IFLA nominate a Panel arbitrator; and email the Form to info@ifla.org.uk (IFLA's preferred method), or send to IFLA, PO Box 302, Orpington, Kent BR6 8QX, or call 01689 820272.	Art 4.1 Art 4.3
3	By their ARB1FS parties agree *inter alia*: • to be **bound** by A's award (subject to court-made amendments) • **not to apply to court** during the arbitration save in connection therewith • if necessary, **to apply to court for an order** in the terms of the award.	Para 6.4 & art 13.3 Para 6.2 Para 6.5 & art 13.4
4	A must disclose any actual or potential **conflict of interest** or any matter raising justifiable doubt as to impartiality.	Art 5.1
5	The arbitration **commences** once A communicates acceptance (following agreement on A's terms and conditions). *Note*: A may convene, in advance of formal appointment, an **exploratory meeting** at which the parties can raise queries about the process, and A can ensure that they have understood their obligations.	Art 4.5
6	Disputes under the Scheme are arbitrated in accordance with: • the provisions of Arbitration Act 1996 ('**AA96**'), both mandatory and non-mandatory • the **Rules**, to the extent that they exclude, replace or modify the non-mandatory provisions of AA96, and • the parties' **agreement**, to the extent that that excludes, replaces or modifies the non-mandatory provisions of AA96 or the Rules. (Art 3, stipulating that the law of England and Wales be applied, is mandatory.)	Art 1.3 Art 1.3(c)
7	On commencement, A is likely to convene a **case management hearing** (in person or by telephone, videolink / Skype or email) and invite submissions as to the issues to be arbitrated, procedure etc. Directions may be given then or subsequently and at any stage in the arbitration.	Art 10.2 Art 11
8	While the parties are free to agree the **form of procedure**, once the arbitration has commenced A's consent is needed. A has wide discretion and extensive case-management powers.	Arts 1.4, 8.1 & 9; ss 33, 34 & 37
9	The Rules offer two **procedural templates**: • a CPR-type procedure ('general procedure') • a financial remedy-type procedure ('alternative procedure'). Variants, or a documents-only procedure or some other simplified or expedited procedure may be adopted.	 Art 10 Art 12 Art 9.1
10	The **court's powers** may be invoked in support of the arbitration.	ss 42 to 45
11	A's **award** must be in writing and contain reasons (unless agreed otherwise or the award is by consent).	Art 13.2
12	In financial remedy proceedings a **reflective court order** will generally be required to give effect to the award and thus a consent application (or if opposed, notice to show cause) should be issued: see *S v S* [2014] EWHC 7 (Fam); *DB v DLJ* [2016] EWHC 324 (Fam); and President's Practice Guidance (23/11/15). In stand-alone TLATA or MWPA proceedings AA96 s. 66 may facilitate **enforcement** of the award.	Art 13.4 s 66
13	Subject to A's overriding discretion to make a conduct-based costs order, there is a **'no order as to costs'** presumption (which may, subject to art 1.4, be disapplied by agreement).	Art 14.4 Art 14.5
14	The arbitration process may be **challenged** under the Act only on the following bases (discussed in *DB v DLJ* [2016] EWHC 324 (Fam)): • A's lack of jurisdiction (unlikely to arise under the Scheme given the clarity of ARB1FS) • a 'serious irregularity' causing substantial injustice • by agreement or with court's leave, on appeal on a point of law (unless expressly excluded by agreement). An award may also be challenged on the basis of a *Barder* event or mistake: *DB v DLJ, above*.	 s 67 s 68 s 69

20

Table 21 Pensions Overview

Pensions are a complex area. This text highlights only the key features of pensions in the family proceedings context. It is not (nor is it intended to be) a sufficient basis upon which to advise clients. Specialist advice from an independent financial adviser and/or an actuary will in most cases be essential.

The current pensions 'simplification' rules for registered pension schemes came into force on 6 April 2006 (**A-Day**) and are found in the Finance Act 2004, Part 4. Significant subsequent changes have been made, notably by the Taxation of Pensions Act 2014 (**TOPA**).

LIFETIME ALLOWANCE

The *lifetime allowance* (**LTA**) is the overall limit on the total amount of tax-relieved pension savings that an individual can have over his/her lifetime, subject however to the various *protection regimes* which have provided opportunities for individuals to enhance their LTA.

2010-11 and 2011-12	£1.8M
2012-13 and 2013-14	£1.5M
2014-15 and 2015-16	£1.25M
2016-17 and 2017-18	£1.0M
2018-19	£1.03M

From 6 April 2018 LTA increases annually in line with CPI.
- The following *protection regimes* can no longer be claimed:
  - *Primary protection* was available to individuals with existing pension funds valued at more than £1.5M on A-Day and gave them their own LTA, and *Enhanced protection* was available to any individual provided they ceased accruing further pension benefits.
  - *Fixed protection 2012* (FP 2012) provided an LTA of £1.8M, but only if contributions to all registered pension schemes ceased before 6 April 2012. And see **Note** *below*.
  - *Fixed protection 2014* (FP 2014) provided an LTA of £1.5M, but only if contributions to all registered pension schemes ceased before 6 April 2014. It was available for individuals who had not already registered for primary, enhanced or FP 2012. And see **Note** *below*.
  - *Individual protection 2014* (IP 2014) for those whose pension rights exceeded £1.25M on 5 April 2014, provided an individual LTA of up to £1.5M while enabling the individual to continue to save towards this limit. There was a 3-year period from 6 April 2014 to register for IP 2014 which could be claimed in addition to either enhanced protection, fixed protection 2012 or fixed protection 2014: but not by anyone holding primary protection.

Note that in the case of FPs 2012, 2014 and 2016 **deferred final salary benefits** may increase in value, but limited to the 'relevant percentage': an increase in the member's pension each year of up to either the rate used in the scheme rules at a specified date, or the CPI increase in each year ending with the previous September.
- These *protection regimes* remain available:
  - *Fixed protection 2016* (FP 2016) is available, whether or not benefits exceed £1M, provided that the individual does not hold primary protection, enhanced protection, fixed protection 2012 or fixed protection 2014. There can be no benefit accruals after 5 April 2016. An individual with FP 2016 has a fixed LTA of £1.25M. And see **Note** *above*.
  - *Individual protection 2016* (IP 2016) is available to an individual who does not have primary protection or IP 2014 and who has benefits worth £1M or more on 5 April 2016. IP 2016 allows for the benefits to continue to accrue. The individual will have a LTA equal to the capital value of benefits as at 5 April 2016 subject to a cap of £1.25M.
- A pension sharing order (**PSO**) pension debit does not reduce the transferor's LTA, permitting pension rebuilding (but where the party suffering the pension debit has elected for any form of protection the position is more complex).
- A pension credit counts towards the recipient's LTA.
- Tax relief on any pension savings above the LTA is recovered by the application of the *lifetime allowance tax charge* upon the excess at a rate of 25% if the excess is taken as a pension or 55% if taken as a lump sum.
- The impact, whether for the transferor or the transferee, that a PSO may have on any of these protections is a complex area requiring specialist advice.

ANNUAL ALLOWANCE

The *annual allowance* (**AA**) is the limit of an individual's annual pension savings which qualify for tax relief.

2010-11	£255,000
2011-12 to 2013-14	£50,000
2014-15 onwards	£40,000* (see note re **PIP** alignment)

* from 2015-16 **MPAA** (*below*) may apply.

- Relief is at an individual's marginal rate of tax up to 100% of an individual's UK taxable income (subject to the AA) or £3,600 (whichever is the greater).
- Carry forward of unused AA (but not MPAA) from up to 3 previous years is available to off-set against excess pension savings.
- From 6 April 2011, the AA limit is extended so as to apply also in the year benefits come into payment.
- AA is measured by reference to an annual *pension input period* (**PIP**) determined by the pension scheme and aligned to the tax year. Previously, PIPs were not necessarily aligned to tax years. During 2015-16 PIP periods were aligned with tax years and AA was increased to £80,000, equally split between 2 mini tax years: until, and from, 9 July 2015.
- From 6 April 2015, if income is taken via either *flexi-access drawdown* or UFPLS (see **Benefits Structure** *below*) a **Money Purchase Annual Allowance** (**MPAA**) of £4,000 replaces the normal AA from 2017-18.
- From 6 April 2016, those with an 'adjusted income' (adding tax relief on pension contributions and the value of employer contributions) of more than £150,000 will have their annual allowance restricted on a tapered basis so that, for every £2 of income exceeding £150,000, £1 of annual allowance is lost. There is a maximum taper of £30,000 so that the minimum tapered annual allowance is £10,000 for an individual with an adjusted income of £210,000 or more.

Table 21 Pensions Overview

- Neither a pension credit nor a pension debit resulting from a PSO counts towards an individual's AA.

MINIMUM BENEFIT AGE

- The Minimum Benefit Age (**MBA**) is 55 (except for incapacity retirement and any who as at 10 December 2003 had a contractual right to early retirement at age 50).
- From 6 April 2028, MBA will increase to age 57 and then be fixed at 10 years prior to state retirement age.
- MBA also applies to pension credit benefits (subject to individual scheme terms).
- Individuals taking pension benefit can continue working.

BENEFITS STRUCTURE

- From 6 April 2015, how benefits may be taken depends upon whether the scheme is defined benefit / final salary (**DB**) *OR* defined contribution / money purchase (**DC**).
- In the case of a DB scheme, a *pension commencement lump sum* of up to 25% of the value of the benefit (normally subject to an overriding limit of 25% of the LTA) may be taken as a tax-free lump sum. Income is provided by means of a scheme pension.
- In the case of a DC scheme, the opportunity to take up to 25% as a tax-free lump sum remains. But since TOPA, there are from 6 April 2015 three primary options available:
  - *Flexi-access drawdown* enables a pension commencement lump sum to be taken with the remainder of the fund paid as income over a period of time, or in one payment with no upper limit subject to tax at the individual's marginal rate.
  - *Uncrystallised funds pension lump sum* (**UFPLS**) can be taken from an uncrystallised pension fund where 25% will be tax-free and the remainder taxed at the individual's marginal rate.
  - A *lifetime annuity* can still be used to provide a secured income for life, although there is now greater flexibility in how income is taken.
- From 6 April 2015, flexi-access drawdown replaced flexible and capped drawdown (which enabled a pension income to be drawn subject to an annual limit). Existing capped drawdown arrangements, with the limit on any pension income drawn, can continue after 5 April 2015 and the standard annual allowance, currently £40,000, is retained.

DEATH BENEFITS

- From 6 April 2015, where death occurs before age 75 the lump sum payable is tax-free. Income payable to any beneficiary is tax-free if taken by way of income drawdown or an annuity.
- After 6 April 2016, where death occurs after age 75 lump sums are taxed as income at the beneficiary's marginal rate of income tax. Income paid to any beneficiary is taxed at their marginal rate of tax. (For payments made between 6 April 2015 and 5 April 2016, any lump sum payable was subject to 45% tax, unless paid as income.)

PENSION SHARING

- Only available upon petitions for divorce or nullity (not judicial separation) issued on or after 1 December 2000.
- A PSO requires an English/Welsh court order: cannot be achieved by agreement alone.
- Must be expressed as a percentage (up to 100%) of the Cash Equivalent (*H v H* [2010] 2 FLR 173) (except that a PSO made against the protected payment of the new state pension is to be expressed as a percentage of the weekly amount: see **State Retirement Pension** *below*).
- A pension in payment may be shared.
- When a person with benefit of pension credit retires at their scheme retirement age part of his/her pension may be commuted, unless the pension out of which the pension credit was carved was already the subject of commutation.
- The same rules apply to PSOs on marriage annulment or civil partnership dissolution.
- Forms: P (Pension Inquiry Form); P1 (Pension Sharing Annex, available to complete in *@eGlance*).
- Equal division of a Cash Equivalent does not achieve equality of outcome in income terms: appropriate specialist pension or actuarial advice is required.
- No pension sharing or attachment order can be made against an overseas pension (*Goyal v Goyal* [2016] EWFC 50).

PENSION PROTECTION FUND

- Provides benefits by way of PPF compensation up to a capped level of certain defined benefit occupational pension schemes, where (broadly) a *qualifying insolvency event* took place on or after 6 April 2005.
- *Pension compensation sharing orders* and *pension compensation attachment orders* became available from 6 April 2011 against PPF.
- If the PPF assumes responsibility for a pension scheme, any outstanding pension sharing / attachment orders are implemented by the PPF.

AUTO-ENROLMENT

- A compulsory pension scheme for employees came into force on 1 October 2012 under the Pensions Act 2008. All eligible employees (but not the self-employed) must be enrolled by their employer in an automatic enrolment scheme, which will be either:
  - their employer's pension scheme (where it is a qualifying scheme); or
  - the national pension scheme called NEST (National Employment Savings Trust).
- The NEST pension may be shared by a PSO.

STATE RETIREMENT PENSION

- The state pension to which a person is entitled depends on the date on which they reach state pension age (SPA).
- An SPA calculator may be found at www.gov.uk.
- The old state pension scheme (the old scheme) applies to those already claiming their state pension and those who reached SPA prior to 6 April 2016, who will not be affected by the new state pension scheme (the new scheme)
- The Pensions Act 2014 introduced the new scheme for those who reach SPA on or after 6 April 2016: see Comparative Table *overleaf.*
- A transitional rate of state pension is payable to a person who falls within the new scheme, has at least 10 qualifying years and at least one qualifying year attributable to tax years prior to the introduction of the new scheme. A person entitled to the transitional rate will receive the higher of their entitlement under either the new scheme or the old scheme: referred to as the 'foundation amount'.
- Where a person has a foundation amount which is less than

21

Table 21 Pensions Overview

State pension arrangements: the old and the new	
The old scheme: for those reaching state pension age prior to 6 April 2016	**The new scheme: for those reaching state pension age on or after 6 April 2016**
A state pension with two components: a basic flat-rate state pension (Category A pension) and an additional state pension, the amounts of which are calculated with reference to the individual's National Insurance contributions.	A flat-rate, single tier state pension for those with the maximum number of qualifying years of National Insurance contributions. Transitional arrangements will allow for 'protected payments' for those who would have received a greater state pension under the current scheme.
A full basic state pension is payable to a person who has 30 qualifying years of contributions if they reach state pension age after 6 April 2010.	A person needs 35 qualifying years of contributions to receive the full flat rate (£159.55 per week for 2017-18) of the single tier pension. For those with fewer than 35 qualifying years, each qualifying year will entitle him or her to one 35th of the full rate (£4.56 per week).
A person may defer claiming their state pension and then choose from either a (taxable) lump sum or a greater weekly pension (10.4% p.a. increase).	A person may defer claiming their state pension in order to receive a greater weekly sum (5.8% p.a. increase), but no lump sum option will be available.
Certain individuals may use the national insurance contributions record of their spouse or civil partner to obtain a full basic state pension (Category B pension), even if not living together.	The state pension is based on an individual's own contribution record alone.
A person whose spouse or civil partner has died may use the National Insurance contributions record of the deceased person to improve their own state pension in certain circumstances, and may inherit some additional state pension.	The state pension is based on an individual's own contribution record alone, subject to transitional arrangements.
A person who is divorced (or whose civil partnership is dissolved) may use the National Insurance contributions record of their former spouse / civil partner to improve their own basic state pension in certain circumstances.	The state pension is based on an individual's own contribution record alone.
A PSO may be made in respect of the additional state pension component of the current state pension.	No PSO may be made in respect of the single tier pension, other than in relation to 'protected payments'.

the full rate of the new state pension, he/she can continue to add qualifying years after 5 April 2016 until he/she reaches the full rate amount or reaches full pension age.

- If the foundation amount is more than the full rate of the new state pension, the difference is paid on top of the full rate payment and is referred to as the 'protected payment'.
- The Pensions Act 2014 allows for pension sharing of the new state pension only in limited circumstances: it will be possible to obtain a PSO under the new scheme in respect of 'protected payments'. However, where the state pension was in payment before 6 April 2016 or where an individual reaches SPA prior to that date but defers taking payment, the Additional State Pension (**ASP**) will be shareable even if the divorce proceedings were commenced after 6 April 2016 (WRPA 1999, s 49).
- The Pensions Act 2014 does not affect the validity of a PSO made before the new scheme came into force in respect of the ASP of a person falling within that scheme.
- From 6 April 2016, the Sharing of State Scheme Rights (Provision of Information and Valuation) (No 2) Regulations 2000 (SI 2000/2914) have been amended by the State Pension Regulations 2015 (SI 2015/173) to distinguish between shareable old (i.e. the ASP and a shared additional pension) and shareable new (i.e. the protected payment) scheme rights. Reg 6 of the 2000 Regulations now sets out the information to be supplied to a person or to the court in relation to sharing new state scheme rights.
- The Pensions Act 2014 provides for a PSO that takes effect on or after 6 April 2016 to be implemented under the new Rules. However, transitional rules in the Pensions Act 2014 (Pension Sharing on Divorce etc (Transitional Provision) Order 2016 (SI 2016/39) ensure that the existing rules in relation to pension sharing of state scheme rights continue to apply where a petition was filed before 6 April 2016.
- The Substitution Rule allowed for a partner's longer NI record to be substituted for their own so that a greater basic state pension became payable. Since 6 April 2016 this only applies in very limited circumstances, and in any event only to recipients who had attained SPA by that date.

QUALIFYING RECOGNISED OVERSEAS PENSION SCHEME (QROPS)

A transfer from a UK tax relieved pension scheme to a *qualifying recognised overseas pension scheme* (QROPS) will be taxable at 25% of its point of transfer value, and within the following 5 years where requested after 9 March 2017, if both the individual and the QROPS are not in the same country, or both are not within the European Economic Area, or the QROPS is not provided by an employer. See, further, *International Pension Orders After Goyal* [2016] Fam Law 1413.

Table 22   Pension Sharing Procedure

Procedure on an application for a pension sharing order

	Step	Timing	FPR/Reg/ WRP Act 1999
1	**Applicant** (party without pension) makes the application for pension sharing order ('**PSO**') in **Form A / D50F**	On or at any time after (a) filing of application for a matrimonial or civil partnership order (Form A) or (b) permission is granted (on application in Form D50E) to apply for a PSO after overseas divorce / dissolution (Form D50F)	9.4 and PD 5A Table 2
	Application must contain / be accompanied by MIAM form (unless by consent: see FPR 9.32)		3.6 to 3.8; PD 3A paras 11, 13, 14
2	Applicant serves the person responsible for each pension arrangement ('**PRPA**') with a copy of Form A / D50F	Upon making the application	9.31
3	PRPA provides prescribed information	Within 21 days of receipt of Form A or as directed	reg 4, 2000 Regs
4	Unless **Respondent** (party with pension) has or has requested a relevant valuation[1] of his pension rights or benefits (ie the CETV or CEB) (and whether or not a PSO has been applied for), he requests PRPA to provide it	Within 7 days of receiving notice of First Appointment	9.30(1), (2) and (4)
5	PRPA provides the information at step 4	If notified that requested for purpose of proceedings, within 6 weeks of request or as directed	reg. 2(5), 2000 Regs
6	Respondent serves the information at step 5 together with name and address of PRPA	Within 7 days of receipt	9.30(3)
7	If / as directed at the First Appointment, Respondent to file and serve a Pension Inquiry Form (**Form P**)[2]	As directed	9.15(7)(c); regs 2, 3, 4, 2000 Regs
8	PRPA provides as directed the information required by Form P	Within 21 days of receipt or as otherwise directed	reg 4(1), 2000 Regs
9	The PSO must include a statement that the order provides for pension sharing in accordance with its annex(es)	When drafting or making the PSO	9.35(a)
10	The PSO must be accompanied by an annex for each pension arrangement in the prescribed form (**Form P1**)[3]	When drafting or making the PSO	9.35(b)
11	Where the PSO is made by consent but no service has been effected under step 2, Respondent must request from PRPA the information in Section C of Form P (unless already provided) and on receipt serve copy on Applicant	On making of order	9.32
12	The PSO and annex(es) are sent to PRPA by one of the parties or by Court, as directed, together with copies of the divorce decrees/ dissolution orders	Within 7 days of the later of the making of the PSO or decree absolute / final order of dissolution	9.36(2), (4) and (5)
13	PSO takes effect	On the later of decree absolute or 7 days from expiry of time for appeal against PSO	MCA s 24B(2); reg 9, D(P)R 2000[4]
14	PRPA implements the PSO	Within EITHER 4 months of date PSO takes effect OR after which PRPA receives the order and annex(es), copies of the divorce decrees / dissolution orders, the information specified in the applicable paragraphs of the annex(es) and payment of its charges (whichever the later) OR as directed by Court[5]	WRPA 1999, s 34(1); reg 5, 2000 Regs WRPA 1999, ss 34(4) and 41(2)(a)

[1]   See reg. 2(2), Pensions on Divorce etc (Provision of Information) Regulations 2000 ('2000 Regs').
[2]   Form P should always be used for significant pensions where an order may be made: *Martin-Dye* [2006] 2 FLR 901.
[3]   PSO of new state pension 'protected payment' is expressed as % of weekly sum. Otherwise, as CE %: *H v H* [2010] 2 FLR 173.
[4]   I.e. reg. 9 of the Divorce etc (Pensions) Regulations 2000.
[5]   Pursuant to Pension Sharing (Implementation and Discharge of Liability) Regulations 2000 or Pensions on Divorce etc (Charging) Regulations 2000.

Note: additional/other steps must be taken in the case of PPF involvement (rule 9.37), and on applications for pension compensation sharing orders (FPR Part 9, Chapter 9), for all of which, and for Forms P and P1, see *@eGlance*.

Table 23 Social Security Benefits

Universal Credit (UC)

Means tested benefit to replace Income-based Jobseeker's Allowance (IBJSA), Income-related Employment and Support Allowance (IRESA), Income Support (IS), Child Tax Credit (CTC), Working Tax Credit (WTC), most Housing Benefit (HB), and some aspects of the Social Fund.

UC rolling out gradually to new claimants. All new claims expected to be for UC by December 2018, except for families with three or more children, who must claim CTC until 1 February 2019, when UC claim restricted to two children only. All remaining existing benefit claimants to start moving over from July 2019; move to be completed by March 2022 (with cash protection on transfer unless new circumstances, subject to Benefits Cap (BC)). Check https://universalcreditinfo.net for availability of UC in your area. Online applications at https://www.universal-credit.service.gov.uk/postcode-checker; telephone applications only in limited circumstances.

For applicants on a low income or out of work 18+ and under Pension Credit (PC) age, mostly for those present and habitually resident in UK, with right to reside and N.I. number, making 'claimant commitment' recording requirements. Not usually available to students. Under 21s claiming UC for 6+ months must apply for training or apprenticeships/ attend work placements unless considered to be vulnerable. If claimant one of couple, must make joint claim; if one of couple fails to meet relevant conditions, ignored when calculating UC maximum amount, but his/her savings/capital/income and earnings taken into account. If one of couple in eligible area over PC age, couple choose whether to claim UC or PC.

Different tests applied depending on individual capability and circumstances. Four groups: i) no work-related requirements (e.g. for those earning above threshold or pregnant or responsible for child under 1) ii) work focused interview requirement (e.g. responsible for child aged 1-3); iii) work preparation requirement (e.g. limited capability for work); iv) all work-related requirements (almost all claimants). Parents whose youngest child 3+ (including lone parents) now expected to work. Work search hours target: usually 35 hours p.w. Volunteer hours permitted and may reduce claimant's relevant work search hours target by up to half. Reductions to target in other circumstances, including caring responsibilities and physical or mental disability.

Entitlement on first day of application; advance payments of up to 100% available with 12 month repayment. Usually one monthly payment, paid into bank account, consisting of basic allowance specific to circumstances, plus up to four of six additional elements: child element/disabled child additions; childcare costs element; carer element or limited capability for work element (abolished for most new claimants from 3 April 2017) or limited capability for work-related activity element; housing costs element. Minimum income floor for self-employed – equivalent to 35 hours p.w. on minimum wage. Sanctions for failure to meet claimant commitment.

Some 'work allowances' before UC award reduced (earnings disregards) if claimant has responsibility for child and/or illness or disability; lower rate if maximum UC award contains housing costs element; only one permitted; £397 p.c.m. for those without housing costs; £192 p.c.m. for those with housing costs.

Statutory sick pay, maternity/paternity/adoption pay, treated as earnings. Some other benefit income taken into account.

• Child element for child or qualifying young person (QYP) who normally lives with claimant; from April 2017 restricted to two children, so not available for third or subsequent child born thereafter; also, first child element not available for new claims from April 2017; addition for disabled child or QYP: paid at lower rate for DLA mobility or care at less than highest rate of care component or for three lower PIP rates; paid at higher rate for DLA highest rate of care component or PIP enhanced rate of daily living component, or registered blind/severely sight impaired. Disabled child addition for third/subsequent child payable even if child element not available for that child.

• Childcare costs element for up to 85% of costs of registered childcare, up to p.m. maximum of £646.35 for one child, £1,108.04 for two or more children; must meet work conditions; if part of couple, both must be in work unless one unable to look after child for recognised reason.

• Carer element for those caring for severely disabled person for 35 hours+ (same conditions as Carer's Allowance (CA), except may earn more than £116 p.w.). Not available with limited capacity for work-related activity element.

• Housing costs element available towards rental costs including some service charges. Those already on housing benefit continue to receive HB award for first 2 weeks of UC claim (not recoverable by government). Mortgage interest support not recoverable from April 2018; claimants who want support with payment of mortgage interest invited to apply for loan, to be repaid on sale of house or return to work, if affordable. For all tenants, rules similar to HB; usually subject to deduction for resident non-dependants. May sometimes be paid directly to landlord for rent. No automatic entitlement to housing costs element for unemployed 18-21 year olds. Discretionary housing payment may also be available from local council. Possible to claim HB and UC (without housing costs element) at same time in some special supported accommodation: hostels, refuges, some temporary accommodation.

UC withdrawn at constant rate of 63p for each £1 of net earnings above allowance. UC reduced by £1 for every £1 of unearned income. Savings/capital limit £16,000 (for both single and joint claimants). Capital over £6,000 subject to tariff income of £4.35 per £250 or part thereof. Capital under £6,000 disregarded. Not taxable. Subject to BC.

	Per month 2018-19
Basic Allowance	
Single claimant under 25	251.77
Single claimant over 25	317.82
Joint claimants both under 25	395.20
Joint claimants one or both over 25	498.89
Child Element	
First child or QYP (not available to new claimants)	277.08
Second and each subsequent child (or QYP)	231.67
Additional amount for disabled child or QYP	
Lower rate	126.11
Higher rate	383.86
Capability for work elements (not available to new claimants)	
Limited capability for work	126.11
Limited capability for work and work-related activity	328.32
Carer element	156.45

Table 23 Social Security Benefits

Work allowances (only one to be claimed)

Higher (UC award without housing element)

Single/joint (no child or QYP)	Nil
Single (child or QYP)	397.00
Couple (child or QYP)	397.00
Single/joint (limited capability)	397.00

Lower (UC award with housing element)

Single/joint (no child or QYP)	Nil
Single (child or QYP)	192.00
Couple (child or QYP)	192.00
Single/joint (limited capability)	192.00

Benefits Cap (BC)

Reducing UC or Housing Benefit (HB), BC imposes a cap on the total of a working-age person's entitlement from these benefits: Bereavement Allowance (BA), Child Benefit (CHB), Child Tax Credit (CTC), Employment and Support Allowance (ESA) (other than support group), HB, Incapacity Benefit, Income Support (IS), Jobseeker's Allowance (JSA), Maternity Allowance, Severe Disablement Allowance, UC, Widowed Parent's Allowance (or Widowed Mother's Allowance or Widow's Pension). If no HB received, BC does not apply until move to UC.

BC worked out weekly for HB and monthly for UC. Total benefits claimed limited to (weekly) £442.31 for single parent or couple in Greater London (GL); £296.35 for single claimant in GL; £384.62 for single parent or couple outside GL; £257.69 for single claimant outside GL; (monthly) £1,916.67 for single parent or couple in GL; £1,284.17 for single claimant in GL; £1,666.67 for single parent or couple outside GL; £1116.67 for single claimant outside GL.

Exempt from BC if claiming UC and household earns at least combined gross income equivalent to 16 hours p.w. at national minimum/living wage (usually £125 pw) or, if claiming HB and household works enough hours to qualify for WTC or if over qualifying age for PC (unless partner not), or if entitled to CA, carer's element of UC, Guardian's Allowance or get DLA or PIP, Attendance Allowance, Armed Forces Compensation Scheme/Independence Payment or Industrial Injuries Benefits/equivalent payments, or support component of ESA or limited capability for work related activity element of UC, or exempt accommodation (supported accommodation). Child maintenance payments not taken into account.

If claimant (and/or partner) worked for 50 weeks in previous year with combined gross income equivalent to 16 hours p.w. at national minimum/living wage (usually £125 pw) and you were not entitled, while in work, to IS, JSA or ESA, then BC not applied for the first 39 weeks after claimant stops work.

Income replacement

1. Retirement

New State Pension   **2018-19**

Up to	164.35

New state pension for people reaching state pension age after 6 April 2016 (women born after 5 April 1953; and men born after 5 April 1951). Simpler system; no right to inherit; no right to pension on basis of spousal contributions; no additional state pension; not entitled to savings credit element of PC; new full rate more than guarantee element of PC. 35+ qualifying years of

N.I. payments required for full rate; less with fewer qualifying years; normal minimum 10 years NI payments; transitional arrangements mean more may be available for those who made full NI payments to get additional state pension, in form of protected pension. Pension sharing of protected pension may be possible. Contributory and taxable. BC does not apply.

Women's state pension age increasing gradually to 65 by November 2018. For both men and women state pension age then gradually increasing to 66 by 2020, 67 by 2028, 68 by 2039. Check at www.gov.uk/calculate-state-pension.

Old State Pension   **2018-19**

Up to	Category A	125.95
	Category B	75.50

Only for those reaching state pension age before 6 April 2016. Either spouse/civil partner qualifies in own right (Category A) or as spouse, civil partner, widow(er) or civil partner (Category B). Additional state pension based on contributions. Highly variable rates according to contribution history. Age addition of 25p p.w. for those 80+. Pension sharing of ex spouse/partner's additional pension/protected payment possible. Contributory and taxable. BC does not apply.

For Form E information submit Form BR20 (for valuation); or Form BR19 (for state pension forecast): both at www.gov.uk.

2. Ill Health

i. Statutory Sick Pay   **2018-19**

Standard rate	92.05

Paid by employer for up to 168 days (28 six-day weeks), to employees (not agricultural workers) earning not less than £116 gross p.w who have been ill for at least 4 days in row. Taxable. Not replaced by UC. BC does not apply.

ii. Employment and Support Allowance (ESA)   **2018-19**

Maximum Basic (Rate	
Single claimant (under 25)	57.90
Single claimant (over 25)	73.10
Couple (means-tested)	114.85
Additional component for those meeting limited capability	
for work test (not available to new claimants)	29.05
Additional support component	
(for those assessed as more severely disabled)	37.65
Premiums (Means-tested)	
Enhanced disability – single	16.40
Enhanced disability – couple	23.55
Severe disability – single/couple (lower rate)	64.30
Severe disability – couple (higher rate)	128.60
Carer premium	36.00

Benefit for people of working age currently unable to work because of sickness or disability. Not available to those getting sick pay or IS or adoption/maternity/paternity pay or JSA. (Remaining Incapacity Benefit claimants being transferred to ESA.) Both contributions-based and 'income-related' (means-tested) benefit, based on either limited capability for work (placed in 'work-related activity group': must attend and take part in work-related activity), or limited capability for work-related activity (not expected to work, placed in 'support group'). New claimants not eligible for limited capability component.

Basic rate during 13-week assessment phase; different rules for terminally ill. Delays may extend assessment period.

Table 23 Social Security Benefits

Contribution-based/'new style' ESA: dependent on NI contributions; limited to 1 year for those in 'work-related activity group'. Taxable. Not replaced by UC; called new style ESA if claimed with UC; payments deducted from UC.

Income-related ESA (IRESA): habitual residence test (including right to reside), assessment, housing costs and capital rules modelled on IS. (ESA not usually affected if earn up to £20 p.w. or do permitted work – must be less than 16 hours p.w. earning up to £120 p.w. Child maintenance disregarded. Passport to other benefits including HB. Not taxable. Gradually being replaced by UC.

BC applies except where support component awarded.

iii. Carer's Allowance	**2018-19**
Claimant	64.60
Adult dependent (not available for new claims)	38.00

Paid to people over 16 who spend at least 35 hours p.w. caring for recipient of: higher or middle rates of DLA care component, PIP daily living component, Attendance Allowance, Constant Attendance Allowance at or above the normal rate with related pension, or Armed Forces Independence Payment. Claimant can earn no more than £116 p.w. net and must not be in full-time education; however, entitled to offset against earnings up to half any sums paid to someone else (not close relative) to care for either recipient of allowances or carer's children under 16. Claimant must be present, have been present in GB for 104 weeks out of previous 156 (2 of last 3 years) and be habitually resident. Benefit usually stops 4 weeks after person cared for enters residential care and 8 weeks after that person dies.

Non-contributory; not means-tested. Taxable. Not replaced by UC. Those receiving PIP not subject to BC.

3. Unemployment – Jobseeker's Allowance (JSA)

i. Contribution-based/'new style' JSA		**2018-19**
Claimant	18-24	57.90
	25 and over	73.10

ii. Income-based JSA (IBJSA)		**2018-19**
Claimant	16-24	57.90
	25 and over	73.10
Couple	Both over 18	114.80
Dependent children (but see Note below)		66.90
Premiums: as for IS		

Benefit for unemployed. Main rates only shown. Includes both contribution-based and 'income-related' (means-tested) benefit. Claimants must be under state pension age, available for and actively seeking work, with current Jobseeker's Agreement. Not usually available for those under 18, full time students, or those working 16+ hours p.w.

Children rate runs only until day before 20th birthday (or end of secondary education, if earlier); and only for existing transferred claimants (for others see CTC).

Contribution-based/'new style' JSA: age-related flat-rate payment; dependent on NI contributions; unaffected by savings or partner's income; reduced by part-time earnings; no dependant allowances; paid for up to 26 weeks. Taxable. Not replaced by UC; called new style JSA if claimed with UC; payments deducted from UC).

Income-based JSA paid with, or from expiry of, contribution-based JSA, with IS-style rules for habitual residence (including right to reside), income, capital and premiums (mortgage interest replaced by loan secured against property). Partner must usually work less than average of 24 hours p.w. Child maintenance disregarded; earnings may be disregarded up to £20 p.w. in some circumstances. Basic payment taxable; premiums not. Being replaced by UC. BC applies.

4. Maternity/paternity/adoption

i. Statutory Maternity Pay[1] (SMP)	**2018-19**
Average earnings threshold	116.00
Higher rate (first 6 weeks)	90%
of average weekly gross wage	
Lower rate (for up to next 33 weeks)	145.18[2]

Paid by employer up to 39 weeks (during which may work up to 10 days). Taxable. Not replaced by UC. BC does not apply.

ii. Statutory Paternity Pay[1] (SPP)	**2018-19**
Average earnings threshold	116.00
Rate	145.18[2]

For fathers, or partners of new mothers/adopters. Payable for up to 2 weeks; leave must have been taken within 56 days of birth. Taxable. Not replaced by UC. BC does not apply.

iii. Statutory Shared Parental Pay[1] (ShPP)	**2018-19**
Average earnings threshold	116.00
Rate	145.18[2]

For fathers, or partners of new mothers/adopters. Mother or adopter must be entitled to, and have given notice to curtail, maternity or adoption entitlements and must share main responsibility for child care with father or her partner. Even if one parent not eligible for ShPP, other eligible parent may still be entitled, provided ineligible parent employed or self-employed for at least 26 weeks in 66 weeks before due date, and average pay over £30 p.w. for 13 of those weeks. Taxable. Not replaced by UC. BC does not apply.

iv. Maternity Allowance (MA)	**2018-19**
Average earnings threshold	30.00
Standard rate	145.18[2]

Paid to claimants not entitled to SMP but employed or self-employed for at least 26 weeks in 66 weeks before due date, and average pay over £30 p.w. Maximum 39 weeks (during which may work up to 10 days). Available for 14 weeks to some people working unpaid for spouse/partner's business. Non-taxable. BC applies. Not replaced by UC.

v. Statutory Adoption Pay[1] (SAP)	**2018-19**
Average earnings threshold	116.00
Standard rate	145.18[2]

For adopters or surrogate parents or partners of adopters. Paid by employer for a maximum of 39 weeks (during which may work up to 10 days). Taxable. Not replaced by UC.

1 Claimant must be employee, working for same employer for at least 26 weeks at end of 15th week before child is due (or by week matched with adopted child) and earning more than threshold earnings.
2 Or (if less) 90% of the parent's weekly average gross earnings.

vi. Surestart Maternity Grant	**2018-19**
Standard one-off payment	500.00

Subject to complex conditions including receipt of means-tested benefits. Now available only for first child or for multiple births. Gradually being replaced by UC.

Table 23 Social Security Benefits

5. Bereavement

Bereavement Benefit	2018-19
i. Bereavement Support Payment	
Recipients not entitled to child benefit	
lump sum	2,500.00
monthly payment	100.00
Recipients entitled to child benefit (or pregnant)	
lump sum	3,500.00
monthly payment	350.00

Replaced Bereavement Payment, Bereavement Allowance and Widowed Parent's Allowance from 6 April 2017.

Available to bereaved spouses/civil partners 45+ but under state pension age. Payable for up to 18 months from date of bereavement, depending on date of claim. Unaffected by remarriage or re-partnering. Contributory. Not taxable. BC does not apply, disregarded in calculation of other benefits.

ii. Widowed Parent's Allowance	113.70

Available only if spouse or civil partner died before 6 April 2017 (claimant must be under state pension age and in receipt of CHB; must not have remarried or be cohabiting). Taxable. BC applies. Not replaced by UC.

Special needs

1. Disability Living Allowance (DLA)

		2018-19
Care Component	Highest	85.60
	Middle	57.30
	Lowest	22.65
Mobility Component	Higher	59.75
	Lower	22.65

New claimants restricted to disabled children under 16 who need help to look after themselves or have mobility problems for 3 months, which are likely to continue for further 6 months (unless terminally ill). Must usually be present, have been present in GB for 104 weeks out of previous 156 (2 of last 3 years) (unless refugee or terminally ill) and be habitually resident. Existing DLA recipients aged 16 to 64 transferring to PIP; transfers due to complete by May 2018.

2. Personal Independence Payment (PIP)

Replaces DLA for new claimants (but see DLA above for limited continuing eligibility). Transfer of all working age DLA recipients to PIP due to complete by May 2018 – DLA recipients invited to apply for PIP and then assessed.

Available to those aged 16 to 64 who satisfy daily living and/or mobility activities test for 3 months prior to claim (qualifying period starts when eligible needs arise) and likely to continue to satisfy test for at least 9 months after claim (prospective test establishing long-term health condition or disability). Terminally ill claimants (death expected within 6 months) exempt from both qualifying period and prospective test. Claimant must be present, have been present in GB (unless terminally ill or refugee) for set periods (depending on age) and be habitually resident.

Made up of two elements: daily living component paid at either standard rate (limited ability to carry out such activities) or enhanced rate (severely limited ability to carry out daily living activities), and mobility component paid at either standard (limited mobility) or enhanced rate (severely limited mobility). Terminally ill claimants automatically receive daily living component enhanced rate, and can apply for mobility component. If in care home paid for by public funds, may be entitled to mobility component, but not daily living component.

		2018-19
Daily living component	Standard rate	57.30
	Enhanced rate	85.60
Mobility component	Standard rate	22.65
	Enhanced rate	59.75

3. Attendance Allowance (AA)

	2018-19
Higher rate	85.60
Lower rate	57.30

Paid for care needs of those 65+ who satisfy one of disability tests for at least 6 months (unless terminally ill). Claimant must be present, have been present in GB for 104 weeks out of previous 156 (2 of last 3 years) (unless terminally ill or refugee) and be habitually resident. Not replaced by PIP.

PIP, DLA and AA all based on physical need, with no money use restrictions. All non-contributory, non-means tested, non-taxable and ignored as income for means-tested benefits. Not replaced by UC. Those receiving not subject to BC.

Children

1. Child Benefit (CHB)

	2018-19
Only/elder/eldest child	20.70
Each subsequent child	13.70

Paid to person responsible for child under 16, or under 20 and in approved education (12 hours p.w+ average; must not be advanced or paid for by employer; may include traineeships). Must live in UK with right to reside (usually not available if subject to immigration control). Tapered income tax charge applies if household receives CHB and parent or partner earns over £50,000 p.a.; tax charge rate 1% of CHB per £100 annual income; full CHB recovered from those earning £60,000 p.a.

Administered by HMRC. Non-contributory and otherwise non-taxable. BC applies. Not replaced by UC.

2. Guardian's allowance

	2018-19
Allowance	17.20

Payable with CHB to those raising children of deceased parents (sometimes if one parent has survived), if one parent born in UK and present in UK for at least 52 weeks in any 2 year period since 16. Administered by HMRC. Non-contributory, non-taxable. Not replaced by UC. GA recipients not subject to BC.

3. Childcare

	2018-19

See also UC and Tax Credits

Childcare vouchers – no new claims for employer childcare vouchers – existing claims will continue until child 15 (or 16 if disabled) or claimant claims under another scheme.

Tax-free childcare costs for under 12s (or under 17s if child disabled) – for families with adult parents in work (both

Table 23 Social Security Benefits

parents living together, single parent or parent and partner living with the child), earning equivalent of average of 16 hours+ on current minimum/living wage p.w. (usually £125 p.w.); some limited exceptions including start-up period of new business, on leave or about to start a new job; neither parent living with child must earn £100,000. Applications online via https://www.childcare-support.tax.service.gov.uk/par/app/ invitedtotrial. Child must usually live with applicant, be under 12 years or registered disabled and under 17. Not available for foster children; nor with childcare vouchers, tax credits or UC. Separate free 15 and 30 hour schemes exist for 3 and 4 year olds.

Pays 20% of first £10,000 of registered childcare costs per child p.a.; up to £2,000 (£4,000 if disabled) per child p.a. (paid per quarter via online Childcare account by government putting in 20% of amount already paid in by parents).

Free childcare entitlement for 3 and 4 year olds – 15 hours p.w. available 38 weeks (or 570 hours) p.a. without conditions. 30 hours p.w. available 38 weeks (or 1,140 hours) p.a. to families with adult parents in work (both parents living together, single parent or parent and partner living with the child), earning equivalent of average of 16 hours+ on current minimum/living wage (usually £125) p.w. Limited exceptions include start-up period of new business, on leave or about to start a new job; must not earn more than £100,000 each. Not for foster children.

Free childcare entitlement for 2 year olds – 15 hours p.w. available 38 weeks (or 570 hours) p.a. to those receiving certain forms of support including IS, JSA, ESA, UC, and Tax Credits whose annual income under £16,190, or receive DLA for child.

Income Support (IS) 2018-19

For those not expected to look for work, under women's state pension age, on low income (e.g. lone parents of young children, carers, very limited range of students; those entitled to statutory sick pay); may not work more than 16 hrs p.w (partner not more than 24 hrs p.w.). Not for unemployed (see JSA) or long-term ill/disabled claimants (see ESA) or most childless people under 18. Children dependent while CHB is paid, but dependants payments only available if already claiming at 8 September 2005; after this CTC instead; no dependents payments payable for third or subsequent child born after April 2017, except in special circumstances. Restricted entitlement for lone parents as youngest child reaches threshold age, 5+ for IS (3+ for UC) – claims thereafter for UC, JSA or ESA unless child disabled). Claimant must be present and habitually resident (with right to reside).

A need level is established from allowances and premiums (below), plus (after 13 week waiting period) ground rent, certain service charges; from April 2018 support for mortgage interest to be paid as loan, repayable on sale or return to work. IS paid to supplement other income to need level. Detailed rules on application of premiums and disregarded income.

Payments from former partner may disqualify, but all child maintenance disregarded. Capital up to £6,000 disregarded (£10,000 if in residential/nursing homes; £3,000 for child). Capital between £6,000 and £16,000 deemed to produce tariff income of £1 for each £250 (or part) over £6,000. No entitlement to IS if capital exceeds £16,000; value of home may be included. BC applies. Gradually being replaced by UC. Non-contributory. Rarely taxable. Main rates:

Personal allowances		p.w.	p.a.
Single person	16-24	57.90	3,010.80
	25 or over	73.10	3,801.20
Lone parent	Under 18	57.90	3,010.80
	Over 18	73.10	3,801.20
Couple	Both over 18	114.85	5,972.20
Dependent children		66.90	3,478.80

Note that dependent child allowance is for existing untransferred claimants only (others see CTC); ceases on earlier of 20th birthday or end of secondary education.

Main premiums

	p.w.	p.a.
Carer	36.00	1,872.00
Disability		
Single	33.55	1,744.60
Couple	47.80	2,485.60
Enhanced disability		
Single	16.40	852.80
Couple	23.55	1,224.60
Severe disability		
Single (or one of couple)	64.30	3,343.60
Couple (both qualifying)	128.60	6,687.20

Existing claimants only (others see CTC)

	p.w.	p.a.
Family/lone parent family	17.45	907.40
Disabled child	62.86	3,268.72
Enhanced disability (child)	25.48	1,324.96

Pension Credit (PC) 2018-19

2 elements: Guarantee Credit (GC) for those of qualifying age with income below 'standard minimum guarantee'; and Savings Credit (SC) for those 65+ with modest savings or income. From April 2016 no new claims to SC. Claimant must be present, habitually resident and with right to reside. Payment normally stops after 4 weeks abroad.

Age at which GC available to men and women rising gradually in line with respective increases in state pension age: for pension age calculator, see https://www.gov.uk/state-pension-age.

Means-tested, up to £20 p.w. income disregarded. £10,000 capital disregarded; thereafter tariff income is £1 for every £500 capital (or part). Child maintenance disregarded; other maintenance disregarded only for SC. Administered by DWP. Not a tax credit. State pension not affected. HB not treated as income. Additional housing costs sometimes recoverable for costs not covered by HB; after UC introduced, housing credit to be added to PC. Mortgage interest support no longer recoverable from April 2018; option of applying for loan, repayable on sale of house or return to work, if borrower can afford it.

Non-contributory. Not taxable. PC recipients not subject to BC.

Standard Minimum Guarantee		p.w.
Single		163.00
Couple		248.80
Additional amount for severe disability		
Single		64.30
Couple (both qualify)		128.60
Additional amount for carers		**36.00**
Savings Credit		
Threshold	Single	140.67
	Couple	223.82
Maximum	Single	13.40
	Couple	14.99

Table 23 Social Security Benefits

Working Tax Credit (WTC) 2018-19

	p.a.
Income threshold	6,420.00
Withdrawal rate	41%
Basic element	1,960.00
Additional couple's/lone parent element	2,010.00
30 hour element	810.00
Disabled worker element	3,090.00
Severe disability element	1,330.00
Childcare element	**p.w.**
Maximum eligible cost	300.00
Maximum eligible cost for one child	175.00
(up to 70% of eligible costs covered)	

Based on gross annual income: in-work support for families with child/children where lone parent (or equivalent) aged 16+ works 16+ hours p.w., or couple's combined work hours total 24 hours p.w. and one parent works 16+ hours p.w. Extra payment for working 30+ hours p.w. Also in-work support for some households without child, including those 25+ working 30+ hours p.w. and those 60+ or with disability working 16+ hours p.w. Includes registered self-employed. Must be present and residing in UK. Up to threshold, claimants receive maximum. Credit then tapers by 41p per £1 of income. Above threshold, claimant loses main element of WTC first, then childcare element, then child element of any CTC, then family element.

Elements cumulative. Complex assessment rules. Maintenance (spousal and child), CHB and some other benefits ignored. Assessed on annual income, joint incomes for couples (disregarding £300 of some unearned income). Awards provisional until end of year notice identifies under/overpayments. Disregard of £2,500 before in-year fall or rise in income affects entitlement. HMRC administered. Gradually being replaced by UC. Visit www.gov.uk/tax-credits-calculator for online help.

Child Tax Credit (CTC) 2018-19

	p.a.
First Income threshold (if only entitled to CTC)	16,105.00
Withdrawal rate	41%
Family element (not available to new claimants)	545.00
Child element (per child) (new claimants restricted to 2 children)	2,780.00
Disabled child additional element	3,275.00
Severely disabled child additional element	1,330.00

Based on gross annual income, support for families with child/children. Must have right to reside. First per child element then family element tapers by 41p per £1 of income once income above £16,105 (WTC abated first).

One family element per family; not available for new claimants from April 2017. Child elements cumulative, including any disabled child or severely disabled child additional elements. If first child born after 6 April 2017 support limited to first two children (some exceptions including multiple births, adopted children, disabled children). Paid to nominated main carer for under 16s or under 19s in full-time non-advanced education (FTNAE), must inform HMRC that child still in FTNAE.

BC applies. UC replacing CTC but until February 2019 all families with 3 or more children must claim CTC instead of UC.

Housing Benefit (HB) 2018-19

Covers 'eligible rent' (and some service charges but not mortgages) of those on low income, present and habitually resident with right to reside. If on IS, IREAS, JSA or GC element of PC, all eligible rent usually covered; for others, income compared to applicable amount (subsistence level set by LA or government). If income exceeds that sum, tapered reduction applies; HB reduced by 63% of excess. Usual upper savings limit £16,000; if on Guarantee PC no upper limit (but tariff income). Capital up to £6,000 disregarded. (£10,000 if above qualifying age for PC or in care home). For claimants under women's pension age: each £250 (or part) over £6,000 is deemed to produce tariff income of £1 p.w.; and for those older: £1 per £500 (or part).

For rental claims, eligible rent based on Local Housing Allowance (LHA) not actual rent. LHA is flat rate based on local area and number of bedrooms needed. 2018 national maximum housing allowance 4 bedroom rate (London) £429.53 p.w., with individual caps dependent on number of bedrooms. Full table available at https://www.gov.uk/government/publications/local-housing-allowance-lha-rates-applicable-from-april-2018-to-march-2019. Most single under 35s restricted to bed-sit/shared accommodation rate. Usually paid to claimant. Backdating possible – for working age claimants 1 month only. Payments usually stop after 4 weeks abroad.

For social housing claimants, LHA size criteria applied to working age claimants (but not state pension credit age), but no 4 bedroom limit, private shared accommodation rate does not apply, and no limits if reasonably occupying supported exempt accommodation. One 'empty' bedroom means loss of 14% of maximum eligible rent; 2 or more loss of 25% of maximum eligible rent. (Can choose to rent out spare room, keeping first £20 p.w.) Otherwise social housing tenants' eligible rent based on contractual rent. Usually paid to social landlord.

Child benefit disregarded. Childcare costs paid by working single parents and working/disabled couples may be disregarded, up to £175 p.w. for one child and £300 p.w. for more than one child. Two child limit on all new claims.

Administered by LAs. Non-contributory and non-taxable. Gradually being replaced by UC. BC applies; HB reduced first.

		p.w.
Claimant	18-24	57.90
	25 or over	73.10
Lone parent	Under 18	57.90
	18 or over	73.10
Couple	Both under 18	87.50
	One or both over 18	114.85
Dependent children to day before 20th birthday		66.90
Pensioner (including qualified for PC but under 65)		
Single/lone parent under 65		163.00
Couple one or both under 65		248.80
Single 65 and over		176.40
Couple one or both 65 and over		263.80
Premiums as for IS, except		
Family/lone parent family premium – withdrawn from 1 May 2016 for new claims/births.		17.45
Protected lone parent family premium		22.20
ESA components		
Work-related activity		29.05
Support		37.65

Table 24 Life Cover

Level Term: per £100,000 of sum assured

Age	Policy length (years)									
	10		**15**		**20**		**25**		**30**	
	NS	S	NS	S	NS	S	NS	S	NS	S
25	4.38	6.17	4.41	5.86	4.97	5.94	4.58	6.98	4.84	6.99
30	4.46	6.60	4.33	6.28	5.00	7.13	5.26	7.99	5.70	9.29
35	5.15	8.41	5.00	7.99	5.97	9.89	6.56	11.44	7.34	13.60
40	6.28	11.82	6.47	12.39	7.82	14.68	8.78	17.56	10.96	21.30
45	8.54	18.14	8.21	17.03	10.70	23.37	12.49	28.09	16.33	34.08
50	11.96	28.13	11.95	29.17	15.93	38.55	21.08	38.27	26.80	57.91

Family Income Benefit: £25,000 income per annum for the balance of the chosen term

Age	Policy length (years)									
	10		**15**		**20**		**25**		**30**	
	NS	S	NS	S	NS	S	NS	S	NS	S
25	7.00	7.80	8.32	11.18	10.19	13.75	11.95	16.90	14.01	20.47
30	7.15	9.39	9.69	12.07	11.26	16.41	13.60	21.19	16.44	26.82
35	8.46	11.09	11.03	16.25	13.85	23.15	17.22	30.78	21.33	39.63
40	10.58	16.25	14.15	25.48	18.70	36.31	23.73	48.76	30.30	68.03
45	13.40	25.52	20.28	40.82	26.43	60.21	35.09	79.78	46.51	106.85
50	19.81	42.07	30.30	72.29	40.67	101.22	56.33	136.28	76.34	183.06

Mortgage Protection: per initial sum assured of £100,000, reducing in line with a 5% interest repayment mortgage

Age	Policy length (years)									
	10		**15**		**20**		**25**		**30**	
	NS	S	NS	S	NS	S	NS	S	NS	S
25	4.51	5.30	4.45	5.53	4.57	5.62	4.61	5.87	4.65	6.05
30	4.57	5.56	4.70	6.04	4.68	6.31	4.80	6.75	4.90	7.20
35	4.99	6.58	5.01	7.32	5.21	7.91	5.54	8.49	5.96	9.75
40	5.86	8.70	6.20	9.51	6.41	10.97	6.96	12.46	8.15	14.07
45	6.99	12.25	7.68	14.42	8.50	16.58	9.48	19.11	10.89	22.90
50	8.86	19.60	10.96	23.01	12.46	27.11	13.76	32.80	17.71	39.04

Policy features

All premiums are monthly, payable throughout the term, for non-smokers and for smokers. All the above quotations are based on guaranteed premium rates for the term of the plan. None of these types of policy achieves a capital or surrender value.

Rates quoted have been unisex since their harmonisation for men and women took effect in December 2012.

A **level term policy** pays out the sum assured should the life assured die or suffer from a terminal illness during the term of the plan.

A **family income benefit policy** pays out a tax free income for the remaining term of the plan from the death or prior terminal illness of the policy holder.

A **mortgage protection policy** is designed so that the sum assured decreases in line with a repayment mortgage: on death the payment is the amount of the loan then outstanding (assuming all payments made in accordance with the mortgage terms).

These rates are as quoted by www.lifeassureonline.co.uk on 19 February 2018.

Table 25 Exchange Rates

Annual average sterling exchange rates of 24 currencies for the past 10 years

	Argentina	Australia	Brazil	Canada	China	Denmark	EMU	H. Kong
	peso	dollar	real	dollar	yuan	krone	euro	dollar
08	5.09	2.19	3.35	1.96	12.92	9.39	1.26	14.43
09	6.18	1.99	3.08	1.78	10.78	8.36	1.12	12.14
10	6.20	1.68	2.72	1.59	10.46	8.69	1.17	12.01
11	6.68	1.55	2.68	1.59	10.38	8.59	1.15	12.48
12	7.21	1.53	3.10	1.58	10.00	9.18	1.23	12.30
13	8.58	1.62	3.38	1.61	9.99	8.78	1.18	12.13
14	13.17	1.83	3.87	1.82	10.15	9.25	1.24	12.78
15	14.13	2.04	5.10	1.96	9.60	10.28	1.39	11.85
16	19.62	1.82	4.75	1.79	9.00	9.11	1.22	10.51
17	21.37	1.68	4.12	1.67	8.70	8.49	1.14	10.04

	India	Israel	Japan	N. Zealand	Norway	Pakistan	Poland	Russia
	rupee	shekel	yen	dollar	krone	rupee	zloty	rouble
08	80.62	6.62	192.36	2.61	10.34	117.33	4.42	45.82
09	75.64	6.15	146.47	2.48	9.81	136.18	4.85	49.57
10	70.57	5.77	135.46	2.14	9.34	133.73	4.66	46.97
11	74.52	5.74	127.75	2.03	8.99	139.59	4.75	47.12
12	84.67	6.11	126.47	1.96	9.22	146.77	5.16	49.23
13	101.89	5.65	152.69	1.91	9.20	157.65	4.94	49.87
14	100.49	5.89	174.16	1.99	10.37	165.03	5.19	63.36
15	98.02	5.94	185.10	2.20	12.34	157.08	5.76	93.50
16	91.06	5.21	147.28	1.95	11.38	141.69	5.35	91.04
17	83.87	4.63	144.54	1.81	10.65	136.91	4.86	75.16

	S. Arabia	Singapore	S. Africa	Sweden	Switzerland	UAE	USA	Vietnam
	riyal	dollar	rand	krona	franc	dirham	dollar	dong
08	6.95	2.61	15.13	12.09	2.00	6.82	1.85	30,452
09	5.88	2.27	13.10	11.93	1.70	5.80	1.57	28,008
10	5.80	2.11	11.31	11.12	1.61	5.68	1.55	29,542
11	6.01	2.02	11.64	10.41	1.42	5.89	1.60	33,020
12	5.94	1.98	13.02	10.73	1.49	5.82	1.59	33,210
13	5.87	1.96	15.11	10.19	1.45	5.75	1.56	32,850
14	6.18	2.09	17.87	11.30	1.51	6.05	1.65	34,823
15	5.73	2.10	19.52	12.89	1.47	5.61	1.53	33,507
16	5.08	1.87	19.95	11.57	1.33	4.98	1.35	30,321
17	4.83	1.78	17.16	11.00	1.27	4.73	1.29	29,264

Month-end data for 36 currencies available and regularly refreshed, plus a converter, with @eGlance

Table 26 International Living Costs

An index of comparative city living costs in September 2017

City	Index	City	Index	City	Index	City	Index
Singapore	132	Tokyo	116	Brussels	98	Moscow	76
Hong Kong	130	Vienna	113	Amsterdam	95	Warsaw	72
Paris	130	Dublin	109	Beijing	90	Johannesburg	67
Copenhagen	123	Frankfurt	108	Istanbul	83	Mumbai	57
Geneva	122	Rome	101	Athens	79	Cairo	55
Sydney	120	**London**	**100**	Prague	78	Karachi	51
New York	116	Madrid	100	Rio de Janeiro	78	Lagos	47

Centred on London at 100, the index illustrates the cost of living in 27 other cities around the world.

The ratings derive from the Worldwide Cost of Living Survey, published in December 2017 by the Economist Intelligence Unit (EIU).

The survey is published 6-monthly, based on over 170 goods and services. Full reports for these and a further 107 cities are available from EIU (☎ 020 7576 8181, email London@eiu.com or visit www.eiu.com).

The index fluctuates readily as cost comparisons are sensitive to exchange rates and inflation.

Table 27 Points of Interest

Statutory Charge Interest Rates

For the period	Rate (%)
From 1 April 2002 to 30 September 2005	5.00
From 1 October 2005	8.00

The legal aid statutory charge is now governed by Legal Aid, Sentencing and Punishment of Offenders Act 2012, s. 25.

Interest is payable where the charge is postponed and the applicable rate is set by Civil Legal Aid (Statutory Charge) Regulations 2013 (S.I. No. 2013/503), reg. 25.

Judgment Debt Interest Rate since April 1993

This judgment debt rate (currently still 8%) is set pursuant to s. 17 of the Judgments Act 1838.

By virtue of art. 1(2) of the County Courts (Interest on Judgment) Debts Order 1991 (S.I. No. 1991/1184) as amended, this rate applies to 'a judgment or order of, or registered in, the family court for the payment of a sum of money of not less than £5,000'.

Reference to registered judgments or orders is included to reflect the fact that various enactments make provision for certain orders or judgments made in different courts or jurisdictions to be registered in the Family Court for enforcement purposes.

For information about **Stamp Duty on residential properties (SDLT)** *and* **Annual Tax on Enveloped Dwellings (ATED)** *see the comprehensive rubric* **Housing Costs**, *at Table 7,* ante, *where the impact of* **mortgage rate changes** *is demonstrated and* **Council Tax Bands** *for England and Wales are set out.*

Other Financial Remedy Materials

Matrimonial Causes Act 1973

21A. Pension sharing orders

(1) For the purposes of this Act, a pension sharing order is an order which –

    (a) provides that one party's –

        (i) shareable rights under a specified pension arrangement, or

        (ii) shareable state scheme rights,

        be subject to pension sharing for the benefit of the other party, and

    (b) specifies the percentage value to be transferred.

(2) In subsection (1) above –

    (a) the reference to shareable rights under a pension arrangement is to rights in relation to which pension sharing is available under Chapter I of Part IV of the Welfare Reform and Pensions Act 1999, or under corresponding Northern Ireland legislation,

    (b) the reference to shareable state scheme rights is to rights in relation to which pension sharing is available under Chapter II of Part IV of the Welfare Reform and Pensions Act 1999, or under corresponding Northern Ireland legislation, and

    (c) 'party' means a party to a marriage.

Sections 21B and 21C (pension compensation sharing orders) are not reproduced.

Ancillary relief in connection with divorce proceedings, etc

22. Maintenance pending suit

(1) On a petition for divorce, nullity of marriage or judicial separation, the court may make an order for maintenance pending suit, that is to say, an order requiring either party to the marriage to make to the other such periodical payments for his or her maintenance and for such term, being a term beginning not earlier than the date of the presentation of the petition and ending with the date of the determination of the suit, as the court thinks reasonable.

(2) An order under this section may not require a party to a marriage to pay to the other party any amount in respect of legal services for the purposes of the proceedings.

(3) In subsection (2) "legal services" has the same meaning as in section 22ZA.

22ZA. Orders for payment in respect of legal services

(1) In proceedings for divorce, nullity of marriage or judicial separation, the court may make an order or orders requiring one party to the marriage to pay to the other ("the applicant") an amount for the purpose of enabling the applicant to obtain legal services for the purposes of the proceedings.

(2) The court may also make such an order or orders in proceedings under this Part for financial relief in connection with proceedings for divorce, nullity of marriage or judicial separation.

(3) The court must not make an order under this section unless it is satisfied that, without the amount, the applicant would not reasonably be able to obtain appropriate legal services for the purposes of the proceedings or any part of the proceedings.

(4) For the purposes of subsection (3), the court must be satisfied, in particular, that-

    (a) the applicant is not reasonably able to secure a loan to pay for the services, and

    (b) the applicant is unlikely to be able to obtain the services by granting a charge over any assets recovered in the proceedings.

(5) An order under this section may be made for the purpose of enabling the applicant to obtain legal services of a specified description, including legal services provided in a specified period or for the purposes of a specified part of the proceedings.

(6) An order under this section may-

    (a) provide for the payment of all or part of the amount by instalments of specified amounts, and

    (b) require the instalments to be secured to the satisfaction of the court.

(7) An order under this section may direct that payment of all or part of the amount is to be deferred.

(8) The court may at any time in the proceedings vary an order made under this section if it considers that there has been a material change of circumstances since the order was made.

(9) For the purposes of the assessment of costs in the proceedings, the applicant's costs are to be treated as reduced by any amount paid to the applicant pursuant to an order under this section for the purposes of those proceedings.

(10) In this section "legal services", in relation to proceedings, means the following types of services-

    (a) providing advice as to how the law applies in the particular circumstances,

    (b) providing advice and assistance in relation to the proceedings,

    (c) providing other advice and assistance in relation to the settlement or other resolution of the dispute that is the subject of the proceedings, and

    (d) providing advice and assistance in relation to the enforcement of decisions in the proceedings or as part of the settlement or resolution of the dispute,

Matrimonial Causes Act 1973

and they include, in particular, advice and assistance in the form of representation and any form of dispute resolution, including mediation.

(11)   In subsections (5) and (6) "specified" means specified in the order concerned.

22ZB. Matters to which court is to have regard in deciding how to exercise power under section 22ZA

(1)   When considering whether to make or vary an order under section 22ZA, the court must have regard to-
- (a)   the income, earning capacity, property and other financial resources which each of the applicant and the paying party has or is likely to have in the foreseeable future,
- (b)   the financial needs, obligations and responsibilities which each of the applicant and the paying party has or is likely to have in the foreseeable future,
- (c)   the subject matter of the proceedings, including the matters in issue in them,
- (d)   whether the paying party is legally represented in the proceedings,
- (e)   any steps taken by the applicant to avoid all or part of the proceedings, whether by proposing or considering mediation or otherwise,
- (f)   the applicant's conduct in relation to the proceedings,
- (g)   any amount owed by the applicant to the paying party in respect of costs in the proceedings or other proceedings to which both the applicant and the paying party are or were party, and
- (h)   the effect of the order or variation on the paying party.

(2)   In subsection (1)(a) "earning capacity", in relation to the applicant or the paying party, includes any increase in earning capacity which, in the opinion of the court, it would be reasonable to expect the applicant or the paying party to take steps to acquire.

(3)   For the purposes of subsection (1)(h), the court must have regard, in particular, to whether the making or variation of the order is likely to-
- (a)   cause undue hardship to the paying party, or
- (b)   prevent the paying party from obtaining legal services for the purposes of the proceedings.

(4)   The Lord Chancellor may by order amend this section by adding to, omitting or varying the matters mentioned in subsections (1) to (3).

(5)   An order under subsection (4) must be made by statutory instrument.

(6)   A statutory instrument containing an order under subsection (4) may not be made unless a draft of the instrument has been laid before, and approved by a resolution of, each House of Parliament.

(7)   In this section "legal services" has the same meaning as in section 22ZA.

23. Financial provision orders in connection with divorce proceedings, etc

(1)   On granting a decree of divorce, a decree of nullity of marriage or a decree of judicial separation or at any time thereafter (whether, in the case of a decree of divorce or of nullity of marriage, before or after the decree is made absolute), the court may make any one or more of the following orders, that is to say –
- (a)   an order that either party to the marriage shall make to the other such periodical payments, for such term, as may be specified in the order;
- (b)   an order that either party to the marriage shall secure to the other to the satisfaction of the court such periodical payments, for such term, as may be so specified;
- (c)   an order that either party to the marriage shall pay to the other such lump sum or sums as may be so specified;
- (d)   an order that a party to the marriage shall make to such person as may be specified in the order for the benefit of a child of the family, or to such a child, such periodical payments, for such term, as may be so specified;
- (e)   an order that a party to the marriage shall secure to such person as may be so specified for the benefit of such a child, or to such a child, to the satisfaction of the court, such periodical payments, for such term, as may be so specified;
- (f)   an order that a party to the marriage shall pay to such person as may be so specified for the benefit of such a child, or to such a child, such lump sum as may be so specified;

subject, however, in the case of an order under paragraph (d), (e) or (f) above, to the restrictions imposed by section 29(1) and (3) below on the making of financial provision orders in favour of children who have attained the age of eighteen.

(2)   The court may also, subject to those restrictions, make any one or more of the orders mentioned in subsection (1)(d), (e) and (f) above –
- (a)   in any proceedings for divorce, nullity of marriage or judicial separation, before granting a decree; and
- (b)   where any such proceedings are dismissed after the beginning of the trial, either forthwith or within a reasonable period after the dismissal.

(3)   Without prejudice to the generality of subsection (1)(c) or (f) above –
- (a)   an order under this section that a party to a marriage shall pay a lump sum to the other party may be made for the purpose of enabling that other party to meet any liabilities or expenses reasonably incurred by him or her in

Matrimonial Causes Act 1973

maintaining himself or herself or any child of the family before making an application for an order under this section in his or her favour;

(b)   an order under this section for the payment of a lump sum to or for the benefit of a child of the family may be made for the purpose of enabling any liabilities or expenses reasonably incurred by or for the benefit of that child before the making of an application for an order under this section in his favour to be met; and

(c)   an order under this section for the payment of a lump sum may provide for the payment of that sum by instalments of such amount as may be specified in the order and may require the payment of the instalments to be secured to the satisfaction of the court.

(4)   The power of the court under subsection (1) or (2)(a) above to make an order in favour of a child of the family shall be exercisable from time to time; and where the court makes an order in favour of a child under subsection (2)(b) above, it may from time to time, subject to the restrictions mentioned in subsection (1) above, make a further order in his favour of any of the kinds mentioned in subsection (1)(d), (e) or (f) above.

(5)   Without prejudice to the power to give a direction under section 30 below for the settlement of an instrument by conveyancing counsel, where an order is made under subsection (1)(a), (b) or (c) above on or after granting a decree of divorce or nullity of marriage, neither the order nor any settlement made in pursuance of the order shall take effect unless the decree has been made absolute.

(6)   Where the court –

(a)   makes an order under this section for the payment of a lump sum; and

(b)   directs –

     (i)   that payment of that sum or any part of it shall be deferred; or

    (ii)   that that sum or any part of it shall be paid by instalments,

the court may order that the amount deferred or the instalments shall carry interest at such rate as may be specified by the order from such date, not earlier than the date of the order, as may be so specified, until the date when payment of it is due.

24. Property adjustment orders in connection with divorce proceedings, etc

(1)   On granting a decree of divorce, a decree of nullity of marriage or a decree of judicial separation or at any time thereafter (whether, in the case of a decree of divorce or of nullity of marriage, before or after the decree is made absolute), the court may make any one or more of the following orders, that is to say –

(a)   an order that a party to the marriage shall transfer to the other party, to any child of the family or to such person as may be specified in the order for the benefit of such a child such property as may be so specified, being property to which the first-mentioned party is entitled, either in possession or reversion;

(b)   an order that a settlement of such property as may be so specified, being property to which a party to the marriage is so entitled, be made to the satisfaction of the court for the benefit of the other party to the marriage and of the children of the family or either or any of them;

(c)   an order varying for the benefit of the parties to the marriage and of the children of the family or either or any of them any ante-nuptial or post-nuptial settlement (including such a settlement made by will or codicil) made on the parties to the marriage, other than one in the form of a pension arrangement (within the meaning of section 25D below);

(d)   an order extinguishing or reducing the interest of either of the parties to the marriage under any such settlement, other than one in the form of a pension arrangement (within the meaning of section 25D below);

subject, however, in the case of an order under paragraph (a) above, to the restrictions imposed by section 29(1) and (3) below on the making of orders for a transfer of property in favour of children who have attained the age of eighteen.

(2)   The court may make an order under subsection (1)(c) above notwithstanding that there are no children of the family.

(3)   Without prejudice to the power to give a direction under section 30 below for the settlement of an instrument by conveyancing counsel, where an order is made under this section on or after granting a decree of divorce or nullity of marriage, neither the order nor any settlement made in pursuance of the order shall take effect unless the decree has been made absolute.

24A. Orders for sale of property

(1)   Where the court makes an order under section 22ZA or makes under section 23 or 24 of this Act a secured periodical payments order, an order for the payment of a lump sum or a property adjustment order, then, on making that order or at any time thereafter, the court may make a further order for the sale of such property as may be specified in the order, being property in which or in the proceeds of sale of which either or both of the parties to the marriage has or have a beneficial interest, either in possession or reversion.

(2)   Any order made under subsection (1) above may contain such consequential or supplementary provisions as the court thinks fit and, without prejudice to the generality of the foregoing provision, may include –

(a)   provision requiring the making of a payment out of the proceeds of sale of the property to which the order relates, and

(b)   provision requiring any such property to be offered for sale to a person, or class of persons, specified in the order.

Matrimonial Causes Act 1973

(3)   Where an order is made under subsection (1) above on or after the grant of a decree of divorce or nullity of marriage, the order shall not take effect unless the decree has been made absolute.

(4)   Where an order is made under subsection (1) above, the court may direct that the order, or such provision thereof as the court may specify, shall not take effect until the occurrence of an event specified by the court or the expiration of a period so specified.

(5)   Where an order under subsection (1) above contains a provision requiring the proceeds of sale of the property to which the order relates to be used to secure periodical payments to a party to the marriage, the order shall cease to have effect on the death or re-marriage of, or formation of a civil partnership by, that person.

(6)   Where a party to a marriage has a beneficial interest in any property, or in the proceeds of sale thereof, and some other person who is not a party to the marriage also has a beneficial interest in that property or in the proceeds of sale thereof, then, before deciding whether to make an order under this section in relation to that property, it shall be the duty of the court to give that other person an opportunity to make representations with respect to the order; and any representations made by that other person shall be included among the circumstances to which the court is required to have regard under section 25(1) below.

24B. Pension sharing orders in connection with divorce proceedings etc

(1)   On granting a decree of divorce or a decree of nullity of marriage or at any time thereafter (whether before or after the decree is made absolute), the court may, on an application made under this section, make one or more pension sharing orders in relation to the marriage.

(2)   A pension sharing order under this section is not to take effect unless the decree on or after which it is made has been made absolute.

(3)   A pension sharing order under this section may not be made in relation to a pension arrangement which –
    (a)   is the subject of a pension sharing order in relation to the marriage, or
    (b)   has been the subject of pension sharing between the parties to the marriage.

(4)   A pension sharing order under this section may not be made in relation to shareable state scheme rights if –
    (a)   such rights are the subject of a pension sharing order in relation to the marriage, or
    (b)   such rights have been the subject of pension sharing between the parties to the marriage.

(5)   A pension sharing order under this section may not be made in relation to the rights of a person under a pension arrangement if there is in force a requirement imposed by virtue of section 25B or 25C below which relates to benefits or future benefits to which he is entitled under the pension arrangement.

24C. Pension sharing orders: duty to stay

(1)   No pension sharing order may be made so as to take effect before the end of such period after the making of the order as may be prescribed by regulations made by the Lord Chancellor.

(2)   The power to make regulations under this section shall be exercisable by statutory instrument which shall be subject to annulment in pursuance of a resolution of either House of Parliament.

24D. Pension sharing orders: apportionment of charges

If a pension sharing order relates to rights under a pension arrangement, the court may include in the order provision about the apportionment between the parties of any charge under section 41 of the Welfare Reform and Pensions Act 1999 (charges in respect of pension sharing costs), or under corresponding Northern Ireland legislation.

Sections 24E to 24G (pension compensation sharing orders) are not reproduced.

25. Matters to which court is to have regard in deciding how to exercise its powers under ss 23, 24, 24A, 24B and 24E

(1)   It shall be the duty of the court in deciding whether to exercise its powers under section 23, 24, 24A, 24B or 24E above and, if so, in what manner, to have regard to all the circumstances of the case, first consideration being given to the welfare while a minor of any child of the family who has not attained the age of eighteen.

(2)   As regards the exercise of the powers of the court under section 23(1)(a), (b) or (c), 24, 24A, 24B or 24E above in relation to a party to the marriage, the court shall in particular have regard to the following matters –
    (a)   the income, earning capacity, property and other financial resources which each of the parties to the marriage has or is likely to have in the foreseeable future, including in the case of earning capacity any increase in that capacity which it would in the opinion of the court be reasonable to expect a party to the marriage to take steps to acquire;
    (b)   the financial needs, obligations and responsibilities which each of the parties to the marriage has or is likely to have in the foreseeable future;
    (c)   the standard of living enjoyed by the family before the breakdown of the marriage;
    (d)   the age of each party to the marriage and the duration of the marriage;
    (e)   any physical or mental disability of either of the parties to the marriage;
    (f)   the contributions which each of the parties has made or is likely in the foreseeable future to make to the welfare of the family, including any contribution by looking after the home or caring for the family;

Matrimonial Causes Act 1973

    (g)   the conduct of each of the parties, if that conduct is such that it would in the opinion of the court be inequitable to disregard it;

    (h)   in the case of proceedings for divorce or nullity of marriage, the value to each of the parties to the marriage of any benefit which, by reason of the dissolution or annulment of the marriage, that party will lose the chance of acquiring.

(3)   As regards the exercise of the powers of the court under section 23(1)(d), (e) or (f), (2) or (4), 24 or 24A above in relation to a child of the family, the court shall in particular have regard to the following matters:

    (a)   the financial needs of the child;

    (b)   the income, earning capacity (if any), property and other financial resources of the child;

    (c)   any physical or mental disability of the child;

    (d)   the manner in which he was being and in which the parties to the marriage expected him to be educated or trained;

    (e)   the considerations mentioned in relation to the parties to the marriage in paragraphs (a), (b), (c) and (e) of subsection (2) above.

(4)   As regards the exercise of the powers of the court under section 23(1)(d), (e) or (f), (2) or (4), 24 or 24A above against a party to a marriage in favour of a child of the family who is not the child of that party, the court shall also have regard –

    (a)   to whether that party assumed any responsibility for the child's maintenance, and, if so, to the extent to which, and the basis upon which, that party assumed such responsibility and to the length of time for which that party discharged such responsibility;

    (b)   to whether in assuming and discharging such responsibility that party did so knowing that the child was not his or her own;

    (c)   to the liability of any other person to maintain the child.

25A. Exercise of court's powers in favour of party to marriage on decree of divorce or nullity of marriage

(1)   Where on or after the grant of a decree of divorce or nullity of marriage the court decides to exercise its powers under section 23(1)(a), (b) or (c), 24, 24A, 24B or 24E above in favour of a party to the marriage, it shall be the duty of the court to consider whether it would be appropriate so to exercise those powers that the financial obligations of each party towards the other will be terminated as soon after the grant of the decree as the court considers just and reasonable.

(2)   Where the court decides in such a case to make a periodical payments or secured periodical payments order in favour of a party to the marriage, the court shall in particular consider whether it would be appropriate to require those payments to be made or secured only for such term as would in the opinion of the court be sufficient to enable the party in whose favour the order is made to adjust without undue hardship to the termination of his or her financial dependence on the other party.

(3)   Where on or after the grant of a decree of divorce or nullity of marriage an application is made by a party to the marriage for a periodical payments or secured periodical payments order in his or her favour, then, if the court considers that no continuing obligation should be imposed on either party to make or secure periodical payments in favour of the other, the court may dismiss the application with a direction that the applicant shall not be entitled to make any future application in relation to that marriage for an order under section 23(1)(a) or (b) above.

25B. Pensions

(1)   The matters to which the court is to have regard under section 25(2) above include –

    (a)   in the case of paragraph (a), any benefits under a pension arrangement which a party to the marriage has or is likely to have, and

    (b)   in the case of paragraph (h), any benefits under a pension arrangement which, by reason of the dissolution or annulment of the marriage, a party to the marriage will lose the chance of acquiring,

and, accordingly, in relation to benefits under a pension arrangement, section 25(2)(a) above shall have effect as if 'in the foreseeable future' were omitted.

(2)   [*repealed*]

(3)   The following provisions apply where, having regard to any benefits under a pension arrangement, the court determines to make an order under section 23 above.

(4)   To the extent to which the order is made having regard to any benefits under a pension arrangement, the order may require the person responsible for the pension arrangement in question, if at any time any payment in respect of any benefits under the arrangement becomes due to the party with pension rights, to make a payment for the benefit of the other party.

(5)   The order must express the amount of any payment required to be made by virtue of subsection (4) above as a percentage of the payment which becomes due to the party with pension rights.

(6)   Any such payment by the person responsible for the arrangement –

    (a)   shall discharge so much of his liability to the party with pension rights as corresponds to the amount of the payment, and

Matrimonial Causes Act 1973

    (b)   shall be treated for all purposes as a payment made by the party with pension rights in or towards the discharge of his liability under the order.

(7)   Where the party with pension rights has a right of commutation under the arrangement, the order may require him to exercise it to any extent; and this section applies to any payment due in consequence of commutation in pursuance of the order as it applies to other payments in respect of benefits under the arrangement.

(7A)   The power conferred by subsection (7) above may not be exercised for the purpose of commuting a benefit payable to the party with pension rights to a benefit payable to the other party.

(7B)   The power conferred by subsection (4) or (7) above may not be exercised in relation to a pension arrangement which –

    (a)   is the subject of a pension sharing order in relation to the marriage, or

    (b)   has been the subject of pension sharing between the parties to the marriage.

(7C)   In subsection (1) above, references to benefits under a pension arrangement include any benefits by way of pension, whether under a pension arrangement or not.

25C. Pensions: lump sums

(1)   The power of the court under section 23 above to order a party to a marriage to pay a lump sum to the other party includes, where the benefits which the party with pension rights has or is likely to have under a pension arrangement include any lump sum payable in respect of his death, power to make any of the following provision by the order.

(2)   The court may –

    (a)   if the person responsible for the pension arrangement in question has power to determine the person to whom the sum, or any part of it, is to be paid, require him to pay the whole or part of that sum, when it becomes due, to the other party,

    (b)   if the party with pension rights has power to nominate the person to whom the sum, or any part of it, is to be paid, require the party with pension rights to nominate the other party in respect of the whole or part of that sum,

    (c)   in any other case, require the person responsible for the pension arrangement in question to pay the whole or part of that sum, when it becomes due, for the benefit of the other party instead of to the person to whom, apart from the order, it would be paid.

(3)   Any payment by the person responsible for the arrangement under an order made under section 23 above by virtue of this section shall discharge so much of his liability in respect of the party with pension rights as corresponds to the amount of the payment.

(4)   The powers conferred by this section may not be exercised in relation to a pension arrangement which –

    (a)   is the subject of a pension sharing order in relation to the marriage, or

    (b)   has been the subject of pension sharing between the parties to the marriage.

25D. Pensions: supplementary

(1)   Where –

    (a)   an order made under section 23 above by virtue of section 25B or 25C above imposes any requirement on the person responsible for a pension arrangement ('the first arrangement') and the party with pension rights acquires rights under another pension arrangement ('the new arrangement') which are derived (directly or indirectly) from the whole of his rights under the first arrangement, and

    (b)   the person responsible for the new arrangement has been given notice in accordance with regulations made by the Lord Chancellor,

the order shall have effect as if it had been made instead in respect of the person responsible for the new arrangement.

(2)   The Lord Chancellor may by regulations –

    (a)   in relation to any provision of sections 25B or 25C above which authorises the court making an order under section 23 above to require the person responsible for a pension arrangement to make a payment for the benefit of the other party, make provision as to the person to whom, and the terms on which, the payment is to be made,

    (ab)   make, in relation to payment under a mistaken belief as to the continuation in force of a provision included by virtue of section 25B or 25C above in an order under section 23 above, provision about the rights or liabilities of the payer, the payee or the person to whom the payment was due,

    (b)   require notices to be given in respect of changes of circumstances relevant to such orders which include provision made by virtue of sections 25B and 25C above,

    (ba)   make provision for the person responsible for a pension arrangement to be discharged in prescribed circumstances from a requirement imposed by virtue of section 25B or 25C above,

    (e)   make provision about calculation and verification in relation to the valuation of –

        (i)   benefits under a pension arrangement, or

        (ii)   shareable state scheme rights,

for the purposes of the court's functions in connection with the exercise of any of its powers under this Part of this Act.

(2A)   Regulations under subsection (2)(e) above may include –

Matrimonial Causes Act 1973

(a)   provision for calculation or verification in accordance with guidance from time to time prepared by a prescribed person, and

(b)   provision by reference to regulations under section 30 or 49(4) of the Welfare Reform and Pensions Act 1999.

(2B) Regulations under subsection (2) above may make different provision for different cases.

(2C) Power to make regulations under this section shall be exercisable by statutory instrument which shall be subject to annulment in pursuance of a resolution of either House of Parliament.

(3)   In this section and sections 25B and 25C above –

'occupational pension scheme' has the same meaning as in the Pension Schemes Act 1993;

'the party with pension rights' means the party to the marriage who has or is likely to have benefits under a pension arrangement and 'the other party' means the other party to the marriage;

'pension arrangement' means –

(a)   an occupational pension scheme,

(b)   a personal pension scheme,

(c)   a retirement annuity contract,

(d)   an annuity or insurance policy purchased, or transferred, for the purpose of giving effect to rights under an occupational pension scheme or a personal pension scheme, and

(e)   an annuity purchased, or entered into, for the purpose of discharging liability in respect of a pension credit under section 29(1)(b) of the Welfare Reform and Pensions Act 1999 or under corresponding Northern Ireland legislation;

'personal pension scheme' has the same meaning as in the Pension Schemes Act 1993;

'prescribed' means prescribed by regulations;

'retirement annuity contract' means a contract or scheme approved under Chapter III of Part XIV of the Income and Corporation Taxes Act 1988;

'shareable state scheme rights' has the same meaning as in section 21A(1) above; and

'trustees or managers', in relation to an occupational pension scheme or a personal pension scheme, means –

(a)   in the case of a scheme established under a trust, the trustees of the scheme, and

(b)   in any other case, the managers of the scheme.

(4)   In this section and sections 25B and 25C above, references to the person responsible for a pension arrangement are –

(a)   in the case of an occupational pension scheme or a personal pension scheme, to the trustees or managers of the scheme,

(b)   in the case of a retirement annuity contract or an annuity falling within paragraph (d) or (e) of the definition of 'pension arrangement' above, the provider of the annuity, and

(c)   in the case of an insurance policy falling within paragraph (d) of the definition of that expression, the insurer.

The former subss. (2)(c) and (2)(d) of section 25D have been repealed. Sections 25E (Pension Protection Fund), 25F (pension compensation attachment orders) and 25G (supplementary) are not reproduced.

*   *   *   *   *

28. Duration of continuing financial provision orders in favour or party to marriage, and effect of remarriage or formation of civil partnership

(1)   Subject in the case of an order made on or after the grant of a decree of a divorce or nullity of marriage to the provisions of sections 25A(2) above and 31(7) below, the term to be specified in a periodical payments or secured periodical payments order in favour of a party to a marriage shall be such term as the court thinks fit, except that the term shall not begin before or extend beyond the following limits, that is to say –

(a)   in the case of a periodical payments order, the term shall begin not earlier than the date of the making of an application for the order, and shall be so defined as not to extend beyond the death of either of the parties to the marriage or, where the order is made on or after the grant of a decree of divorce or nullity of marriage, the remarriage of, or formation of a civil partnership by, the party in whose favour the order is made; and

(b)   in the case of a secured periodical payments order, the term shall begin not earlier than the date of the making of an application for the order, and shall be so defined as not to extend beyond the death or, where the order is made on or after the grant of such a decree, the remarriage of, or formation of a civil partnership by, the party in whose favour the order is made.

(1A) Where a periodical payments or secured periodical payments order in favour of a party to a marriage is made on or after the grant of a decree of divorce or nullity of marriage, the court may direct that that party shall not be entitled to apply under section 31 below for the extension of the term specified in the order.

(2)   Where a periodical payments or secured periodical payments order in favour of a party to a marriage is made otherwise than on or after the grant of a decree of divorce or nullity of marriage, and the marriage in question is subsequently dissolved or annulled but the order continues in force, the order shall, notwithstanding anything in it, cease to have

Matrimonial Causes Act 1973

effect on the remarriage of, or formation of a civil partnership by, that party, except in relation to any arrears due under it on the date of the remarriage or formation of the civil partnership.

(3)   If after the grant of a decree dissolving or annulling a marriage either party to that marriage remarries whether at any time before or after the commencement of this Act or forms a civil partnership, that party shall not be entitled to apply, by reference to the grant of that decree, for a financial provision order in his or her favour, or for a property adjustment order, against the other party to that marriage.

29. Duration of continuing financial provision orders in favour of children, and age limit on making certain orders in their favour

(1)   Subject to subsection (3) below, no financial provision order and no order for a transfer of property under section 24(1)(a) above shall be made in favour of a child who has attained the age of eighteen.

(2)   The term to be specified in a periodical payments or secured periodical payments order in favour of a child may begin with the date of the making of an application for the order in question or any later date or a date ascertained in accordance with subsection (5) or (6) below but –

(a)   shall not in the first instance extend beyond the date of the birthday of the child next following his attaining the upper limit of the compulsory school age (construed in accordance with section 8 of the Education Act 1996) unless the court considers that in the circumstances of the case the welfare of the child requires that it should extend to a later date; and

(b)   shall not in any event, subject to subsection (3) below, extend beyond the date of the child's eighteenth birthday.

(3)   Subsection (1) above, and paragraph (b) of subsection (2), shall not apply in the case of a child, if it appears to the court that –

(a)   the child is, or will be, or if an order were made without complying with either or both of those provisions would be, receiving instruction at an educational establishment or undergoing training for a trade, profession or vocation, whether or not he is also, or will also be, in gainful employment; or

(b)   there are special circumstances which justify the making of an order without complying with either or both of those provisions.

(4)   Any periodical payments order in favour of a child shall, notwithstanding anything in the order, cease to have effect on the death of the person liable to make payments under the order, except in relation to any arrears due under the order on the date of the death.

(5)   Where –

(a)   a maintenance calculation ('the current calculation') is in force with respect to a child; and

(b)   an application is made under Part II of this Act for a periodical payments or secured periodical payments order in favour of that child –

(i)   in accordance with section 8 of the Child Support Act 1991, and

(ii)   before the end of the period of 6 months beginning with the making of the current calculation,

the term to be specified in any such order made on that application may be expressed to begin on, or at any time after, the earliest permitted date.

(6)   For the purposes of subsection (5) above, 'the earliest permitted date' is whichever is the later of–

(a)   the date 6 months before the application is made; or

(b)   the date on which the current calculation took effect or, where successive maintenance calculations have been continuously in force with respect to a child, on which the first of those calculations took effect.

(7)   Where –

(a)   a maintenance calculation ceases to have effect by or under any provision of the Child Support Act 1991; and

(b)   an application is made, before the end of the period of 6 months beginning with the relevant date, for a periodical payments or secured periodical payments order in favour of a child with respect to whom that maintenance calculation was in force immediately before it ceased to have effect,

the term to be specified in any such order made on that application may begin with the date on which that maintenance calculation ceased to have effect, or any later date.

(8)   In subsection (7)(b) above –

(a)   where the maintenance calculation ceased to have effect, the relevant date is the date on which it so ceased;

(b)   [*repealed*].

*   *   *   *   *

31. Variation, discharge, etc, of certain orders for financial relief

(1)   Where the court has made an order to which this section applies, then, subject to the provisions of this section and of section 28(1A) above, the court shall have power to vary or discharge the order or to suspend any provision thereof temporarily and to revive the operation of any provision so suspended.

(2)   This section applies to the following orders, that is to say –

(a)   any order for maintenance pending suit and any interim order for maintenance;

Matrimonial Causes Act 1973

(b)   any periodical payments order;

(c)   any secured periodical payments order;

(d)   any order made by virtue of section 23(3)(c) or 27(7)(b) above (provision for payment of a lump sum by instalments);

(dd) any deferred order made by virtue of section 23(1)(c) (lump sums) which includes provision made by virtue of –
- (i)   section 25B(4),
- (ii)   section 25C, or
- (iii) section 25F(2),

    (provision in respect of pension rights or pension compensation rights);

(e)   any order for a settlement of property under section 24(1)(b) or for a variation of settlement under section 24(1)(c) or (d) above, being an order made on or after the grant of a decree of judicial separation;

(f)   any order made under section 24A(1) above for the sale of property;

(g)   a pension sharing order under section 24B above, or a pension compensation sharing order under section 24E above, which is made at a time before the decree has been made absolute.

(2A) Where the court has made an order referred to in subsection (2)(a), (b) or (c) above, then, subject to the provisions of this section, the court shall have power to remit the payment of any arrears due under the order or of any part thereof.

(2B) Where the court has made an order referred to in subsection (2)(dd)(ii) above, this section shall cease to apply to the order on the death of either of the parties to the marriage.

(3)   The powers exercisable by the court under this section in relation to an order shall be exercisable also in relation to any instrument executed in pursuance of the order.

(4)   The court shall not exercise the powers conferred by this section in relation to an order for a settlement under section 24(1)(b) or for a variation of settlement under section 24(1)(c) or (d) above except on an application made in proceedings –

(a)   for the rescission of the decree of judicial separation by reference to which the order was made, or

(b)   for the dissolution of the marriage in question.

(4A) In relation to an order which falls within paragraph (g) of subsection (2) above ('the subsection (2) order') –

(a)   the powers conferred by this section may be exercised –
- (i)   only on an application made before the subsection (2) order has or, but for paragraph (b) below, would have taken effect; and
- (ii)   only if, at the time when the application is made, the decree has not been made absolute; and

(b)   an application made in accordance with paragraph (a) above prevents the subsection (2) order from taking effect before the application has been dealt with.

(4B) No variation of a pension sharing order, or a pension compensation sharing order, shall be made so as to take effect before the decree is made absolute.

(4C) The variation of a pension sharing order, or a pension compensation sharing order, prevents the order taking effect before the end of such period after the making of the variation as may be prescribed by regulations made by the Lord Chancellor.

(5)   Subject to subsections (7A) to (7G) below and without prejudice to any power exercisable by virtue of subsection (2)(d), (dd), (e) or (g) above or otherwise than by virtue of this section, no property adjustment order or pension sharing order, or pension compensation sharing order, shall be made on an application for the variation of a periodical payments or secured periodical payments order made (whether in favour of a party to a marriage or in favour of a child of the family) under section 23 above, and no order for the payment of a lump sum shall be made on an application for the variation of a periodical payments or secured periodical payments order in favour of a party to a marriage (whether made under section 23 or under section 27 above).

(6)   Where the person liable to make payments under a secured periodical payments order has died, an application under this section relating to that order (and to any order made under section 24A(1) above which requires the proceeds of sale of property to be used for securing those payments) may be made by the person entitled to payments under the periodical payments order or by the personal representatives of the deceased person, but no such application shall, except with the permission of the court, be made after the end of the period of six months from the date on which representation in regard to the estate of that person is first taken out.

(7)   In exercising the powers conferred by this section the court shall have regard to all the circumstances of the case, first consideration being given to the welfare while a minor of any child of the family who has not attained the age of eighteen, and the circumstances of the case shall include any change in any of the matters to which the court was required to have regard when making the order to which the application relates, and –

(a)   in the case of a periodical payments or secured periodical payments order made on or after the grant of a decree of divorce or nullity of marriage, the court shall consider whether in all the circumstances and after having regard to any such change it would be appropriate to vary the order so that payments under the order are required to be made or secured only for such further period as will in the opinion of the court be sufficient (in the light of any proposed exercise by the court, where the marriage has been dissolved, of its powers under subsection (7B)

Matrimonial Causes Act 1973

below) to enable the party in whose favour the order was made to adjust without undue hardship to the termination of those payments;

(b)   in a case where the party against whom the order was made has died, the circumstances of the case shall also include the changed circumstances resulting from his or her death.

(7A) Subsection (7B) below applies where, after the dissolution of a marriage, the court –

(a)   discharges a periodical payments order or secured periodical payments order made in favour of a party to the marriage; or

(b)   varies such an order so that payments under the order are required to be made or secured only for such further period as is determined by the court.

(7B) The court has power, in addition to any power it has apart from this subsection, to make supplemental provision consisting of any of –

(a)   an order for the payment of a lump sum in favour of a party to the marriage;

(b)   one or more property adjustment orders in favour of a party to the marriage;

(ba) one or more pension sharing orders;

(bb) a pension compensation sharing order;

(c)   a direction that the party in whose favour the original order discharged or varied was made is not entitled to make any further application for –

(i)   a periodical payments or secured periodical payments order, or

(ii)   an extension of the period to which the original order is limited by any variation made by the court.

(7C) An order for the payment of a lump sum made under subsection (7B) above may –

(a)   provide for the payment of that sum by instalments of such amount as may be specified in the order; and

(b)   require the payment of the instalments to be secured to the satisfaction of the court.

(7D) Section 23(6) above applies where the court makes an order for the payment of a lump sum under subsection (7B) above as it applies where the court makes such an order under section 23 above.

(7E) If under subsection (7B) above the court makes more than one property adjustment order in favour of the same party to the marriage, each of those orders must fall within a different paragraph of section 21(2) above.

(7F) Sections 24A and 30 above apply where the court makes a property adjustment order under subsection (7B) above as they apply where it makes such an order under section 24 above.

(7G) Subsections (3) to (5) of section 24B above apply in relation to a pension sharing order under subsection (7B) above as they apply in relation to a pension sharing order under that section.

(7H) Subsections (3) to (10) of section 24E above apply in relation to a pension compensation sharing order under subsection (7B) above as they apply in relation to a pension compensation sharing order under that section.

(8)   The personal representatives of a deceased person against whom a secured periodical payments order was made shall not be liable for having distributed any part of the estate of the deceased after the expiration of the period of six months referred to in subsection (6) above on the ground that they ought to have taken into account the possibility that the court might permit an application under this section to be made after that period by the person entitled to payments under the order; but this subsection shall not prejudice any power to recover any part of the estate so distributed arising by virtue of the making of an order in pursuance of this section.

(9)   The following are to be left out of account when considering for the purposes of subsection (6) above when representation was first taken out –

(a)   a grant limited to settled land or to trust property,

(b)   any other grant that does not permit any of the estate to be distributed,

(c)   a grant limited to real estate or to personal estate, unless a grant limited to the remainder of the estate has previously been made or is made at the same time,

(d)   a grant, or its equivalent, made outside the United Kingdom (but see subsection (9A) below).

(9A) A grant sealed under section 2 of the Colonial Probates Act 1892 counts as a grant made in the United Kingdom for the purposes of subsection (9) above, but is to be taken as dated on the date of sealing.

(10) Where the court, in exercise of its powers under this section, decides to vary or discharge a periodical payments or secured periodical payments order, then, subject to section 28(1) and (2) above, the court shall have power to direct that the variation or discharge shall not take effect until the expiration of such period as may be specified in the order.

Subss. (11) to (15) of section 31 have not been reproduced.

32. Payment of certain arrears unenforceable without the leave of the court

(1)   A person shall not be entitled to enforce through the High Court or the family court the payment of any arrears due under an order for maintenance pending suit, an interim order for maintenance or any financial provision order without the leave of that court if those arrears became due more than twelve months before proceedings to enforce the payment of them are begun.

(2)   The court hearing an application for the grant of leave under this section may refuse leave, or may grant leave subject

Matrimonial Causes Act 1973

to such restrictions and conditions (including conditions as to the allowing of time for payment or the making of payment by instalments) as that court thinks proper, or may remit the payment of the arrears or of any part thereof.

(3)　An application for the grant of leave under this section shall be made in such manner as may be prescribed by rules of court.

*　　*　　*　　*　　*

34. Validity of maintenance agreements

(1)　If a maintenance agreement includes a provision purporting to restrict any right to apply to a court for an order containing financial arrangements, then –

　　(a)　that provision shall be void; but

　　(b)　any other financial arrangements contained in the agreement shall not thereby be rendered void or unenforceable and shall, unless they are void or unenforceable for any other reason (and subject to sections 35 and 36 below), be binding on the parties to the agreement.

(2)　In this section and in section 35 below –

'maintenance agreement' means any agreement in writing made, whether before or after the commencement of this Act, between the parties to a marriage, being

　　(a)　an agreement containing financial arrangements, whether made during the continuance or after the dissolution or annulment of the marriage; or

　　(b)　a separation agreement which contains no financial arrangements in a case where no other agreement in writing between the same parties contains such arrangements;

'financial arrangements' means provisions governing the rights and liabilities towards one another when living separately of the parties to a marriage (including a marriage which has been dissolved or annulled) in respect of the making or securing of payments or the disposition or use of any property, including such rights and liabilities with respect to the maintenance or education of any child, whether or not a child of the family.

35. Alteration of agreements by court during lives of parties

(1)　Where a maintenance agreement is for the time being subsisting and each of the parties to the agreement is for the time being either domiciled or resident in England and Wales, then, subject to subsections (1A) and (3) below, either party may apply to the court for an order under this section.

(1A)　If an application or part of an application relates to a matter where jurisdiction falls to be determined by reference to the jurisdictional requirements of the Maintenance Regulation and Schedule 6 to the Civil Jurisdiction and Judgments (Maintenance) Regulations 2011—

　　(a)　the requirement as to domicile or residence in subsection (1) does not apply to the application or that part of it, but

　　(b)　the court may not entertain the application or that part of it unless it has jurisdiction to do so by virtue of that Regulation and that Schedule.

(2)　If the court is satisfied either –

　　(a)　that by reason of a change in the circumstances in the light of which any financial arrangements contained in the agreement were made or, as the case may be, financial arrangements were omitted from it (including a change foreseen by the parties when making the agreement), the agreement should be altered so as to make different, or, as the case may be, so as to contain, financial arrangements, or

　　(b)　that the agreement does not contain proper financial arrangements with respect to any child of the family,

　　then subject to subsections (4) and (5) below, the court may by order make such alterations in the agreement –

　　(i)　by varying or revoking any financial arrangements contained in it, or

　　(ii)　by inserting in it financial arrangements for the benefit of one of the parties to the agreement or of a child of the family,

　　as may appear to the court to be just having regard to all the circumstances, including, if relevant, the matters mentioned in section 25(4) above;

　　and the agreement shall have effect thereafter as if any alteration made by the order had been made by agreement between the parties and for valuable consideration.

(3)　*[repealed]*

(4)　Where the court decides to alter, by order under this section, an agreement by inserting provision for the making or securing by one of the parties to the agreement of periodical payments for the maintenance of the other party or by increasing the rate of the periodical payments which the agreement provides shall be made by one of the parties for the maintenance of the other, the term for which the payments or, as the case may be, the additional payments attributable to the increase are to be made under the agreement as altered by the order shall be such term as the court may specify, subject to the following limits, that is to say –

Matrimonial Causes Act 1973

(a)   where the payments will not be secured, the term shall be so defined as not to extend beyond the death of either of the parties to the agreement or the remarriage of, or formation of a civil partnership by, the party to whom the payments are to be made;

(b)   where the payments will be secured, the term shall be so defined as not to extend beyond the death or remarriage of, or formation of a civil partnership by, that party.

(5)   Where the court decides to alter, by order under this section, an agreement by inserting provision for the making or securing by one of the parties to the agreement of periodical payments for the maintenance of a child of the family or by increasing the rate of the periodical payments which the agreement provides shall be made or secured by one of the parties for the maintenance of such a child, then, in deciding the term for which under the agreement as altered by the order the payments, or as the case may be, the additional payments attributable to the increase are to be made or secured for the benefit of the child, the court shall apply the provisions of section 29(2) and (3) above as to age limits as if the order in question were a periodical payments or secured periodical payments order in favour of the child.

(6)   For the avoidance of doubt it is hereby declared that nothing in this section or in section 34 above affects any power of a court before which any proceedings between the parties to a maintenance agreement are brought under any other enactment (including a provision of this Act) to make an order containing financial arrangements or any right of either party to apply for such an order in such proceedings.

*   *   *   *   *

37. Avoidance of transactions intended to prevent or reduce financial relief

(1)   For the purposes of this section 'financial relief' means relief under any of the provisions of sections 22, 23, 24, 24B, 27, 31 (except subsection (6)) and 35 above, and any reference in this section to defeating a person's claim for financial relief is a reference to preventing financial relief from being granted to that person, or to that person for the benefit of a child of the family, or reducing the amount of any financial relief which might be so granted, or frustrating or impeding the enforcement of any order which might be or has been made at his instance under any of those provisions.

(2)   Where proceedings for financial relief are brought by one person against another, the court may, on the application of the first-mentioned person –

(a)   if it is satisfied that the other party to the proceedings is, with the intention of defeating the claim for financial relief, about to make any disposition or to transfer out of the jurisdiction or otherwise deal with any property, make such order as it thinks fit for restraining the other party from so doing or otherwise for protecting the claim;

(b)   if it is satisfied that the other party has, with that intention, made a reviewable disposition and that if the disposition were set aside financial relief or different financial relief would be granted to the applicant, make an order setting aside the disposition;

(c)   if it is satisfied, in a case where an order has been obtained under any of the provisions mentioned in subsection (1) above by the applicant against the other party, that the other party has, with that intention, made a reviewable disposition, make an order setting aside the disposition;

and an application for the purposes of paragraph (b) above shall be made in the proceedings for the financial relief in question.

(3)   Where the court makes an order under subsection (2)(b) or (c) above setting aside a disposition it shall give such consequential directions as it thinks fit for giving effect to the order (including directions requiring the making of any payments or the disposal of any property).

(4)   Any disposition made by the other party to the proceedings for financial relief in question (whether before or after the commencement of those proceedings) is a reviewable disposition for the purposes of subsection (2)(b) and (c) above unless it was made for valuable consideration (other than marriage) to a person who, at the time of the disposition, acted in relation to it in good faith and without notice of any intention on the part of the other party to defeat the applicant's claim for financial relief.

(5)   Where an application is made under this section with respect to a disposition which took place less than three years before the date of the application or with respect to a disposition or other dealing with property which is about to take place and the court is satisfied –

(a)   in a case falling within subsection (2)(a) or (b) above, that the disposition or other dealing would (apart from this section) have the consequence, or

(b)   in a case falling within subsection (2)(c) above, that the disposition has had the consequence,

of defeating the applicant's claim for financial relief, it shall be presumed, unless the contrary is shown, that the person who disposed of or is about to dispose of or deal with the property did so or, as the case may be, is about to do so, with the intention of defeating the applicant's claim for financial relief.

(6)   In this section 'disposition' does not include any provision contained in a will or codicil but, with that exception, includes any conveyance, assurance or gift of property of any description, whether made by an instrument or otherwise.

(7)   This section does not apply to a disposition made before 1st January 1968.

Financial Remedy Rules

Mainly derived from FPR 2010 Part 9 and PD 9A, these extracts represent only a portion (though intended to be the most significant portion in daily use) of the rules governing financial remedy applications issued in the High Court and the Family Court.

Case allocation within the Family Court is governed by the Family Court (Composition and Distribution of Business) Rules 2014.

The procedural requirements of these rules are set out in tabular form at Table 19 and (in relation to pension sharing) at Table 22.

For a note on pre-action steps, venue and allocation, bundles and transitional provisions, see the introduction to Table 19.

For all 2010 (and subsequent Amendment) Rules and PDs affecting financial cases use @eGlance, which also contains all variants of the ancillary relief rules in force prior to 6 April 2011, and transitional provisions.

The overriding objective

1.1.—(1) These rules are a new procedural code with the overriding objective of enabling the court to deal with cases justly, having regard to any welfare issues involved.

(2) Dealing with a case justly includes, so far as is practicable—

(a) ensuring that it is dealt with expeditiously and fairly;

(b) dealing with the case in ways which are proportionate to the nature, importance and complexity of the issues;

(c) ensuring that the parties are on an equal footing;

(d) saving expense; and

(e) allotting to it an appropriate share of the court's resources, while taking into account the need to allot resources to other cases.

Application by the court of the overriding objective

1.2. The court must seek to give effect to the overriding objective when it—

(a) exercises any power given to it by these rules; or

(b) interprets any rule.

Duty of the parties

1.3. The parties are required to help the court to further the overriding objective.

Court's duty to manage cases

1.4.—(1) The court must further the overriding objective by actively managing cases.

(2) Active case management includes—

(a) setting timetables or otherwise controlling the progress of the case;

(b) identifying at an early stage—

(i) the issues; and

(ii) who should be a party to the proceedings;

(c) deciding promptly—

(i) which issues need full investigation and hearing and which do not; and

(ii) the procedure to be followed in the case;

(d) deciding the order in which issues are to be resolved;

(e) controlling the use of expert evidence;

(f) encouraging the parties to use a non-court dispute resolution procedure if the court considers that appropriate and facilitating the use of such procedure;

(g) helping the parties to settle the whole or part of the case;

(h) encouraging the parties to co-operate with each other in the conduct of proceedings;

(i) considering whether the likely benefits of taking a particular step justify the cost of taking it;

(j) dealing with as many aspects of the case as it can on the same occasion;

(k) dealing with the case without the parties needing to attend at court;

(l) making use of technology; and

(m) giving directions to ensure that the case proceeds quickly and efficiently.

* * * * * *

2.3.—(1) In these rules …

"financial order" means—

(a) an avoidance of disposition order;

(b) an order for maintenance pending suit;

(c) an order for maintenance pending outcome of proceedings;

(d) an order for periodical payments or lump sum provision as mentioned in section 21(1) of the 1973 Act, except an order under section 27(6) of that Act;

(e) an order for periodical payments or lump sum provision as mentioned in paragraph 2(1) of Schedule 5 to the 2004 Act, made under Part 1 of Schedule 5 to that Act;

(f) a property adjustment order;

(g) a variation order;

(h) a pension sharing order;

(i) a pension compensation sharing order; or

(j) an order for payment in respect of legal services.

("variation order", "pension compensation sharing order" and "pension sharing order" are defined in rule 9.3.)

"financial remedy" means—

(a) a financial order;

(b) an order under Schedule 1 to the 1989 Act;

(c) an order under Part 3 of the 1984 Act except an application under section 13 of the 1984 Act for permission to apply for a financial remedy;

(d) an order under Schedule 7 to the 2004 Act except an application under paragraph 4 of Schedule 7 to the 2004 Act for permission to apply for an order under paragraph 9 or 13 of that Schedule;

(e) an order under section 27 of the 1973 Act;

(f) an order under Part 9 of Schedule 5 to the 2004 Act;

(g) an order under section 35 of the 1973 Act;

(h) an order under paragraph 69 of Schedule 5 to the 2004 Act;

(i) an order under Part 1 of the 1978 Act;

(j) an order under Schedule 6 to the 2004 Act;

(k) an order under section 10(2) of the 1973 Act; or

(l) an order under section 48(2) of the 2004 Act;

* * * * * *

Where to start proceedings

5.4.—(1) Where both the family court and the High Court have jurisdiction to deal with a matter, the proceedings relating to that matter must be started in the family court.

(2) Paragraph (1) does not apply where—

(a) proceedings relating to the same parties are already being heard in the High Court;

(b) any rule, other enactment or Practice Direction provides otherwise; or

(c) the court otherwise directs.

* * * * * *

Financial Remedy Rules

Application

9.1 The rules in this Part apply to an application for a financial remedy.

("Financial remedy" and "financial order" are defined in rule 2.3)

PD 9A: Introduction

1.1 Part 9 of the Family Procedure Rules sets out the procedure applicable to the financial proceedings that are included in the definition of a "financial remedy".

1.2 The shorter procedure set out in Chapter 5 of Part 9 of the Family Procedure Rules applies in respect of –

(a) proceedings under –
(i) the 1978 Act,
(ii) Schedule 6 to the 2004 Act,
(iii)Schedule 1 to the 1989 Act;
(iv) Article 56 of the Maintenance Regulation; and
(v) Article 10 of the 2007 Hague Convention
any application for the variation of an order for a financial remedy.

(b) The longer procedure set out in Chapter 4 of Part 9 applies in respect of all other applications for a financial remedy. In a case to which the shorter Chapter 5 procedure applies, the initial application can include a request for the court instead to apply the longer Chapter 4 procedure. Examples of cases in which it may be appropriate to make such a request include an application under Schedule 1 to the 1989 Act in which there are contested issues about the settlement of property, or a variation application in which a capital payment or pension sharing order is proposed.

1.3 Where an application for a financial remedy includes an application relating to land, details of any mortgagee must be included in the application.

Pre-application protocol

2.1 The "pre-application protocol" annexed to this Direction outlines the steps parties should take to seek and provide information from and to each other prior to the commencement of any application for a financial remedy. The court will expect the parties to comply with the terms of the protocol.

* * * * * *

When an Application for a financial order may be made

9.4. An application for a financial order may be made—
(a) in an application for a matrimonial or civil partnership order; or
(b) at any time after an application for a matrimonial or civil partnership order has been made.

Where to start proceedings

9.5.—(1) An application for a financial remedy must be filed-
(a) if there are proceedings for a matrimonial order or a civil partnership order which are proceeding in the family court, in that court; or
(b) if there are proceedings for a matrimonial order or a civil partnership order which are proceeding in the High Court, in the registry in which those proceedings are taking place.
[(2) and (3) revoked.]

Application for an order preventing a disposition

9.6.— The Part 18 procedure applies to an application for an order preventing a disposition.
(2) An application for an order preventing a disposition may be made without notice to the respondent.

("Order preventing a disposition" is defined in rule 9.3.)

Application for interim orders

9.7.—(1) A party may apply at any stage of the proceedings for—
(a) an order for maintenance pending suit;
(b) an order for maintenance pending outcome of proceedings;
(c) an order for interim periodical payments;
(d) an interim variation order;
(da) an order for payment in respect of legal services; or
(e) any other form of interim order.
(2) An application for an order mentioned in paragraph (1) shall be made using the Part 18 procedure.
(3) Where a party makes an application before filing a financial statement, the written evidence in support must—
(a) explain why the order is necessary; and
(b) give up to date information about that party's financial circumstances.
(4) Unless the respondent has filed a financial statement, the respondent must, at least 7 days before the court is to deal with the application, file a statement of his means and serve a copy on the applicant.
(5) An application for an order mentioned in paragraph (1)(e) may be made without notice.

PD 9A: Orders for payment in respect of legal services

12.1 An application for an order for payment in respect of legal services under section 22ZA of the 1973 Act or paragraph 38A of Part 8 of Schedule 5 to the 2004 Act must be made in accordance with FPR 9.7 using the Part 18 procedure. Where the application is made at the same time as an application for an order for maintenance pending suit or maintenance pending outcome, the applications may be included in one application notice, and evidence in support of or in response to the applications may be contained in one witness statement.

(Where an application is made for an order under FPR 9.7, a copy of the application notice must be served in accordance with the provisions of FPR Part 6 at least 14 days before the court is to deal with the application: FPR 18.8(1)(b).)

12.2 The evidence filed in support of an application for an order for payment in respect of legal services must, in addition to the matters referred to in rule 9.7(3), include a concise statement of the applicant's case on –
(a) the criteria set out in section 22ZA(3) and (4) of the 1974 Act or paragraph 38A(3) and (4) of Part 8 of Schedule 5 to the 2004 Act as applicable; and
(b) the matters set out in section 22ZB(1) of the 1973 Act or paragraph 38B(1) of Part 8 of Schedule 5 to the 2004 Act as applicable.

* * * * * *

Application to set aside a financial remedy order

9.9A.–(1) In this rule—

Financial Remedy Rules

    (a) "financial remedy order" means an order or judgment that is a financial remedy, and includes—
        (i) part of such an order or judgment; or
        (ii) a consent order; and
    (b) "set aside" means—
        (i) in the High Court, to set aside a financial remedy order pursuant to section 17(2) of the Senior Courts Act 1981 and this rule;
        (ii) in the family court, to rescind or vary a financial remedy order pursuant to section 31F(6) of the 1984 Act.

(2) A party may apply under this rule to set aside a financial remedy order where no error of the court is alleged.

(3) An application under this rule must be made within the proceedings in which the financial remedy order was made.

(4) An application under this rule must be made in accordance with the Part 18 procedure, subject to the modifications contained in this rule.

(5) Where the court decides to set aside a financial remedy order, it shall give directions for the rehearing of the financial remedy proceedings or make such other orders as may be appropriate to dispose of the application.

PD 9A: Applications to set aside a financial remedy

13.1 As set out in rule 9.9A(4), the Part 18 procedure applies to applications to set aside a financial remedy. Where such an application was made before rule 9.9A came into force, the Part 18 procedure will still apply subject to any directions that the court might make for the purpose of ensuring the proceedings are dealt with fairly (see the Family Procedure (Amendment No. 2) Rules 2016, rule 5).

13.2 If the financial remedy order was made before 22 April 2014, by any court, an application to set it aside under rule 9.9A is to be made to the family court. This is the combined effect of rule 9.9A(3), which provides that the application is made within the original proceedings, and the Crime and Courts Act 2013 (Family Court: Transitional and Savings Provision) Order 2014, which provides that any such proceedings became family court proceedings as of 22 April 2014.

13.3 If the financial remedy order was made on or after 22 April 2014, an application to set it aside under rule 9.9A is to be made to the court that made the order.

13.4 An application under rule 9.9A is to be dealt with by the same level of judge that dealt with the original application, by virtue of rule 17 of the Family Court (Composition and Distribution of Business) Rules 2014. Where reasonably possible, the application will be dealt with by the same judge that dealt with the original application.

13.5 An application to set aside a financial remedy order should only be made where no error of the court is alleged. If an error of the court is alleged, an application for permission to appeal under Part 30 should be considered. The grounds on which a financial remedy order may be set aside are and will remain a matter for decisions by judges. The grounds include (i) fraud; (ii) material non-disclosure; (iii) certain limited types of mistake; (iv) a subsequent event, unforeseen and unforeseeable at the time the order was made, which invalidates the basis on which the order was made.

13.6 The effect of rules 9.9A(1)(a) and (2) is that an application may be made to set aside all or only part of a financial remedy order, including a financial remedy order that has been made by consent.

13.7 The family court has the power under section 31F(6) of the Matrimonial and Family Proceedings Act 1984 to vary or set aside a financial remedy order. The High Court has the power under rule 9.9A and section 17(2) of the Senior Courts Act 1981 to set aside a financial remedy order. The difference in the wording of the legislative provisions is the reason that "set aside" has been defined as it has in rule 9.9A(1)(b).

13.8 In applications under rule 9.9A, the starting point is that the order which one party is seeking to have set aside was properly made. A mere allegation that it was obtained by, e.g., non-disclosure, is not sufficient for the court to set aside the order. Only once the ground for setting aside the order has been established (or admitted) can the court set aside the order and rehear the original application for a financial remedy. The court has a full range of case management powers and considerable discretion as to how to determine an application to set aside a financial remedy order, including where appropriate the power to strike out or summarily dispose of an application to set aside. If and when a ground for setting aside has been established, the court may decide to set aside the whole or part of the order there and then, or may delay doing so, especially if there are third party claims to the parties' assets. Ordinarily, once the court has decided to set aside a financial remedy order, the court would give directions for a full rehearing to re-determine the original application. However, if the court is satisfied that it has sufficient information to do so, it may proceed to re-determine the original application at the same time as setting aside the financial remedy order.

13.9 The effect of rule 28.3(9) is that the Part 28 rules relating to costs do not apply to applications under rule 9.9A.

Application by parent, guardian etc for financial remedy in respect of children

9.10.—(1) The following people may apply for a financial remedy in respect of a child—
    (a) a parent, guardian or special guardian of any child of the family;
    (b) any person who is named in a child arrangements order as a person with whom a child of the family is to live, and any applicant for such an order;
    (c) any other person who is entitled to apply for a child arrangements order which names that person as a person with whom a child is to live;
    (d) a local authority, where an order has been made under section 31(1)(a) of the 1989 Act placing a child in its care;
    (e) the Official Solicitor, if appointed the children's guardian of a child of the family under rule 16.24; and
    (f) subject to paragraph (1A), a child of the family who has been given permission to apply for a financial remedy.

(1A) Where the application is—
    (a) for the variation of an order under section 2(1)(c), 6 or 7 of the 1978 Act or paragraph 2(1)(c) of, or Part 2 or 3 of, Schedule 6 to the 2004 Act for periodical payments in respect of a child;
    (b) the application is made by the child in question; and
    (c) the child in question is aged 16 or over,

Financial Remedy Rules

the child does not require permission to make the application.

Children to be separately represented on certain applications

9.11.—(1) Where an application for a financial remedy includes an application for an order for a variation of settlement, the court must, unless it is satisfied that the proposed variation does not adversely affect the rights or interests of any child concerned, direct that the child be separately represented on the application.

(2) On any other application for a financial remedy the court may direct that the child be separately represented on the application.

(3) Where a direction is made under paragraph (1) or (2), the court may if the person to be appointed so consents, appoint—

(a) a person other than the Official Solicitor; or

(b) the Official Solicitor,

to be a children's guardian and rule 16.24(5) and (6) and rules 16.25 to 16.28 apply as appropriate to such an appointment.

CHAPTER 4

Duties of the court and the applicant upon issuing an application

9.12.—(1) When an application under this Part is issued, except where Chapter 5 of this Part applies—

(a) the court will fix a first appointment not less than 12 weeks and not more than 16 weeks after the date of the filing of the application; and

(b) subject to paragraph (2), within 4 days beginning with the date on which the application was filed, a court officer will—

(i) serve a copy of the application on the respondent; and

(ii) give notice of the date of the first appointment to the applicant and the respondent.

(2) Where the applicant wishes to serve a copy of the application on the respondent and on filing the application so notifies the court—

(a) paragraph (1)(b) does not apply;

(b) a court officer will return to the applicant the copy of the application and the notice of the date of the first appointment; and

(c) the applicant must,—

(i) within 4 days beginning with the date on which the copy of the application is received from the court, serve the copy of the application and notice of the date of the first appointment on the respondent; and

(ii) file a certificate of service at or before the first appointment.

(Rule 6.37 sets out what must be included in a certificate of service.)

(3) The date fixed under paragraph (1), or for any subsequent appointment, must not be cancelled except with the court's permission and, if cancelled, the court must immediately fix a new date.

(4) In relation to an application to which the Maintenance Regulation or the 2007 Hague Convention applies, where the applicant does not already know the address of the respondent at the time the application is issued, paragraph

(2) does not apply and the court will serve the application in accordance with paragraph (1).

Service of application on mortgagees, trustees etc

9.13.—(1) Where an application for a financial remedy includes an application for an order for a variation of settlement, the applicant must serve copies of the application on—

(a) the trustees of the settlement;

(b) the settlor if living; and

(c) such other persons as the court directs.

(2) In the case of an application for an avoidance of disposition order, the applicant must serve copies of the application on the person in whose favour the disposition is alleged to have been made.

(3) Where an application for a financial remedy includes an application relating to land, the applicant must serve a copy of the application on any mortgagee of whom particulars are given in the application.

(4) Any person served under paragraphs (1), (2) or (3) may make a request to the court in writing, within 14 days beginning with the date of service of the application, for a copy of the applicant's financial statement or any relevant part of that statement.

(5) Any person who—

(a) is served with copies of the application in accordance with paragraphs (1), (2) or (3); or

(b) receives a copy of a financial statement, or a relevant part of that statement, following an application made under paragraph (4),

may within 14 days beginning with the date of service or receipt file a statement in answer.

(6) Where a copy of an application is served under paragraphs (1), (2) or (3), the applicant must file a certificate of service at or before the first appointment.

(7) A statement in answer filed under paragraph (5) must be verified by a statement of truth.

Procedure before the first appointment

9.14.—(1) Not less than 35 days before the first appointment both parties must simultaneously exchange with each other and file with the court a financial statement in the form referred to in Practice Direction 5A.

(2) The financial statement must—

(a) be verified by a statement of truth; and

(b) accompanied by the following documents only—

(i) any documents required by the financial statement;

(ii) any other documents necessary to explain or clarify any of the information contained in the financial statement; and

(iii) any documents provided to the party producing the financial statement by a person responsible for a pension arrangement, either following a request under rule 9.30 or as part of a relevant valuation; and

(iv) any notification or other document referred to in rule 9.37(2), (4) or (5) which has been received by the party producing the financial statement.

(2ZA) Paragraph (2A) applies where the court has determined that the procedure in this Chapter should apply to an application under Article 56 of the Maintenance Regulation or Article 10 of the 2007 Hague Convention.

(2A) The requirement of paragraph (2)(a) relating to verification by a statement of truth does not apply to the financial

Financial Remedy Rules

statement of either party where the application has been made under—

(a) Article 56 of the Maintenance Regulation, using the form in Annex VII to that Regulation; or

(b) Article 10 of the 2007 Hague Convention, using the Financial Circumstances Form,

and the relief sought is limited to a type to which that Regulation or that Convention, as appropriate, applies, but the court may at any time direct that the financial statement of either party shall be verified by a statement of truth.

(3) Where a party was unavoidably prevented from sending any document required by the financial statement, that party must at the earliest opportunity—

(a) serve a copy of that document on the other party; and

(b) file a copy of that document with the court, together with a written explanation of the failure to send it with the financial statement.

(4) No disclosure or inspection of documents may be requested or given between the filing of the application for a financial remedy and the first appointment, except—

(a) copies sent with the financial statement, or in accordance with paragraph (3); or

(b) in accordance with paragraphs (5) and (6).

(Rule 21.1 explains what is meant by disclosure and inspection.)

(5) Not less than 14 days before the hearing of the first appointment, each party must file with the court and serve on the other party—

(a) a concise statement of the issues between the parties;

(b) a chronology;

(c) a questionnaire setting out by reference to the concise statement of issues any further information and documents requested from the other party or a statement that no information and documents are required; and

(d) a notice stating whether that party will be in a position at the first appointment to proceed on that occasion to a FDR appointment.

(6) Not less than 14 days before the hearing of the first appointment, the applicant must file with the court and serve on the respondent confirmation—

(a) of the names of all persons served in accordance with rule 9.13(1) to (3); and

(b) that there are no other persons who must be served in accordance with those paragraphs.

PD 9A: *Procedure before the first appointment*

4.1 In addition to the matters listed at rule 9.14(5), the parties should, if possible, with a view to identifying and narrowing any issues between the parties, exchange and file with the court—

(a) a summary of the case agreed between the parties;

(b) a schedule of assets agreed between the parties; and

(c) details of any directions that they seek, including, where appropriate, the name of any expert they wish to be appointed.

4.2 Where a party is prevented from sending the details referred to in (c) above, the party should make that information available at the first appointment.

PD 9A: *Financial Statements and other documents*

5.1 Practice Direction 22A (Written Evidence) applies to any financial statement filed in accordance with rules 9.14 or 9.19 and to any exhibits to a financial statement. In preparing a bundle of documents to be exhibited to or attached to a financial statement, regard must be had in particular to paragraphs 11.1 to 11.3 and 13.1 to 13.4 of that Direction. Where on account of their bulk, it is impracticable for the exhibits to a financial statement to be retained on the court file after the First Appointment, the court may give directions as to their custody pending further hearings.

5.2 Where the court directs a party to provide information or documents by way of reply to a questionnaire or request by another party, the reply must be verified by a statement of truth. Unless otherwise directed, a reply to a questionnaire or request for information and documents shall not be filed with the court.

(Part 17 and Practice Direction 17A make further provision about statements of truth)

Duties of the court at the first appointment

9.15.—(1) The first appointment must be conducted with the objective of defining the issues and saving costs.

(2) At the first appointment the court must determine—

(a) the extent to which any questions seeking information under rule 9.14(5)(c) must be answered; and

(b) what documents requested under rule 9.14(5)(c) must be produced,

and give directions for the production of such further documents as may be necessary.

(3) The court must give directions where appropriate about—

(a) the valuation of assets (including the joint instruction of joint experts);

(b) obtaining and exchanging expert evidence, if required;

(c) the evidence to be adduced by each party; and

(d) further chronologies or schedules to be filed by each party.

(4) The court must direct that the case be referred to a FDR appointment unless—

(a) the first appointment or part of it has been treated as a FDR appointment and the FDR appointment has been effective; or

(b) there are exceptional reasons which make a referral to a FDR appointment inappropriate.

(5) If the court decides that a referral to a FDR appointment is not appropriate it must direct one or more of the following—

(a) that a further directions appointment be fixed;

(b) that an appointment be fixed for the making of an interim order;

(c) that the case be fixed for a final hearing and, where that direction is given, the court must determine the judicial level at which the case should be heard.

(Under Part 3 the court may also direct that the case be adjourned if it considers that non-court dispute resolution is appropriate.)

(6) In considering whether to make a costs order under rule 28.3(5), the court must have particular regard to the extent to which each party has complied with the requirement to send documents with the financial statement and the explanation given for any failure to comply.

(7) The court may—

(a) where an application for an interim order has been listed for consideration at the first appointment, make an interim order;

(b) having regard to the contents of the notice filed by the parties under rule 9.14(5)(d), treat the appointment (or

Financial Remedy Rules

part of it) as a FDR appointment to which rule 9.17 applies;

(c) in a case where a pension sharing order or a pension attachment order is requested, direct any party with pension rights to file and serve a Pension Inquiry Form, completed in full or in part as the court may direct; and

(d) in a case where a pension compensation sharing order or a pension compensation attachment order is requested, direct any party with PPF compensation rights to file and serve a Pension Protection Fund Inquiry Form, completed in full or in part as the court may direct.

(8) Both parties must personally attend the first appointment unless the court directs otherwise.

After the first appointment

9.16.—(1) Between the first appointment and the FDR appointment, a party is not entitled to the production of any further documents except—

(a) in accordance with directions given under rule 9.15(2); or

(b) with the permission of the court.

(2) At any stage—

(a) a party may apply for further directions or a FDR appointment;

(b) the court may give further directions or direct that parties attend a FDR appointment.

The FDR appointment

9.17.—(1) The FDR appointment must be treated as a meeting held for the purposes of discussion and negotiation.

(2) The judge hearing the FDR appointment must have no further involvement with the application, other than to conduct any further FDR appointment or to make a consent order or a further directions order.

(3) Not less than 7 days before the FDR appointment, the applicant must file with the court details of all offers and proposals, and responses to them.

(4) Paragraph (3) includes any offers, proposals or responses made wholly or partly without prejudice, but paragraph (3) does not make any material admissible as evidence if, but for that paragraph, it would not be admissible.

(5) At the conclusion of the FDR appointment, any documents filed under paragraph (3), and any filed documents referring to them, must, at the request of the party who filed them, be returned to that party and not retained on the court file.

(6) Parties attending the FDR appointment must use their best endeavours to reach agreement on matters in issue between them.

(7) The FDR appointment may be adjourned from time to time.

(8) At the conclusion of the FDR appointment, the court may make an appropriate consent order.

(9) If the court does not make an appropriate consent order as mentioned in paragraph (8), the court must give directions for the future course of the proceedings including, where appropriate—

(a) the filing of evidence, including up to date information; and

(b) fixing a final hearing date.

(10)Both parties must personally attend the FDR appointment unless the court directs otherwise.

PD 9A: Financial Dispute Resolution (FDR) Appointment

6.1 A key element in the procedure is the Financial Dispute Resolution (FDR) appointment. Rule 9.17 provides that the FDR appointment is to be treated as a meeting held for the purposes of discussion and negotiation. Such meetings have been developed as a means of reducing the tension which inevitably arises in family disputes and facilitating settlement of those disputes.

6.2 In order for the FDR to be effective, parties must approach the occasion openly and without reserve. Non-disclosure of the content of such meetings is vital and is an essential prerequisite for fruitful discussion directed to the settlement of the dispute between the parties. The FDR appointment is an important part of the settlement process. As a consequence of **Re D (Minors) (Conciliation: Disclosure of Information)** *[1993] Fam 231, evidence of anything said or of any admission made in the course of an FDR appointment will not be admissible in evidence, except at the trial of a person for an offence committed at the appointment or in the very exceptional circumstances indicated in* **Re D**.

6.3 Courts will therefore expect—

(a) parties to make offers and proposals;

(b) recipients of offers and proposals to give them proper consideration; and

(c) (subject to paragraph 6.4), that parties, whether separately or together, will not seek to exclude from consideration at the appointment any such offer or proposal.

6.4 Paragraph 6.3(c) does not apply to an offer or proposal made during non-court dispute resolution.

6.5 In order to make the most effective use of the first appointment and the FDR appointment, the legal representatives attending those appointments will be expected to have full knowledge of the case.

Editors' note:

For practical advice on the FDR Appointment see the *Financial Dispute Resolution Appointments: Best Practice Guidance* produced by the Family Justice Council in December 2012 (available online and in *@eGlance*).

* * * * * *

CHAPTER 5

Duties of the court and the applicant upon filing an application

9.18.—(A1) This Chapter applies where an application is made—

(a) under—

(i) the 1978 Act;

(ii) Schedule 6 to the 2004 Act;

(iii)Schedule 1 to the 1989 Act;

(iv)Article 56 of the Maintenance Regulation; or

(v) Article 10 of the 2007 Hague Convention.

(b) for the variation of an order for a financial remedy.

(1) Where an application is issued-

(a) the court will fix a first hearing date not less than 4 weeks and not more than 8 weeks after the date of the filing of the application; and

(b) subject to paragraph (2), within 4 days beginning with the date on which the application was filed, a court officer will-

Financial Remedy Rules

(i) serve a copy of the application on the respondent;

(ii) give notice of the date of the first hearing to the applicant and the respondent; and

(iii) send a blank financial statement to both the applicant and the respondent.

(2) Where the applicant wishes to serve a copy of the application on the respondent and, on filing the application, so notifies the court-

(a) paragraph (1)(b) does not apply;

(b) a court officer will return to the applicant the copy of the application and the notice of the date of the first hearing; and

(c) the applicant must-

(i) within 4 days beginning with the date on which the copy of the application is received from the court, serve the copy of the application and notice of the date of the first hearing on the respondent;

(ii) send a blank financial statement to the respondent; and

(iii) file a certificate of service at or before the first hearing.

(3) The date fixed under paragraph (1), or for any other subsequent hearing or appointment must not be cancelled except with the court's permission and, if cancelled, the court must immediately fix a new date.

(4) The requirement in paragraph (1)(b)(iii) for the court officer to send a blank financial statement to the applicant does not apply where the application has been made under—

(a) Article 56 of the Maintenance Regulation, using the form in Annex VII to that Regulation; or

(b) Article 10 of the 2007 Hague Convention, using the Financial Circumstances Form.

(5) In relation to an application to which the Maintenance Regulation or the 2007 Hague Convention applies, where the applicant does not already know the address of the respondent at the time the application is issued, paragraph (2) does not apply and the court will serve the application in accordance with paragraph (1).

Request for change of procedure

9.18A.—(1) This rule applies if the applicant wishes to seek a direction from the court that the procedure in Chapter 4 of this Part should apply to an application for an order in proceedings referred to in rule 9.18(A1).

(2) The application for the order must state—

(a) that the applicant seeks a direction that the procedure in Chapter 4 of this Part should apply; and

(b) the applicant's reasons for seeking such a direction.

(3) The court will—

(a) determine without notice to the parties and before the first hearing whether the procedure in Chapter 4 or Chapter 5 of this Part should apply to the application; and

(b) notify the parties of its determination and any directions made in consequence of that determination.

Procedure before the first hearing

9.19.—(1) Not more than 14 days after the date of the issue of the application both parties must simultaneously exchange with each other and file with the court a financial statement referred to in Practice Direction 5A.

(2) The financial statement must—

(a) be verified by a statement of truth; and

(b) contain the following documents only—

(i) any documents required by the financial statement; and

(ii) any other documents necessary to explain or clarify any of the information contained in the financial statement.

(2A) The requirement of paragraph (2)(a) relating to verification by statement of truth does not apply to the financial statement of either party where the application has been made under—

(a) Article 56 of the Maintenance Regulation, using the form in Annex VII to that Regulation; or

(b) Article 10 of the 2007 Hague Convention, using the Financial Circumstances Form,

but the court may at any time direct that the financial statement of either party shall be verified by a statement of truth..

(3) Where a party was unavoidably prevented from sending any document required by the financial statement, that party must at the earliest opportunity-

(a) serve a copy of that document on the other party; and

(b) file a copy of that document with the court, together with a statement explaining the failure to send it with the financial statement.

(4) No disclosure or inspection of documents may be requested or given between the filing of the application for a financial remedy and the first hearing except copies sent with the financial statement or in accordance with paragraph (3).

(Rule 21.1 explains what is meant by disclosure and inspection.)

Power of the court to direct filing of evidence and set dates for further hearings

9.20. Unless the court is able to determine the application at the first hearing the court may direct that further evidence be filed and set a date for a directions hearing or appointment or final hearing.

* * * * * *

Power to order delivery up of possession etc.

9.24.—(1) This rule applies where the court has made an order under—

(a) section 24A of the 1973 Act;

(b) section 17(2) of the 1984 Act;

(c) Part 3 of Schedule 5 to the 2004 Act; or

(d) paragraph 9(4) of Schedule 7 to the 2004 Act.

(2) When the court makes an order mentioned in paragraph (1), it may order any party to deliver up to the purchaser or any other person—

(a) possession of the land, including any interest in, or right over, land;

(b) receipt of rents or profits relating to it; or

(c) both.

* * * * * *

Applications for consent orders for financial remedy

9.26.—(1) Subject to paragraph (5) and to rule 35.2, in relation to an application for a consent order—

(a) the applicant must file two copies of a draft of the order in the terms sought, one of which must be endorsed with a statement signed by the respondent to the application signifying agreement; and

(b) each party must file with the court and serve on the other

Financial Remedy Rules

party, a statement of information in the form referred to in Practice Direction 5A.

(2) Where each party's statement of information is contained in one form, it must be signed by both the applicant and respondent to certify that they have read the contents of the other party's statement.

(3) Where each party's statement of information is in a separate form, the form of each party must be signed by the other party to certify that they have read the contents of the statement contained in that form.

(4) Unless the court directs otherwise, the applicant and the respondent need not attend the hearing of an application for a consent order.

(5) Where all or any of the parties attend the hearing of an application for a financial remedy the court may—
   (a) dispense with the filing of a statement of information; and
   (b) give directions for the information which would otherwise be required to be given in such a statement in such a manner as it thinks fit.

(6) In relation to an application for a consent order under Part 3 of the 1984 Act or Schedule 7 to the 2004 Act, the application for permission to make the application may be heard at the same time as the application for a financial remedy if evidence of the respondent's consent to the order is filed with the application.

(The following rules contain provision in relation to applications for consent orders – rule 9.32 (pension sharing order), rule 9.34 (pension attachment order), rule 9.41 (pension compensation sharing orders) and rule 9.43 (pension compensation attachment orders.)

PD 9A: Consent orders

7.1 Rule 9.26(1)(a) requires an application for a consent order to be accompanied by two copies of the draft order in the terms sought, one of which must be endorsed with a statement signed by the respondent to the application signifying the respondent's agreement. The rule is considered to have been properly complied with if the endorsed statement is signed by solicitors on record as acting for the respondent; but where the consent order applied for contains undertakings, it should be signed by the party giving the undertakings as well as by that party's solicitor.
(Provision relating to the enforcement of undertakings is contained in the Practice Direction 33A supplementing Part 33 of the FPR)

7.2 Rule 9.26(1)(b) requires each party to file with the court and serve on the other party a statement of information. Where this is contained in one form, both parties must sign the statement to certify that each has read the contents of the other's statement.

7.3 Rule 35.2 deals with applications for a consent order in respect of a financial remedy where the parties wish to have the content of a written mediation agreement to which the Mediation Directive applies made the subject of a consent order.

Questions as to the court's jurisdiction or whether the proceedings should be stayed

9.26A.—(1) This rule applies to applications for maintenance where a question as to jurisdiction arises under—
   (a) the 1968 Convention;
   (b) the 1988 Convention;
   (c) the Lugano Convention;
   (d) the Maintenance Regulation; or
   (e) Article 18 of the 2007 Hague Convention.

(2) If at any time after the issue of the application it appears to the court that it does not or may not have jurisdiction to hear an application, or that under the instruments referred to in paragraph (1) it is or may be required to stay the proceedings or to decline jurisdiction, the court must—
   (a) stay the proceedings, and
   (b) fix a date for a hearing to determine jurisdiction or whether there should be a stay or other order.

(3) The court officer will serve notice of the hearing referred to at paragraph (2)(b) on the parties to the proceedings.

(4) The court must, in writing—
   (a) give reasons for its decision under paragraph (2), and
   (b) where it makes a finding of fact, state such finding.

(5) The court may with the consent of all the parties deal with any question as to the jurisdiction of the court, or as to whether the proceedings should be stayed, without a hearing.

(6) In this rule—
   (a) "the 1968 Convention" has the meaning given to it in the Civil Jurisdiction and Judgments Act 1982;
   (b) "the 1988 Convention" and "the Lugano Convention" have the meanings given to them in rule 34.1(2).

* * * * * *

Adding or removing parties

9.26B.—(1) The court may direct that a person or body be added as a party to proceedings for a financial remedy if—
   (a) it is desirable to add the new party so that the court can resolve all the matters in dispute in the proceedings; or
   (b) there is an issue involving the new party and an existing party which is connected to the matters in dispute in the proceedings, and it is desirable to add the new party so that the court can resolve that issue.

(2) The court may direct that any person or body be removed as a party if it is not desirable for that person or body to be a party to the proceedings.

(3) If the court makes a direction for the addition or removal of a party under this rule, it may give consequential directions about—
   (a) the service of a copy of the application form or other relevant documents on the new party; and
   (b) the management of the proceedings.

(4) The power of the court under this rule to direct that a party be added or removed may be exercised either on the court's own initiative or on the application of an existing party or a person or body who wishes to become a party.

(5) An application for an order under this rule must be made in accordance with the Part 18 procedure and, unless the court directs otherwise, must be supported by evidence setting out the proposed new party's interest in or connection with the proceedings or, in the case of removal of a party, the reasons for removal.

* * * * * *

Estimates of Costs

9.27.—(1) Subject to paragraph (2), at every hearing or appointment each party must produce to the court an

Financial Remedy Rules

estimate of the costs incurred by that party up to the date of that hearing or appointment.

(2) Not less than 14 days before the date fixed for the final hearing of an application for a financial remedy, each party ("the filing party") must (unless the court directs otherwise) file with the court and serve on each other party a statement giving full particulars of all costs in respect of the proceedings which the filing party has incurred or expects to incur, to enable the court to take account of the parties' liabilities for costs when deciding what order (if any) to make for a financial remedy.

(3) *[Revoked.]*

PD 9A: Costs

3.1 Rule 9.27 requires each party to produce to the court, at every hearing or appointment, an estimate of the costs incurred by the party up to the date of that hearing or appointment.

3.2 The purpose of this rule is to enable the court to take account of the impact of each party's costs liability on their financial situations. Parties should ensure that the information contained in the estimate is as full and accurate as possible and that any sums already paid in respect of a party's financial remedy costs are clearly set out. Where relevant, any liability arising from the costs of other proceedings between the parties should continue to be referred to in the appropriate section of a party's financial statement; any such costs should not be included in the estimates under rule 9.27.

* * * * * *

3.4 Any breach of this practice direction or the pre-application protocol annexed to it will be taken into account by the court when deciding whether to depart from the general rule as to costs.

Duty to make open proposals

9.28.—(1) Not less than 14 days before the date fixed for the final hearing of an application for a financial remedy, the applicant must (unless the court directs otherwise) file with the court and serve on the respondent an open statement which sets out concise details, including the amounts involved, of the orders which the applicant proposes to ask the court to make.

(2) Not more than 7 days after service of a statement under paragraph (1), the respondent must file with the court and serve on the applicant an open statement which sets out concise details, including the amounts involved, of the orders which the respondent proposes to ask the court to make.

CHAPTER 8

Application and interpretation of this Chapter

9.29.—(1) This Chapter applies

  (a) where an application for a financial remedy has been made; and

  (b) the applicant or respondent is the party with pension rights.

(2) In this Chapter—

  (a) in proceedings under the 1973 Act and the 1984 Act, all words and phrases defined in sections 25D(3) and (4) of the 1973 Act have the meaning assigned by those subsections;

  (b) in proceedings under the 2004 Act—

    (i) all words and phrases defined in paragraphs 16(4) to (5) and 29 of Schedule 5 to that Act have the meanings assigned by those paragraphs; and

    (ii) "the party with pension rights" has the meaning given to "civil partner with pension rights" by paragraph 29 of Schedule 5 to the 2004 Act;

  (c) all words and phrases defined in section 46 of the Welfare Reform and Pensions Act 1999 have the meanings assigned by that section.

PD 9A: Pensions

10.1 The phrase "party with pension rights" is used in FPR Part 9, Chapter 8. For matrimonial proceedings, this phrase has the meaning given to it by section 25D(3) of the Matrimonial Causes Act 1973 and means "the party to the marriage who has or is likely to have benefits under a pension arrangement". There is a definition of "civil partner with pension rights" in paragraph 29 of Schedule 5 to the Civil Partnership Act 2004 which mirrors the definition of "party with pension rights" in section 25D(3) of the 1973 Act. The phrase "is likely to have benefits" in these definitions refers to accrued rights to pension benefits which are not yet in payment.

What the party with pension rights must do when the court fixes a first appointment

9.30.—(1) Where the court fixes a first appointment as required by rule 9.12(1)(a) the party with pension rights must request the person responsible for each pension arrangement under which the party has or is likely to have benefits to provide the information referred to in regulation 2(2) of the Pensions on Divorce etc (Provision of Information) Regulations 2000.

(The information referred to in regulation 2 of the Pensions on Divorce etc (Provision of Information) Regulations 2000 relates to the valuation of pension rights or benefits.)

(2) The party with pension rights must comply with paragraph (1) within 7 days beginning with the date on which that party receives notification of the date of the first appointment.

(3) Within 7 days beginning with the date on which the party with pension rights receives the information under paragraph (1) that party must send a copy of it to the other party, together with the name and address of the person responsible for each pension arrangement.

(4) A request under paragraph (1) need not be made where the party with pension rights is in possession of, or has requested, a relevant valuation of the pension rights or benefits accrued under the pension arrangement in question.

Applications for pension sharing orders

9.31. Where an application for a financial remedy includes an application for a pension sharing order, or where a request for such an order is added to an existing application for a financial remedy, the applicant must serve a copy of the application on the person responsible for the pension arrangement concerned.

Applications for consent orders for pension sharing

9.32.—(1) This rule applies where—

  (a) the parties have agreed on the terms of an order and the agreement includes a pension sharing order;

  (b) service has not been effected under rule 9.31; and

  (c) the information referred to in paragraph (2) has not otherwise been provided.

Financial Remedy Rules

(2) The party with pension rights must—
- (a) request the person responsible for the pension arrangement concerned to provide the information set out in Section C of the Pension Inquiry Form; and
- (b) on receipt, send a copy of the information referred to in sub-paragraph (a) to the other party.

Applications for pension attachment orders

9.33. *(Not reproduced in this text)*

Applications for consent orders for pension attachment

9.34. *(Not reproduced in this text)*

Pension sharing orders or pension attachment orders

9.35. An order for a financial remedy, whether by consent or not, which includes a pension sharing order or a pension attachment order, must—
- (a) in the body of the order, state that there is to be provision by way of pension sharing or pension attachment in accordance with the annex or annexes to the order; and
- (b) be accompanied by a pension sharing annex or a pension attachment annex as the case may require, and if provision is made in relation to more than one pension arrangement there must be one annex for each pension arrangement.

Duty of the court upon making a pension sharing order or a pension attachment order

9.36.—(1) A court which varies or discharges a pension sharing order or a pension attachment order, must send, or direct one of the parties to send—
- (a) to the person responsible for the pension arrangement concerned; or
- (b) where the Board has assumed responsibility for the pension scheme or part of it, the Board;

the documents referred to in paragraph (4).
- (2) A court which makes a pension sharing order or pension attachment order, must send, or direct one of the parties to send to the person responsible for the pension arrangement concerned, the documents referred to in paragraph (4).
- (3) Where the Board has assumed responsibility for the pension scheme or part of it after the making of a pension sharing order or attachment order but before the documents have been sent to the person responsible for the pension arrangement in accordance with paragraph (2), the court which makes the pension sharing order or the pension attachment order, must send, or direct one of the parties to send to the Board the documents referred to in paragraph (4).
- (4) The documents to be sent in accordance with paragraph (1) to (3) are—
  - (a) in the case of—
    - (i) proceedings under the 1973 Act, a copy of the decree of judicial separation;
    - (ii) proceedings under Schedule 5 to the 2004 Act, a copy of the separation order;
    - (iii) proceedings under Part 3 of the 1984 Act, a copy of the document of divorce, annulment or legal separation;
    - (iv) proceedings under Schedule 7 to the 2004 Act, a copy of the document of dissolution, annulment or legal separation;
  - (b) in the case of divorce or nullity of marriage, a copy of the decree absolute under rule 7.31 or 7.32; or
  - (c) in the case of dissolution or nullity of civil partnership, a copy of the order making the conditional order final under rule 7.31 or 7.32; and
  - (d) a copy of the pension sharing order or the pension attachment order, or as the case may be of the order varying or discharging that order, including any annex to that order relating to that pension arrangement but no other annex to that order.
- (5) The documents referred to in paragraph (4) must be sent—
  - (a) in proceedings under the 1973 Act and the 1984 Act, within 7 days beginning with the date on which—
    - (i) the relevant pension sharing or pension attachment order, or any order varying or discharging such an order, is made; or
    - (ii) the decree absolute of divorce or nullity or decree of judicial separation is made,

    whichever is the later; and
  - (b) in proceedings under the 2004 Act, within 7 days beginning with the date on which—
    - (i) the relevant pension sharing or pension attachment order, or any order varying or discharging such an order, is made; or
    - (ii) the final order of dissolution or nullity or separation order is made,

    whichever is the later.

* * * * * *

Transfer of proceedings

29.17.—(1) Subject to paragraph (3), a court may transfer a case to another court, either of its own initiative or on the application of one of the parties if—
- (a) the parties consent to the transfer;
- (b) the court has held a hearing to determine whether a transfer should be ordered; or
- (c) paragraph (2) applies.
- (2) A court may transfer a case without a hearing if—
  - (a) the court has notified the parties in writing that it intends to order a transfer; and
  - (b) no party has, within 14 days of the notification being sent, requested a hearing to determine whether a transfer should be ordered.
- (3) A case may not be transferred from the family court to the High Court unless—
  - (a) the decision to transfer was made by a judge sitting in the family court who is a person to whom paragraph (4) applies; or
  - (b) one or more of the circumstances specified in Practice Direction 29C applies.
- (4) This paragraph applies to a person who is—
  - (a) the President of the Family Division;
  - (b) an ordinary judge of the Court of Appeal (including the vice-president, if any, of either division of that court);
  - (c) a puisne judge of the High Court.

Efficient Conduct of Financial Hearings

Statement on the Efficient Conduct of Financial Remedy Hearings allocated to a High Court Judge whether sitting at the Royal Courts of Justice or elsewhere

1. I am authorised by the President to release this statement.
2. In order to enhance efficiency in the disposal of financial remedy cases allocated to be heard by a High Court Judge, and to ensure that such cases are allotted an appropriate share of the court's resources, the following standards and procedures must be observed.
3. **Principles of allocation: The governing principle is that a case should only be allocated for hearing by a High Court judge if it is exceptionally complex or there is another substantial ground for the case being heard at that level <u>and that</u> allocation to that level is proportionate. Such allocation is rarely likely to be proportionate unless the net assets exceed £7.5m.**

   In determining whether the governing principle is satisfied the following are relevant considerations:

   (1) The overall net assets exceed £15m; and/or

   (2) The overall net earned annual income exceeds £1m.

   In a case falling within (1) or (2) the governing principle will likely, but not necessarily, be satisfied. There will be some relatively straightforward cases falling within (1) or (2) where a transfer to High Court judge level will nevertheless not be proportionate.

   In a case not falling within (1) or (2) above but where the net assets are said to exceed £7.5m:

   (3) There is a serious case advanced of non-disclosure of assets.

   (4) Substantial assets are held offshore either directly or through the medium of trust or corporate entities and there may be issues as to the enforceability of any award.

   (5) Substantial assets are held in trusts which are said to be variable nuptial settlements.

   (6) Substantial assets are held through the medium of unquoted corporate entities and detailed expert valuation evidence will be required.

   (7) A serious, carefully considered and potentially influential argument is being advanced of
      a. compensation,
      b. non-matrimonial property, or
      c. conduct.

   (8) There are serious, substantial third party claims to the assets otherwise subject to the dispositive powers of the court.

   (9) There is a serious, carefully considered and potentially influential issue as to the effect of a nuptial agreement.

   (10) The application involves a novel and important point of law.

   Where, on any view, the net assets do not exceed £7.5m allocation to a High Court Judge is only likely to be proportionate where the application involves a novel and important point of law.

4. Every case will be allocated to an individual High Court Judge at the earliest opportunity. He or she will, unless this is completely impracticable, conduct all future hearings, including the final hearing, apart from the FDR. Early allocation is essential to achieve judicial continuity which is to be regarded as a critically important objective.
5. Allocation will be undertaken as follows:
   a. If the case is at High Court Judge level by virtue of the self-certification procedure (see para 20 below) then the allocated judge will be determined by the judge in charge of the money list (presently Mostyn J) when granting the certificate. For this purpose it is vital that the available dates of counsel for the First Appointment are stated on the certificate.
   b. If the case has been transferred to High Court Judge level by a district or circuit judge sitting in the Family Court in London or elsewhere on the South-Eastern Circuit the order for transfer, together with available dates of counsel for the next hearing, must be emailed to the judge in charge of the money list (c/o his clerk) who will determine the allocated judge.
   c. If the case has been transferred to High Court Judge level by a district or circuit judge sitting in the Family Court on circuit (other than the South-Eastern Circuit) the order for transfer, together with available dates of counsel for the next hearing, must be emailed to the relevant FDLJ (c/o his or her clerk) who will determine the allocated judge.
   d. If the case has been transferred to High Court Judge level by a High Court Judge (for example on or following an early application for a freezing injunction) that judge will normally allocate the case to himself or herself. If he or she does not do so the procedure in (b) or (c) should apply depending on whether the case was heard in London or on circuit.
6. If the allocated Judge deems it appropriate, the date for the final hearing may be fixed at the First Appointment.
7. The FDR will be listed with a time estimate of 1 day unless (i) the parties certify, giving written reasons, that a lesser period is sufficient and (ii) obtain the written permission of the FDR Judge (before whom the case is listed for hearing) for the reduced time estimate.
8. Any interlocutory application in the course of the proceedings must be made to the allocated Judge, unless to do so would be impracticable or would cause undue delay.
9. Every case allocated to a High Court Judge must be the subject of a Pre-Trial Review before that judge held approximately 4 weeks before the final hearing. If the case is to be heard on circuit the Pre-Trial Review may be heard before the allocated judge sitting in London by video-link.

Efficient Conduct of Financial Hearings

10. At the Pre-Trial Review a final hearing template must be prepared. This should: a. allow a reasonable and realistic time for judicial reading and judgment writing; b. not normally allow longer than one hour for opening; and c. not allow for any evidence-in-chief unless the court has expressly authorised this at the Pre-Trial Review within the terms of FPR rules 22.6(2)–(4). Pursuant to rule 22.6(2) the parties' section 25 statements will almost invariably stand as their evidence-in-chief.

11. The parties' section 25 statements must only contain evidence. By virtue of FPR PD22A para 4.3(b) the statement must indicate the source for any matters of information and belief. On no account should a section 25 statement contain argument or other rhetoric.

12. If a direction for a discussion between experts has not previously been made pursuant to FPR rule 25.16 and PD 25E then that matter must be raised at the Pre-Trial Review. There would have to be very good reasons why such a direction should not be made at the Pre-Trial Review.

13. At the Pre-Trial Review a direction should be made which ensures compliance with the indispensable requirement in FPR PD27A para 4.3(b) of provision of an agreed statement of the issues to be determined at the final hearing. To the statement of issues must be attached:

    a. an agreed schedule of assets on which any un-agreed items must be clearly denoted; and

    b. an agreed chronology on which any un-agreed events must be clearly denoted.

    It is absolutely unacceptable for the court to be presented at the final hearing with competing asset schedules and chronologies.

14. The court bundle for the final hearing must scrupulously comply with FPR PD27A. This limits the size of the bundle to a single file containing no more than 350 pages: a specific prior direction from the court must be obtained at the Pre-Trial Review if the bundle is to exceed that limit (PD27A para 5.1). The limit of 350 pages includes the skeleton arguments (see para 15 below) and the agreed documents under para 13 above. Only those documents which are relevant to the hearing and which it is necessary for the court to read, or which will actually be referred to during the hearing, may be included: correspondence (including with experts), bank or credit card statements and other financial records must not be included unless a specific prior direction of the court at the Pre-Trial Review has been obtained (PD27A para 4.1). A separate bundle of all authorities relied on must be prepared and this must be agreed between the advocates (PD27A para 4.3). That bundle should not contain more than an absolute maximum of 10 authorities. Practitioners are specifically referred to the decision of the President in Re L (A Child) [2015] EWFC 15, paras 9–25, and to the earlier pronouncements referred to there, all of which apply fully to financial hearings.

15. Skeleton arguments must:

    a. be concise and not exceed

        i. for the first appointment, or any other interim hearing, 10 pages (including any attached schedules);

        ii. for the FDR, 15 pages (excluding agreed documents but including any other appended schedules);

        iii. for the final hearing, 20 pages (excluding agreed documents under para 13 above, but including any other appended schedules);

    b. be printed on A4 paper in not less than 12 point font and 1.5 line spacing;

    c. both define and confine the areas of controversy;

    d. be set out in numbered paragraphs;

    e. be cross-referenced to any relevant documents in the bundle;

    f. be self-contained and not incorporate by reference material from previous skeleton arguments; and

    g. not include extensive quotations from documents.

    Where it is necessary to refer to an authority, a skeleton argument must first state the proposition of law the authority demonstrates; and then identify the parts of the authority that support the proposition, *but without extensive quotation from it.*

16. If a skeleton argument for the final hearing is intended to exceed the limit of 20 pages a direction to that effect should be sought at the Pre-Trial Review. Very good reasons would have to be shown for such a direction to be made. A skeleton argument which breaches the limit will be returned unread for abridgement.

17. At the final hearing the parties' advocates will be expected to adhere to the hearing template. Slippage will not be tolerated unless there are very good reasons. When conducting cross-examination advocates must have in mind the strictures of Lord Judge LCJ in R v Farooqi & Ors [2013] EWCA Crim 1649 at para 113, where he stated "what ought to be avoided is the increasing modern habit of assertion, (often in tendentious terms or incorporating comment), which is not true cross-examination".

18. If advocates unreasonably fail to comply with paras 13 (provision of agreed statement of issues, schedule of assets and chronology), 15 (length and content of skeleton argument) or 17 (adherence to hearing template) they will risk an order being made disallowing a proportion of their fees pursuant to CPR 44.11(1)(b) and/or section 51(6) Senior Courts Act 1981. In this regard attention is drawn to the comparable warning in CPR PD 52C para 31(4).

19. If, following receipt of a draft written judgment either party wishes to seek permission to appeal, grounds of appeal must be filed at court and served on the other

Efficient Conduct of Financial Hearings

party at least one clear business day before the hearing of the application for permission.

20. The self-certification procedure concerning the allocation of financial remedy cases to a High Court Judge is set out below.

Guidance: Financial Proceedings: cases to be allocated to a judge of the High Court by self-certification

1. This Guidance takes effect from 1 July 2015 and applies, as far as practicable, to cases commenced before, as well as those commenced on or after, that date. It applies to financial remedy applications pending in the Family Court where the parties seek allocation to a judge of the High Court. It is no longer confined to cases proceeding in the CFC.

2. An application for a financial remedy will normally only be considered suitable for hearing by a High Court judge if it is exceptionally complex or there is another substantial ground for the case being heard by a High Court judge.

3. Where the parties seek the allocation of the proceedings to a High Court judge before an allocation direction has been made both counsel or, if counsel are not instructed, solicitor(s) for the parties must complete and file a certificate in the form annexed to this Guidance, stating concisely the reasons for certifying that the application is suitable for determination by a Judge of the Family Division. The completed certificate must be filed with the Clerk of the Rules not less than 21 days before the date fixed for the First Appointment in the Family Court.

4. The completed certificate will be referred to and considered by the Judge of the Family Division in charge of the money list who will determine whether the certificate indicates that the case is suitable for hearing by a High Court judge. If so determined, the case will be allocated to a Judge of the Family Division. A date will be fixed for the First Appointment before the allocated Judge and the merits of the certification will be further considered at that appointment.

5. If, at the First Appointment, the allocated Judge considers that the certification was not appropriate, the proceedings will be re-allocated within the Family Court and the allocated Judge may give directions as to case management, including the level of judiciary before whom the case should be listed. The allocated Judge may make such orders as to costs as considered appropriate.

6. Where proceedings are allocated to a High Court judge under paragraph 3, it is the responsibility of the solicitor for the applicant to ensure that the First Appointment fixed in the Family Court is vacated.

1 February 2016
Mr Justice Mostyn

Certificate
[Heading]

Outline facts:
a. The parties married on **[Date]**
b. The parties separated on **[Date]**
c. There are **[Number]** children of the family
d. The **[Petition/Answer]** was issued on **[Date]**
e. The Decree Nisi was pronounced on **[Date]**
f. The Decree Absolute was granted on **[Date]**
g. There is **[not]** a dispute about the jurisdiction of the High Court of England and Wales.

The reason for the dispute is **[Give short reasons]**

[Name] being **[Counsel/solicitor]** for the Applicant **[Wife/Husband]**

[Name] being **[Counsel/solicitor]** for the respondent **[Wife/Husband]**

We certify that this application should be allocated to a judge of the High Court because:

Delete/complete as appropriate

(1) The assets in this case are currently estimated to be in the order of:
   (a) £10 – £15 million
   (b) £15 – £25 million
   (c) £25 – £50 million
   (d) £50 million plus **[State the figure]**
   (e) Other **[State the figure]**

If the assets are less than the figures set out in (a) to (d) above state the reasons why the case is fit for allocation to a judge of the High Court. **[State reasons]**

Potential allegations/issues may arise which include:

(2) Non disclosure of assets. **[Yes / No]**
(3) Assets are/were held through the medium of offshore trusts/settlements. **[Yes / No]**
(4) Assets are/were held through the medium of family/unquoted corporate entities. **[Yes / No]**
(5) The value of family assets, trust and/or corporate entities. **[Yes / No]**
(6) A nuptial agreement is relied on. **[Yes / No]**
(7) Assets are held offshore. **[Yes / No]**
(8) The parties' respective contributions. **[Yes / No]**
Give brief details of the potential dispute. **[Yes / No]**
[Details of potential dispute]
(9) There are/may be disputed allegations of 'obvious and gross' conduct. Give brief outline of potential matters that may be in dispute.
[Details of conduct allegations]
(10) There are substantial arguments concerning the illiquidity of assets. Give brief details of potential matters that may be in dispute.
[Details of illiquidity of assets disputes]
(11) There may be substantial arguments about:
   (a) which assets are 'matrimonial assets' or 'non matrimonial assets'. **[Yes / No]**
   (b) assets that were owned prior to the marriage. **[Yes / No]**
   (c) assets acquired after the parties separated. **[Yes / No]**
   (d) other – give brief details of matters that may be in dispute. **[Yes / No] [Details of dispute]**
(12) The application involves a novel point of law. Specifically…(set out in outline the proposition of law that may be involved).

We certify that this case is suitable for transfer to be heard by a High Court Judge. The dates mutually convenient to the advocates for the first appointment are …………

Signed [Counsel/solicitors]

Court Bundles: PD 27A

Practice Direction 27A – Family Proceedings: Court Bundles
(Universal Practice To Be Applied In The High Court And Family Court)

1.1 The President of the Family Division has issued this practice direction to achieve consistency across the country in the Family Court and the Family Division of the High Court in the preparation of court bundles and in respect of other related matters.

Application of the practice direction
2.1 Except as specified in paragraph 2.4, and subject to specific directions given in any particular case, the following practice applies to:
  (a)   all hearings before a judge sitting in the Family Division of the High Court wherever the court may be sitting; and
  (b)   all hearings in the Family Court.
2.2 'Hearing' includes all appearances before the court, whether with or without notice to other parties and whether for directions or for substantive relief.
2.3 This practice direction applies whether a bundle is being lodged for the first time or is being re-lodged for a further hearing (see paragraph 9.2).
2.4 This practice direction does not apply to the hearing of any urgent application if and to the extent that it is impossible to comply with it.

Responsibility for the preparation of the bundle
3.1 A bundle for the use of the court at the hearing shall be provided by the party in the position of applicant at the hearing (or, if there are cross-applications, by the party whose application was first in time) or, if that person is a litigant in person, by the first listed respondent who is not a litigant in person. Where all the parties are litigants in person none of them shall, unless the court otherwise directs, be obliged to provide a bundle, but any bundle which they choose to lodge must be prepared and lodged so as to comply with this practice direction.
3.2 The party preparing the bundle shall paginate it using Arabic numbering throughout. If possible the contents of the bundle shall be agreed by all parties.

Contents of the bundle
4.1 The bundle shall contain copies of only those documents which are relevant to the hearing and which it is necessary for the court to read or which will actually be referred to during the hearing. In particular, copies of the following classes of documents must not be included in the bundle unless specifically directed by the court:
  (a)   correspondence (including letters of instruction to experts);
  (b)   medical records (including hospital, GP and health visitor records);
  (c)   bank and credit card statements and other financial records;
  (d)   notes of contact visits;
  (e)   foster carer logs;
  (f)   social services files (with the exception of any assessment being relied on by any of the parties);
  (g)   police disclosure.
This does not prevent the inclusion in the bundle of specific documents which it is necessary for the court to read or which will actually be referred to during the hearing.
4.2 The documents in the bundle shall be arranged in chronological order from the front of the bundle, paginated individually and consecutively (starting with page 1 and using Arabic numbering throughout), indexed and divided into separate sections (each section being separately paginated) as follows:
  (a)   preliminary documents (see paragraph 4.3) and any other case management documents required by any other practice direction;
  (b)   applications and orders;
  (c)   statements and affidavits (which must be dated in the top right corner of the front page) but without exhibiting or duplicating documents referred to in para 4.1;
  (d)   care plans (where appropriate);
  (e)   experts' reports and other reports (including those of a guardian, children's guardian or litigation friend); and
  (f)   other documents, divided into further sections as may be appropriate.
All statements, affidavits, care plans, experts' reports and other reports included in the bundle must be copies of originals which have been signed and dated.
4.3 At the commencement of the bundle there shall be inserted the following documents (the preliminary documents):
  (a)   an up to date case summary of the background to the hearing confined to those matters which are relevant to the hearing and the management of the case and limited, if practicable, to four A4 pages;
  (b)   a statement of the issue or issues to be determined (1) at that hearing and (2) at the final hearing;
  (c)   a position statement by each party including a summary of the order or directions sought by that party (1) at that hearing and (2) at the final hearing;
  (d)   an up to date chronology, if it is a final hearing or if the summary under (i) is insufficient;
  (e)   skeleton arguments, if appropriate;
  (f)   a list of essential reading for that hearing; and
  (g)   the time estimate (see paragraph 10.1).
Copies of all authorities relied on must be contained in a separate composite bundle agreed between the advocates.
4.4 Each of the preliminary documents shall be as short and succinct as possible and shall state on the front page

Court Bundles: PD 27A

immediately below the heading the date when it was prepared and the date of the hearing for which it was prepared. Where proceedings relating to a child are being heard by magistrates the summary of the background shall be prepared in anonymised form, omitting the names and identifying information of every person referred to other than the parties' legal representatives, and stating the number of pages contained in the bundle. Identifying information can be contained in all other preliminary documents.

4.5 The summary of the background, statement of issues, chronology, position statement and any skeleton arguments shall be cross-referenced to the relevant pages of the bundle.

4.6 The summary of the background, statement of issues, chronology and reading list shall in the case of a final hearing, and shall so far as practicable in the case of any other hearing, each consist of a single document in a form agreed by all parties. Where the parties disagree as to the content the fact of their disagreement and their differing contentions shall be set out at the appropriate places in the document.

4.7 Where the nature of the hearing is such that a complete bundle of all documents is unnecessary, the bundle (which need not be repaginated) may comprise only those documents necessary for the hearing, but

(a)   the summary of the background must commence with a statement that the bundle is limited or incomplete; and

(b)   the bundle shall if reasonably practicable be in a form agreed by all parties.

4.8 Where the bundle is re-lodged in accordance with paragraph 9.2, before it is re-lodged:

(a)   the bundle shall be updated as appropriate; and

(b)   all superseded documents (and in particular all outdated summaries, statements of issues, chronologies, skeleton arguments and similar documents) shall be removed from the bundle.

Format of the bundle

5.1 Unless the court has specifically directed otherwise, being satisfied that such direction is necessary to enable the proceedings to be disposed of justly, the bundle shall be contained in one A4 size ring binder or lever arch file limited to no more than 350 sheets of A4 paper and 350 sides of text.

5.2 All documents in the bundle shall (a) be copied on one side of paper only, unless the court has specifically directed otherwise, and (b) be typed or printed in a font no smaller than 12 point and with 1½ or double spacing.

5.3 The ring binder or lever arch file shall have clearly marked on the front and the spine:

(a)   the title and number of the case;

(b)   the place where the case has been listed;

(c)   the hearing date and time;

(d)   if known, the name of the judge hearing the case; and

(e)   where in accordance with a direction of the court there is more than one ring binder or lever arch file, a distinguishing letter (A, B, C etc).

Timetable for preparing and lodging the bundle

6.1 The party preparing the bundle shall, whether or not the bundle has been agreed, provide a paginated index to all other parties not less than 4 working days before the hearing.

6.2 Where counsel is to be instructed at any hearing, a paginated bundle shall (if not already in counsel's possession) be delivered to counsel by the person instructing that counsel not less than 3 working days before the hearing.

6.3 The bundle (with the exception of the preliminary documents if and insofar as they are not then available) shall be lodged with the court not less than 2 working days before the hearing, or at such other time as may be specified by the court.

6.4 The preliminary documents shall be lodged with the court no later than 11 am on the day before the hearing and, where the hearing is before a judge of the High Court and the name of the judge is known, shall (with the exception of the authorities, which are to be lodged in hard copy and not sent by email) at the same time be sent by email to the judge's clerk.

Lodging the bundle

7.1 The bundle shall be lodged at the appropriate office. If the bundle is lodged in the wrong place the court may:

(a)   treat the bundle as having not been lodged; and

(b)   take the steps referred to in paragraph 12.

7.2 Unless the court has given some other direction as to where the bundle in any particular case is to be lodged (for example a direction that the bundle is to be lodged with the judge's clerk) the bundle shall be lodged:

(a)   for hearings at the RCJ, in the office of the Clerk of the Rules, 1st Mezzanine (Rm 1M), Queen's Building, Royal Courts of Justice, Strand, London WC2A 2LL (DX 44450 Strand);

(b)   for hearings at any other place, at such place as may be designated by the designated family judge responsible for that place and in default of any such designation at the court office for the place where the hearing is to take place.

7.3 Any bundle sent to the court by post, DX or courier shall be clearly addressed to the appropriate office and shall show the date and place of the hearing on the outside of any packaging as well as on the bundle itself.

7.4 Unless the court has given some other direction or paragraph 7.5 applies only one copy of the bundle shall be lodged with the court but the party who is responsible for lodging the bundle shall bring to court at each hearing at which oral evidence may be called a copy of the bundle for use by the witnesses.

7.5 In the case of a hearing listed before a bench of magistrates four copies of the bundle shall be lodged with the court.

7.6 In the case of hearings at the RCJ or at any other place where the designated family judge responsible for that place has directed that this paragraph shall apply, parties shall:

Court Bundles: PD 27A

(a) if the bundle or preliminary documents are delivered personally, ensure that they obtain a receipt from the clerk accepting it or them; and

(b) if the bundle or preliminary documents are sent by post or DX, ensure that they obtain proof of posting or despatch.

The receipt (or proof of posting or despatch, as the case may be) shall be brought to court on the day of the hearing and must be produced to the court if requested. If the receipt (or proof of posting or despatch) cannot be produced to the court the judge may: (a) treat the bundle as having not been lodged; and (b) take the steps referred to in paragraph 12.

Lodging the bundle – additional requirements for Family Division or Family Court cases being heard at the RCJ

8.1 Bundles or preliminary documents delivered after 11 am on the day before the hearing may not be accepted by the Clerk of the Rules and if not shall be delivered:

(a) in a case where the hearing is before a judge of the High Court, directly to the clerk of the judge hearing the case;

(b) in a case where the hearing is before any other judge, to such place as may be specified by the Clerk of the Rules.

8.2 Upon learning before which judge a hearing is to take place, the clerk to counsel, or other advocate, representing the party in the position of applicant shall no later than 3 pm the day before the hearing:

(a) in a case where the hearing is before a judge of the High Court, telephone the clerk of the judge hearing the case;

(b) in a case where the hearing is before any other judge email the Clerk of the Rules at RCJ.familyhighcourt@hmcts .gsi.gov.uk;

to ascertain whether the judge has received the bundle (including the preliminary documents) and, if not, shall organise prompt delivery by the applicant's solicitor.

Removing and re-lodging the bundle

9.1 Unless either the court wishes to retain the bundle or specific alternative arrangements have been agreed with the court, the party responsible for the bundle shall, following completion of the hearing, retrieve the bundle from the court immediately or, if that is not practicable, collect it from the court within 5 working days. Bundles which are not collected in due time are liable to be destroyed without further notice.

9.2 The bundle shall be re-lodged for the next and any further hearings in accordance with the provisions of this practice direction and in a form which complies with para 4.7.

Time estimates

10.1 In every case a time estimate (which shall be inserted at the front of the bundle) shall be prepared which shall so far as practicable be agreed by all parties and shall:

(a) specify separately: (i) the time estimated to be required for judicial pre- reading; and (ii) the time required for hearing all evidence and submissions; and (iii) the time estimated to be required for preparing and delivering judgment;

(b) be prepared on the basis that before they give evidence all witnesses will have read all relevant filed statements and reports; and

(c) take appropriate account of any additional time likely to be incurred by the use of interpreters or intermediaries.

10.2 Once a case has been listed, any change in time estimates shall be notified immediately by telephone (and then immediately confirmed in writing):

(a) in the case of hearings in the RCJ, to the Clerk of the Rules; and

(b) in the case of hearings elsewhere, to the relevant listing officer.

Taking cases out of the list

11.1 As soon as it becomes known that a hearing will no longer be effective, whether as a result of the parties reaching agreement or for any other reason, the parties and their representatives shall immediately notify the court by telephone and email which shall be confirmed by letter. The letter, which shall wherever possible be a joint letter sent on behalf of all parties with their signatures applied or appended, shall include:

(a) a short background summary of the case;

(b) the written consent of each party who consents and, where a party does not consent, details of the steps which have been taken to obtain that party's consent and, where known, an explanation of why that consent has not been given;

(c) a draft of the order being sought; and

(d) enough information to enable the court to decide (i) whether to take the case out of the list and (ii) whether to make the proposed order.

Penalties for failure to comply with the practice direction

12.1 Failure to comply with any part of this practice direction may result in the judge removing the case from the list or putting the case further back in the list and may also result in a 'wasted costs' order or some other adverse costs order.

Commencement of the practice direction and application of other practice directions

13.1 Subject to paragraph 13.2 this practice direction shall have effect from 22 April 2014.

13.2 Sub-paragraphs (a)-(c) and (e)-(g) of paragraph 4.1 and paragraphs 5.1 and 5.3(e) shall have effect from 31 July 2014. In the meantime paragraphs 5.1 and 5.3(e) shall have effect as if:

(a) paragraph 5.1 read 'The bundle shall be contained in one or more A4 size ring binders or lever arch files (each lever arch file being limited to no more than 350 pages).'; and

Court Bundles: PD 27A

(b)   in paragraph 5.3(e) the words 'in accordance with a direction of the court' were omitted.

This Practice Direction is issued:

(a)   in relation to family proceedings, by the President of the Family Division, as the nominee of the Lord Chief Justice, with the agreement of the Lord Chancellor; and

(b)   to the extent that it applies to proceedings to which section 5 of the Civil Procedure Act 1997 applies, by the Master of the Rolls as the nominee of the Lord Chief Justice, with the agreement of the Lord Chancellor.

Practitioners' Commentary

*PD 27A applies **to all hearings at all Family Court venues**.*

*The agreed hearing bundle must be contained within a single file comprising **no more than 350 pages**: a specific prior direction from the court **must be obtained** if the bundle is to exceed that limit (para 5.1). The bundle may only be in A4 size (ibid). Double-sided printing is forbidden (para 5.2). Only those documents which are relevant to the particular hearing and which it is necessary for the court to read, or which will actually be referred to during the hearing, may be included: correspondence (including with experts), bank or credit card statements and other financial records **must not be included unless a specific prior direction of the court has been obtained** (para 4.1). **These are fundamental requirements.***

The bundle must be lodged two working days before the hearing (para 6.3). For hearings at the RCJ (and at any other place where the DFJ has so directed) a receipt (or proof of posting) must be obtained (para 7.6).

*A separate bundle of all authorities relied on must be prepared and **this must be agreed between the advocates** (para 4.3). It should not contain more than 10 authorities: see **Seagrove v Sullivan** [2014] EWHC 4110 (Fam) at [21]. It is good practice for the relevant passages of a report to be sidelined.*

*Strict compliance with paras 4.3 and 4.6 requires six separate preliminary documents to be prepared **and lodged by 11 am on the day before the hearing** and that the parties should if practicable agree the content of the most potentially contentious of them. A further requirement prior to First Appointment is to agree if possible a case summary and schedule of assets as well as the directions sought (PD 9A para 4.1). Experience in financial remedy cases has been that attempts to agree content are costly but almost always fail. Judges often accept a composite note from each side containing the information specified in para 4.3(a) to (g). However, some judges require an agreed chronology, schedule of assets and bundle of authorities. Whilst an agreed bundle of authorities must be produced, agreed chronologies and asset schedules remain impracticable for the reasons suggested. Most judges welcome email filing (referred to in para 6.4).*

The Efficiency Statement for cases allocated to High Court judge level (page 72, ante) provides that skeleton arguments are limited to 10 pages for the first appointment and any other interim hearing; to 15 pages for the FDR; and to 20 pages for the final hearing. It is suggested that these limits should be observed for all cases.

*For cases at the RCJ, the clerk to the applicant's advocate must **by 3 pm on the day before the hearing** telephone the clerk to the High Court judge allocated to hear the case (or in the case of a hearing before any other judge at the RCJ email the Clerk of the Rules) to ascertain whether the judge has received the bundle and the preliminary documents and if not must organise their prompt delivery (para 8.2).*

In the case of an FDR hearing in the Financial Remedies Unit of the Central Family Court, that court requires that the FDR core bundle must be lodged by 11 am on the preceding day.

***It cannot sufficiently be emphasised that non-compliance with the requirement to file preliminary documents by 11 am the day before the hearing is totally unacceptable.** Persistent or blatant offenders risk naming and shaming, disallowance of fees, wasted costs orders, and disciplinary complaint to regulatory bodies. For fair warning of the potential sanctions for non-compliance see the extremely strong judgment of the President in **Re L (A Child)** [2015] EWFC 15 where he stated at [25] 'the judges of the Family Division and the Family Court have had enough. The professions have been warned'.*

*Where one party is represented and the other party is a litigant in person, the court should normally direct as a matter of course that the documents mentioned in para 6 of PD 27A (i.e. the bundle, and the skeleton argument) are to be served on the litigant in person at least three days before the final hearing, especially where the litigant in person is not fluent in English: **Re B (Litigants In Person: Timely Service of Documents)** [2016] EWHC 2365 (Fam), [2016] 4 WLR 158.*

*See also the section **Court bundles and retention of documents** within the Commentary on Part 27 of the FPR in **@eGlance** for a more detailed exposition of the chorus of judicial excoriations on these topics.*

Costs: FPR 2010 Part 28 and PD 28A

What follow are **key *but not comprehensive* extracts** from the FPR 2010 costs regime as applicable to all applications for financial remedies. Transitional provisions regulate the costs of any applications launched before 6 April 2011: see PD 36A, para 4.5.

Application of CPR regime to family proceedings

FPR 2010 Part 28 applies swathes (but by no means all) of the CPR costs regime, but a number of parts of the relevant CPR rules are omitted or amended.

On 1 April 2013 the provisions of the CPR were comprehensively overhauled and rewritten in order to implement the recommendations of the Review of Civil Litigation Costs. The old CPR Parts 43 to 48 and the Costs Practice Direction were revoked. The current rules are contained in Parts 44 to 47, each with its own Practice Direction. Part 48 contains the transitional provisions.

By FPR 28.2 the following parts of the CPR as amended are applied generally to family proceedings (but subject to FPR 28.3: *below*): Part 44 – General rules about costs (except rules 44.2(2) and (3) and 44.10(2) and (3)); rule 45.8 – Fixed enforcement costs; Part 46 – Special cases; and Part 47 – Procedure for detailed assessment. These CPR provisions as amended for FPR use are conveniently accessible in *@eGlance*.

PD 28A applies the CPR Costs PDs with modifications that do no more than reflect that certain parts of the CPR regime have not been applied.

A most important change introduced in the CPR, so far as financial remedy proceedings are concerned, is the requirement of proportionality in the assessment of costs. To this end CPR rule 44.3(5) has been introduced. Further, the old procedure of certifying a case as fit for one or more counsel is now reintroduced by CPR PD 44 para 5.1.

Special treatment of some financial remedy applications

This application of the CPR regime is subject to FPR rule 28.3, retaining the 'no order' principle for a limited class of financial remedy proceedings. The financial remedies subject to rule 28.3 are as follows:

- a financial order, except an order for maintenance pending suit (or an order for maintenance pending outcome of proceedings), an interim periodical payments order, a legal services payment order or any other interim order made within financial order proceedings (apart from an interim variation order)
- an order under Part 3 of MFPA 1984 or under Schedule 7 to CPA 2004
- an order under section 10(2) MCA 1973 or under section 48(2) CPA 2004.

The **financial applications not covered by rule 28.3**, and which are therefore subject to the modified CPR regime are:

- an order for maintenance pending suit (or pending outcome of proceedings)
- an interim periodical payments order
- a legal services payment order under sections 22ZA and 22ZB MCA 1973 or paras 38A and 38B of Schedule 5 to CPA 2004
- any other interim order (for example, on a preliminary issue) made within financial order proceedings (apart from an interim variation order)
- an order under Schedule 1 to CA 1989
- an order under section 27 MCA 1973 or under Part 9 of Schedule 5 to CPA 2004 (failure to maintain)
- an order under section 35 MCA 1973 or under para 69 of Schedule 5 to CPA 2004 (variation of maintenance agreement)
- an order under Part 1 of DPMCA 1978 or under Schedule 6 to CPA 2004 (maintenance proceedings before lay justices)
- an order under section 36 MCA 1973 or para 73 of Schedule 5 to CPA 2004 (alteration of maintenance agreement after death of one party)
- an order under section 17 MWPA 1882 or section 66 CPA 2004 (question as to property to be decided in summary way)
- an order under section 13 MFPA 1984 or para 4 of Schedule 7 to CPA 2004 (permission to apply for a financial remedy after overseas proceedings)
- an order for the transfer of a tenancy under section 53 of and Schedule 7 to FLA 1996
- an order preventing avoidance under section 32L CSA 1991.

*See also the **Editors' Note** which follows these extracts.*

RELEVANT EXTRACTS

Estimates of Costs

FPR 9.27

(1) Subject to paragraph (2), at every hearing or appointment each party must produce to the court an estimate of the costs incurred by that party up to the date of that hearing or appointment *[in Form H]*.

(2) Not less than 14 days before the date fixed for the final hearing of an application for a financial remedy, each party ('the filing party') must (unless the court directs otherwise) file with the court and serve on each other party a statement giving full particulars of all costs in respect of the proceedings which the filing party has incurred or expects to incur, to enable the court to take account of the parties' liabilities for costs when deciding what order (if any) to make for a financial remedy *[in Form H1]*.

* * * * *

Costs: FPR 2010 Part 28 and PD 28A

Costs

FPR 28.1

The court may at any time make such order as to costs as it thinks just.

Application of other rules

FPR 28.2

(1) Subject to rule 28.3, Parts 44 (except rules 44.2(2) and (3) and 44.10(2) and (3)), 46 and 47 and rule 45.8 of the CPR apply to costs in proceedings, with the following modifications –

   (a) in the definition of "authorised court officer" in rule 44.1(1), for the words in sub-paragraph (i) substitute "the family court";

   (b) *[omitted]*

   (c) in accordance with any provisions in Practice Direction 28A; and

   (d) any other necessary modifications.

Costs in financial remedy proceedings

FPR 28.3

(1) This rule applies in relation to financial remedy proceedings

(2) Rule 44.2(1), (4) and (5) of the CPR do not apply to financial remedy proceedings.

(3) Rules 44.2(6) to (8) and 44.12 of the CPR apply to an order made under this rule as they apply to an order made under rule 44.3 of the CPR.

(4) In this rule –

   (a) 'costs' has the same meaning as in rule 44.1(1)(c) of the CPR; and

   (b) 'financial remedy proceedings' means proceedings for –

      (i) a financial order except an order for maintenance pending suit, an order for maintenance pending outcome of proceedings, an interim periodical payments order, an order for payment in respect of legal services or any other form of interim order for the purposes of rule 9.7(1)(a), (b), (c) and (e);

      (ii) an order under Part 3 of the 1984 Act;

      (iii) an order under Schedule 7 to the 2004 Act;

      (iv) an order under section 10(2) of the 1973 Act;

      (v) an order under section 48(2) of the 2004 Act.

(5) Subject to paragraph (6), the general rule in financial remedy proceedings is that the court will not make an order requiring one party to pay the costs of another party.

(6) The court may make an order requiring one party to pay the costs of another party at any stage of the proceedings where it considers it appropriate to do so because of the conduct of a party in relation to the proceedings (whether before or during them).

(7) In deciding what order (if any) to make under paragraph (6), the court must have regard to–

   (a) any failure by a party to comply with these rules, any order of the court or any practice direction which the court considers relevant;

   (b) any open offer to settle made by a party;

   (c) whether it was reasonable for a party to raise, pursue or contest a particular allegation or issue;

   (d) the manner in which a party has pursued or responded to the application or a particular allegation or issue;

   (e) any other aspect of a party's conduct in relation to proceedings which the court considers relevant; and

   (f) the financial effect on the parties of any costs order.

(8) No offer to settle which is not an open offer to settle is admissible at any stage of the proceedings, except as provided by rule 9.17.

(9) For the purposes of this rule "financial remedy proceedings" do not include an application under rule 9.9A.

PD 28A Costs in financial remedy proceedings

4.1 Rule 28.3 relates to the court's power to make costs orders in financial remedy proceedings. For the purposes of rule 28.3, 'financial remedy proceedings' are defined in accordance with rule 28.3(4)(b). That definition, which is more limited than the principal definition in rule 2.3(1), includes –

(a) an application for a financial order, except –

   (i) an order for maintenance pending suit or an order for maintenance pending outcome of proceedings;

   (ii) an interim periodical payments order or any other form of interim order for the purposes of rule 9.7(1)(a),(b),(c) and (e);

   (iii) an order for payment in respect of legal services;

(b) an application for an order under Part 3 of the Matrimonial and Family Proceedings Act 1984 or Schedule 7 to the Civil Partnership Act 2004; and

(c) an application under section 10(2) of the Matrimonial Causes Act 1973 or section 48(2) of the Civil Partnership Act 2004.

4.2 Accordingly, it should be noted that –

(a) while most interim financial applications are excluded from rule 28.3, the rule does apply to an application for an interim variation order within rule 9.7(1)(d),

(b) rule 28.3 does not apply to an application for any of the following financial remedies –

   (i) an order under Schedule 1 to the Children Act 1989;

   (ii) an order under section 27 of the Matrimonial Causes Act 1973 or Part 9 of Schedule 5 to the Civil Partnership Act 2004;

   (iii) an order under section 35 of the Matrimonial Causes Act 1973 or paragraph 69 of Schedule 5 to the Civil Partnership Act 2004; or

   (iv) an order under Part 1 of the Domestic Proceedings and Magistrates' Courts Act 1978 or Schedule 6 to the Civil Partnership Act 2004.

Costs: FPR 2010 Part 28 and PD 28A

4.3 Under rule 28.3 the court only has the power to make a costs order in financial remedy proceedings when this is justified by the litigation conduct of one of the parties. When determining whether and how to exercise this power the court will be required to take into account the list of factors set out in that rule. The court will not be able to take into account any offers to settle expressed to be 'without prejudice' or 'without prejudice save as to costs' in deciding what, if any, costs orders to make.

4.4 In considering the conduct of the parties for the purposes of rule 28.3(6) and (7) (including any open offers to settle), the court will have regard to the obligation of the parties to help the court to further the overriding objective (see rules 1.1 and 1.3) and will take into account the nature, importance and complexity of the issues in the case. This may be of particular significance in applications for variation orders and interim variation orders or other cases where there is a risk of the costs becoming disproportionate to the amounts in dispute.

4.5 Parties who intend to seek a costs order against another party in proceedings to which rule 28.3 applies should ordinarily make this plain in open correspondence or in skeleton arguments before the date of the hearing. In any case where summary assessment of costs awarded under rule 28.3 would be appropriate parties are under an obligation to file a statement of costs in CPR Form N260.

4.6 An order for payment in respect of legal services under section 22ZA of the Matrimonial Causes Act 1973 or paragraph 38A of Part 8 of Schedule 5 to the Civil Partnership Act 2004 is not a 'costs order' within the meaning of rule 28.3.

4.7 By virtue of rule 28.2(1), where rule 28.3 does not apply, the exercise of the court's discretion as to costs is governed by the relevant provisions of the CPR and in particular rule 44.2 (excluding r 44.2(2) and (3)).

* * * * *

Civil Procedure Rules 1998

44.2 Court's discretion as to costs

(1) The court has discretion as to –
   (a) whether costs are payable by one party to another;
   (b) the amount of those costs; and
   (c) when they are to be paid.

[(2) and (3) are disapplied for FPR purposes]

(4) In deciding what order (if any) to make about costs, the court will have regard to all the circumstances, including:
   (a) the conduct of all the parties;
   (b) whether a party has succeeded on part of its case, even if that party has not been wholly successful; and
   (c) any admissible offer to settle made by a party which is drawn to the court's attention, and which is

not an offer to which costs consequences under Part 36 apply.
(5) The conduct of the parties includes:
   (a) conduct before, as well as during, the proceedings and in particular the extent to which the parties followed the Practice Direction – Pre-Action Conduct or any relevant pre-action protocol;
   (b) whether it was reasonable for a party to raise, pursue or contest a particular allegation or issue;
   (c) the manner in which a party has pursued or defended its case or a particular allegation or issue; and
   (d) whether a claimant who has succeeded in the claim, in whole or in part, exaggerated its claim.
(6) The orders which the court may make under this rule include an order that a party must pay:
   (a) a proportion of another party's costs;
   (b) a stated amount in respect of another party's costs;
   (c) costs from or until a certain date only;
   (d) costs incurred before proceedings have begun;
   (e) costs relating to particular steps taken in the proceedings;
   (f) costs relating only to a distinct part of the proceedings; and
   (g) interest on costs from or until a certain date, including a date before judgment.
(7) Before the court considers making an order under paragraph (6)(f), it will consider whether it is practicable to make an order under paragraph (6)(a) or (c) instead.
(8) Where the court orders a party to pay costs subject to detailed assessment, it will order that party to pay a reasonable sum on account of costs, unless there is good reason not to do so.

44.3 Basis of assessment
(1) Where the court is to assess the amount of costs (whether by summary or detailed assessment) it will assess those costs:
   (a) on the standard basis; or
   (b) on the indemnity basis,
but the court will not in either case allow costs which have been unreasonably incurred or are unreasonable in amount.

(Rule 44.5 sets out how the court decides the amount of costs payable under a contract.)

(2) Where the amount of costs is to be assessed on the standard basis, the court will:
   (a) only allow costs which are proportionate to the matters in issue. Costs which are disproportionate in amount may be disallowed or reduced even if they were reasonably or necessarily incurred; and
   (b) resolve any doubt which it may have as to whether costs were reasonably and proportionately incurred or were reasonable and proportionate in amount in favour of the paying party.

Costs: FPR 2010 Part 28 and PD 28A

(Factors which the court may take into account are set out in rule 44.4.)

(3) Where the amount of costs is to be assessed on the indemnity basis, the court will resolve any doubt which it may have as to whether costs were reasonably incurred or were reasonable in amount in favour of the receiving party.

(4) Where:

(a) the court makes an order about costs without indicating the basis on which the costs are to be assessed; or

(b) the court makes an order for costs to be assessed on a basis other than the standard basis or the indemnity basis,

the costs will be assessed on the standard basis.

(5) Costs incurred are proportionate if they bear a reasonable relationship to:

(a) the sums in issue in the proceedings;

(b) the value of any non-monetary relief in issue in the proceedings;

(c) the complexity of the litigation;

(d) any additional work generated by the conduct of the paying party; and

(e) any wider factors involved in the proceedings, such as reputation or public importance.

...

(7) Paragraphs (2)(a) and (5) do not apply in relation to—

(a) cases commenced before 1st April 2013; or

(b) costs incurred in respect of work done before 1st April 2013,

and in relation to such cases or costs, rule 44.4.(2)(a) as it was in force immediately before 1st April 2013 will apply instead.

44.4 Factors to be taken into account in deciding the amount of costs

(1) The court will have regard to all the circumstances in deciding whether costs were:

(a) if it is assessing costs on the standard basis:

(i) proportionately and reasonably incurred; or

(ii) proportionate and reasonable in amount, or

(b) if it is assessing costs on the indemnity basis:

(i) unreasonably incurred; or

(ii) unreasonable in amount.

(2) In particular, the court will give effect to any orders which have already been made.

(3) The court will also have regard to:

(a) the conduct of all the parties, including in particular:

(i) conduct before, as well as during, the proceedings; and

(ii) the efforts made, if any, before and during the proceedings in order to try to resolve the dispute;

(b) the amount or value of any money or property involved;

(c) the importance of the matter to all the parties;

(d) the particular complexity of the matter or the difficulty or novelty of the questions raised;

(e) the skill, effort, specialised knowledge and responsibility involved;

(f) the time spent on the case;

(g) the place where and the circumstances in which work or any part of it was done; and

(h) the receiving party's last approved or agreed budget.

(Rule 35.4(4) gives the court power to limit the amount that a party may recover with regard to the fees and expenses of an expert.)

44.6 Procedure for assessing costs

(1) Where the court orders a party to pay costs to another party (other than fixed costs) it may either:

(a) make a summary assessment of the costs; or

(b) order detailed assessment of the costs by a costs officer,

unless any rule, practice direction or other enactment provides otherwise.

(Practice Direction 44 – General rules about costs sets out the factors which will affect the court's decision under paragraph (1).)

(2) A party may recover the fixed costs specified in Part 45 in accordance with that Part.

44.7 Time for complying with an order for costs

A party must comply with an order for the payment of costs within 14 days of:

(a) the date of the judgment or order if it states the amount of those costs;

(b) if the amount of those costs (or part of them) is decided later in accordance with Part 47, the date of the certificate which states the amount; or

(c) in either case, such other date as the court may specify.

(Part 47 sets out the procedure for detailed assessment of costs.)

CPR Costs PD 44 – General rules about costs

Fees of Counsel

5.1

(1) When making an order for costs the court may state an opinion as to whether or not the hearing was fit for the attendance of one or more counsel, and, if it does so, the court conducting a detailed assessment of those costs will have regard to the opinion stated.

(2) The court will generally express an opinion only where:

(a) the paying party asks it to do so;

(b) more than one counsel appeared for a party; or

(c) the court wishes to record its opinion that the case was not fit for the attendance of counsel.

Costs: FPR 2010 Part 28 and PD 28A

Summary assessment: general provisions

9.1 Whenever a court makes an order about costs which does not provide only for fixed costs to be paid the court should consider whether to make a summary assessment of costs.

Timing of summary assessment

9.2 The general rule is that the court should make a summary assessment of the costs:

... (b) at the conclusion of any other hearing, which has lasted not more than one day, in which case the order will deal with the costs of the application or matter to which the hearing related. If this hearing disposes of the claim, the order may deal with the costs of the whole claim, unless there is good reason not to do so, for example where the paying party shows substantial grounds for disputing the sum claimed for costs that cannot be dealt with summarily.

Consent orders

9.4 Where an application has been made and the parties to the application agree an order by consent without any party attending, the parties should seek to agree a figure for costs to be inserted in the consent order or agree that there should be no order for costs.

Duty of parties and legal representatives

9.5

(1) It is the duty of the parties and their legal representatives to assist the judge in making a summary assessment of costs in any case to which paragraph 9.2 above applies, in accordance with the following subparagraphs.

(2) Each party who intends to claim costs must prepare a written statement of those costs showing separately in the form of a schedule:
(a) the number of hours to be claimed;
(b) the hourly rate to be claimed;
(c) the grade of fee earner;
(d) the amount and nature of any disbursement to be claimed, other than counsel's fee for appearing at the hearing;
(e) the amount of legal representative's costs to be claimed for attending or appearing at the hearing;
(f) counsel's fees; and
(g) any VAT to be claimed on these amounts.
(3) The statement of costs should follow as closely as possible Form N260 and must be signed by the party or the party's legal representative. Where a party is:
(a) an assisted person;
(b) a LSC funded client; ... or
(d) represented by a person in the party's employment, the statement of costs need not include the certificate appended at the end of Form N260.
(4) The statement of costs must be filed at court and copies of it must be served on any party against whom an order for payment of those costs is intended to be sought as soon as possible and in any event: ...
(b) for all other hearings, not less than 24 hours before the time fixed for the hearing.

9.6 The failure by a party, without reasonable excuse, to comply with paragraph 9.5 will be taken into account by the court in deciding what order to make about the costs of the claim, hearing or application, and about the costs of any further hearing or detailed assessment hearing that may be necessary as a result of that failure.

No summary assessment by a costs officer

9.7 The court awarding costs cannot make an order for a summary assessment of costs by a costs officer. If a summary assessment of costs is appropriate but the court awarding costs is unable to do so on the day, the court may give directions as to a further hearing before the same judge.

Assisted persons etc

9.8 The court will not make a summary assessment of the costs of a receiving party who is an assisted person or LSC funded client ...

Children or protected parties

9.9

(1) The court will not make a summary assessment of the costs of a receiving party who is a child or protected party within the meaning of Part 21 unless the legal representative acting for the child or protected party has waived the right to further costs (see Practice Direction 46 paragraph 2.1).
(2) The court may make a summary assessment of costs payable by a child or protected party.

Disproportionate or unreasonable costs

9.10 The court will not give its approval to disproportionate or unreasonable costs. When the amount of the costs to be paid has been agreed between the parties the order for costs must state that the order is by consent.

Costs: Editors' Note

CPR rule 44.2(4)(c) makes **Calderbank letters** admissible in the costs phase of the proceedings listed above **other than** those covered by FPR rule 28.3; and, following well understood principle, they should then strongly influence if not dictate the outcome of the costs application: see **KS v ND (Schedule 1: Appeal: Costs)** [2013] EWHC 464 (Fam), [2013] 2 FLR 698 at [20]. Thus Calderbank offers may not be referred to nor relied upon when costs are considered in proceedings governed by rule 28.3. 'Without Prejudice' offers can still be made but can only be referred to at the FDR hearing. Calderbank offers are admissible at the conclusion of an appeal: see **WD v HD** [2015] EWHC 1547 (Fam), [2016] Fam Law 160.

The terms of open proposals to settle are however expressly to be considered in determining whether or not litigation misconduct has occurred.

The removal of maintenance pending suit and comparable orders from the 'no order as to costs' regime is a significant change designed to meet the complaint that the 'no order' principle effectively emasculated the economic value of many such orders. It is somewhat surprising that the same distinction has not been carried through to variation orders, whether interim or final, where similar concerns have been raised, although PD 28A para 4.4 supplies a strong steer in favour of making orders for costs in such proceedings.

The application under CPR rule 44.3(5) of the new proportionality principle in an assessment of standard costs can result in a dramatic reduction in the claimed sum: see **K v K** [2016] EWHC 2002 (Fam), [2017] 1 FCR 144 and **May v Wavell Group plc** [2016] EWHC B16 (Costs). In **Kazakhstan Kagazy PLC v Zhunus** [2015] EWHC 404 (Comm) it was held that the touchstone is the lowest amount which a party could reasonably have been expected to spend in order to have its case conducted and presented proficiently: expenditure over that level is not recoverable.

Reported cases and practitioners' experience demonstrate that **the 'no order' principle in rule 28.3 is by no means absolute and does not apply across the board**.

The starting point is that at the final hearing unpaid costs will be 'taken off the top' as a debt of the party in question. For this purpose a detailed costs estimate in Form H1 is required at trial.

Where there is a striking disparity in the costs each party incurs the court may, when fairly calculating the relevant assets, disregard unpaid costs and/or add back costs already paid: see **RH v RH** [2008] 2 FLR 2142, **LS v JS (Appeal: Costs)** [2012] EWHC 2960 (Fam), and **J v J** [2014] EWHC 3654 (Fam) at [27].

Clearly the court in determining the substantive outcome should be ready to penalise in costs a party who has adopted an open position that is manifestly unreasonable or who has failed to make an open offer at all: see **Evans v Evans** [2013] EWHC 506 (Fam), [2013] 2 FLR 999, at [178] to [204] and **SR v RS** [2014] EWHC 4305 (Fam). For a number of other cases where adverse costs orders have been made applying FPR 28.3(6) and (7) and PD 28A para 4.4, see the section *Costs in (some) financial remedy proceedings* in the Commentary on Part 28 of the FPR in *@eGlance*.

Importantly, rule 28.3(7)(f) requires the court to have regard to the financial effect of a costs order upon a party: for instance where an adverse costs order might undermine the judicial objective of the order, such as to provide secure housing: see **KS v ND (Schedule 1: Appeal: Costs)** at [25] to [27] and **J v J** [2014] EWHC 3654 (Fam) at [55] to [58].

For the principles to be applied on an application for indemnity costs see **M v M and Others (Costs)** [2013] EWHC 3372 (Fam), [2014] 1 FLR 499 and **AB v CD** [2016] EWHC 2482 (Fam), [2017] 1 FLR 13.

The 'no order' principle in rule 28.3 only applies to mainstream final financial remedy applications between the two principal parties. The principle has (so far) been held **not to** apply in the following situations:

- to the costs of a person joined to proceedings against his will (**KSO v MJO and JMO (PSO intervening)** [2009] 1 FLR 1036); or who intervenes in proceedings (**Baker v Rowe** [2010] 1 FLR 761)
- to the costs of civil proceedings heard together with financial remedy proceedings (**Ben Hashem v Ali Shayif and Radfan Ltd** [2009] 2 FLR 896)
- to an application made to set aside a financial remedy order on the grounds of mistake and/or non-disclosure (**Judge v Judge** [2009] 1 FLR 1287)
- to an application that a concluded agreement be made an order of the court (**T v T** [2013] EWHC B3 (Fam))
- to a financial remedy appeal (**H v W (cap on wife's share of bonus payments) (No 2)** [2014] EWHC 2846 (Fam)).

The powers of the court to award a legal services payment order in relation to divorce proceedings are now contained in ss. 22ZA and 22ZB of the Matrimonial Causes Act 1973. **Rubin v Rubin** [2014] EWHC 611 (Fam), [2014] 2 FLR 1018, at [13] contains guidance as to the governing principles on an application for a costs allowance. In principle (xii) it was stated that monthly instalments are to be preferred to a single lump sum payment. In **Re F (A Child) (Financial Provision: Legal Costs Funding)** [2016] 1 WLR 4720 it was held that principle (iv) of **Rubin** (proscription on payment of historic costs) did not apply where the legal costs funding claim arises within ongoing proceedings in relation to costs reasonably and legitimately incurred prior to the determination of the legal costs funding application, and where a clear case is shown that the applicant's solicitors were reaching the end of their tolerance in carrying the debt.

These legal services payment order provisions do not extend to proceedings under Schedule 1 of the Children Act 1989, the Inheritance (Provision for Family and Dependants) Act 1975 or Part III MFPA 1984. In such cases the application will continue to be for an interim order for costs funding. **Rubin** at [15] suggests that the principles there set out should, with the necessary modifications, also apply to such applications. For the application of the principles in a Schedule 1 case see **MG and JG v JF** [2015] EWHC 564 (Fam).

For in-depth coverage on costs, with links to the relevant rules and periodical updating to include new cases and developments, see the Commentary on Part 28 and PD 28A (and the relevant CPR provisions) in *@eGlance*.

Leading Citations

The court's objective in applying MCA 1973 Part II is to achieve a fair outcome: *White* [2000] UKHL 54 at [1]. There is no place for discrimination between husband and wife and their respective roles and there should thus be no bias in favour of the money-earner and against the home-maker and the child-carer: *ibid.* [24]. As a general guide, equality should be departed from only if, and to the extent that, there is good reason for doing so: *ibid.* [25].

There is no hierarchy in the section 25 factors; which will carry most weight depends upon the facts of the particular case: *Piglowska* [1999] 3 All ER 632 at 642.

In addition to the welfare of minor children, the court is guided by the three 'strands' of needs, sharing and compensation: *Miller; McFarlane* [2006] UKHL 24 at [10] to [16] and [138] to [143].

The **needs** principle requires consideration of the financial needs, obligations and responsibilities of the parties, the standard of living enjoyed by the family before the breakdown of the marriage; the age of each party; and any physical or mental disability: *Charman* [2007] EWCA Civ 503 at [70]. In a case where the magnetic factor is needs, the court's first concern will be to provide a home for the primary carer and the children and then if possible for the other parent: *M v B (lump sum)* [1998] 1 FLR 53 at 60 (in any case where there is, by stretch and a degree of risk-taking, the possibility of a division to enable both parties to rehouse themselves, that is an exceptionally important consideration and one which will almost invariably have a decisive impact on outcome), *H v H* [1998] 1 FLR 971, *Cordle* [2001] EWCA Civ 1791 at [33]. The 'needs' discretion is almost unbounded: *FF v KF* [2017] EWHC 1093 (Fam) at [18].

The enquiry required by **sharing** is dictated by reference to the contributions of each party to the welfare of the family and the duration of the marriage: *Charman, above* at [72]. The sharing principle applies to all the parties' property; but to the extent that their property is non-matrimonial there is likely to be better reason for departure from equality: *ibid.* [66]. There is no reported case where non-matrimonial property has been 'shared' (*Hart* [2017] EWCA Civ 1306 at [66]). When the result suggested by needs is an award less than the result suggested by sharing, the latter result should in principle prevail, and *vice versa*: *ibid.* [65]. The importance of the source of non-marital assets (and thus the extent to which they are subject to the sharing principle) may diminish over time: because the significance of their value is reduced in relation to the overall value of marital assets accrued, by virtue of mingling with marital assets or otherwise being treated as marital, and/or by their application to the purchase of a matrimonial home: *K v L* [2011] EWCA Civ 550 at [18]. On the facts of a particular case, however, the family home may be divided unequally under the sharing principle: *Vaughan* [2007] EWCA Civ 1085, *S v AG* [2011] EWHC 2637 (Fam), *JL v SL (No 2)* [2014] EWHC 360 (Fam). The court is not required to adopt a formulaic approach when determining whether property is matrimonial or non-matrimonial or its impact on outcome. Having made such factual determination as is appropriate in the light of the overriding objective the court must fit its determination into the exercise of its discretion, having regard to all the relevant factors in the case (*Hart, above*, at [83] to [97]). Departure from equal sharing may also be justified because of 'special contribution' (*Work v Gray* [2017] EWCA Civ 270); illiquidity of assets (*G v G* [2002] EWHC 1339 (Fam)); the need to achieve a balance in the award between safe and risky assets (*Wells* [2002] EWCA Civ 476); delay (*Wyatt v Vince* [2015] UKSC 14); and where the marriage is short, childless and dual-income, with separate finances (*Sharp* [2017] EWCA Civ 408).

The principle of **compensation** relates to prospective financial disadvantage which upon divorce some parties face as a result of decisions which they took for the benefit of the family during the marriage, for example in sacrificing or not pursuing a career: *Charman, above* at [71]. See also (compensatory element included): *Miller; McFarlane, above, Lauder* [2007] EWHC 1227 (Fam), *H v H* [2014] EWHC 760 (Fam); and (compensatory element not included): *RP v RP* [2006] EWHC 3409 (Fam), *S v S* [2006] EWHC 2793 (Fam), *H v H* [2007] EWHC 459 (Fam), *CR v CR* [2007] EWHC 3206 (Fam), *VB v JP* [2008] EWHC 112 (Fam), *McFarlane* [2009] EWHC 891 (Fam), *SA v PA* [2014] EWHC 392 (Fam).

The principles set out above were neatly summarised by Lord Wilson in *Scatliffe (British Virgin Islands)* [2016] UKPC 36 at [25(x)]: 'in an ordinary case the proper approach is to apply the sharing principle to the matrimonial property and then to ask whether, in the light of all the matters specified in section 26(1) [*of the local Act, corresponding to section 25(2), MCA 1973*] and of its concluding words, the result of so doing represents an appropriate overall disposal. In particular it should ask whether the principles of need and/or of compensation, best explained in the speech of Lady Hale in the *Miller* case at paras 137 to 144, require additional adjustment in the form of transfer to one party of further property, even of non-matrimonial property, held by the other.'

The court's enquiry is in two stages, **computation** and **distribution**: *Charman, above*, at [67]. When computing resources, the court may add back assets to the pool where there has been wanton or reckless dissipation (although it will not reattribute notional assets to meet needs): *Vaughan* [2007] EWCA Civ 1085; see also *MAP v MFP (financial remedies add back)* [2015] EWHC 627 (Fam), *BD v FD (No 2)* [2016] EWHC 594 (Fam). The court may infer the existence of assets where a party's disclosure has been materially deficient *(NG v AG (appeal: non-disclosure)* [2011] EWHC 3270 (Fam)).

Periodical payments should be awarded only by reference to needs, save in a most exceptional case where it can be said that the sharing or compensation principle applies (*SS v NS* [2014] EWHC 4183 (Fam) at [46]). In considering the imposition of a 'clean break' as required under MCA 1973 s. 25A, the court applies the principles set out in *C v C* [1997] 2 FLR 26 at 47.

On a **variation** application, the court is not required to consider the matter *de novo* but must conduct an exercise proportionate to the requirements of the case, which may be a complete or a 'light touch' review. In the latter case the court may confine its consideration to factors relevant to the variation application: *Morris* [2016] EWCA Civ 812 at [87].

On a **capitalisation** application the court (1) determines the appropriate current quantum of periodical payments, (2) fixes the termination date and (3) quantifies the substituted capital payment by reference to the *Duxbury* tables (with a narrow discretion to depart from the latter to reflect special factors). The court should look first to making a pension sharing order: *Pearce* [2003] EWCA Civ 1054. Depending on the circumstances, the court may require a capitalisation payee to amortise assets: *Vaughan* [2010] EWCA Civ 349 at [42], *H v H* [2014] EWHC 760 (Fam).

The court encourages and upholds the expression of **party autonomy** in the form of agreements (*Radmacher v Granatino* [2010] UKSC 42); the collaborative process (*S v P (settlement by collaborative process)* [2008] 2 FLR 2040); mediation (*Mann* [2014] EWHC 537 (Fam)); and arbitration (*S v S* [2014] EWHC 7 (Fam)).

Leading Cases

<table>
<tr><td>

Adjournment of claims
Agreements
Appealing out of time
Appeals
Arbitration
Arrears, enforcement/remission
Avoidance of dispositions
Bankruptcy
Children
  capital provision
  income provision, marital
  income provision, non-marital
Child Support Act
Clean break/termination
Companies
Compensation
  compensatory element included
  compensatory element not included
Conduct
  financial misconduct
  misconduct of proceedings
  sexual
  violence, etc
  other
Contributions
Costs
  inter partes
  orders against lawyers and others
Delay
Duxbury income capitalisation

</td><td>

Enforcement
Equality of division
  departure from
  principle applied
Experts
Farms
Financial relief after overseas divorce
Forum conveniens
Inheritance (Provision for Family and
  Dependants) Act 1975
Injunctions in support of financial
  remedies
  section 37 injunctions
  freezing and mandatory injunctions
  search (Anton Piller) orders
  writ ne exeat regno, etc
  anti-suit / Hemain injunctions
Interim capital orders/orders for sale
Jurisdiction
  EU Regulations
  domicile
  habitual residence
Legal Aid
Length of marriage
  cohabitation before
  short
Lump sums
Maintenance pending suit/LSPO
Media access, etc
Money: small

</td><td>

Negligence (by lawyers and others)
Non-disclosure/discovery
Non-parties, disclosure by
Orders over property
Pensions
  military
  other
Periodical payments
  capitalisation of
  principles of award
  variation of
Practice and procedure
Proceeds of Crime Act
Property, beneficial interest in
Remarriage and cohabitation
  prospects
  actual remarriage
  cohabitation
Resources
  computation and extent of
  (il)liquidity of
Resources, non-matrimonial
  pre-marital
  acquired during marriage
  acquired post-separation
Third parties, claims by/against
Trusts
Variation of final orders

</td></tr>
</table>

Adjournment of claims

MT v MT (financial provision: lump sum)　　[1992] 1 FLR 362
G (financial claims: liberty to restore
  application for lump sum), Re　　[2004] EWHC 88 (Fam), [2004] 1 FLR 997

Agreements

Hyman v Hyman　　[1929] AC 601, [1929] All ER Rep 245, (1929) FLR Rep 342, HL
Dean v Dean　　[1978] Fam 161, [1978] 3 All ER 758, [1978] 3 WLR 288, (1978) FLR Rep 234
Edgar v Edgar　　[1980] 3 All ER 887, [1980] 1 WLR 1410, (1981) FLR 19, CA
Camm v Camm　　(1983) FLR 577, CA
Pounds v Pounds　　[1994] 4 All ER 777, [1994] 1 WLR 1535, [1994] 1 FLR 775, CA
Richardson v Richardson (No. 2)　　[1996] 2 FLR 617, CA
Harris (formerly Manahan) v Manahan　　[1996] 4 All ER 454, [1997] 1 FLR 205, CA
Xydhias v Xydhias　　[1999] 2 All ER 386, [1999] 1 FLR 683, CA
X v X (Y and Z intervening)　　[2002] 1 FLR 508
Rose v Rose (No 1)　　[2002] EWCA Civ 208, [2002] 1 FLR 978
NA v MA　　[2006] EWHC 2900 (Fam), [2007] 1 FLR 1760
Soulsbury v Soulsbury　　[2007] EWCA Civ 969, [2008] Fam 1, [2008] 2 WLR 834, [2008] 1 FLR 90
Crossley v Crossley　　[2007] EWCA Civ 1491, [2008] 1 FLR 1467
Radmacher (formerly Granatino) v Granatino　　[2010] UKSC 42, [2011] 1 All ER 373, [2010] 2 FLR 1900; sub nom Granatino v
    Radmacher (formerly Granatino) [2011] 1 AC 534, [2010] 3 WLR 1367
Z v Z (No 2) (financial remedy:
  marriage contract)　　[2011] EWHC 2878 (Fam), [2012] 1 FLR 1100
GS v L (financial remedies:
  pre-acquired assets: needs)　　[2011] EWHC 1759 (Fam), [2013] 1 FLR 300
V v V (prenuptial agreement)　　[2011] EWHC 3230 (Fam), [2012] 1 FLR 1315
Kremen v Agrest (financial remedy:
  non-disclosure: post-nuptial agreement)　　[2012] EWHC 45 (Fam), [2012] 2 FLR 414
B v S (financial remedy:
  marital property regime)　　[2012] EWHC 265 (Fam), [2012] 2 FLR 502

Z v A (financial remedies: overseas divorce)　　[2012] EWHC 467 (Fam), [2012] 2 FLR 667
AH v PH (Scandinavian marriage settlement)　　[2013] EWHC 3873 (Fam), [2013] All ER (D) 296 (Jun), [2014] 2 FLR 251
Luckwell v Limata　　[2014] EWHC 502 (Fam), [2014] 2 FLR 168
Y v Y (financial remedy: marriage contract)　　[2014] EWHC 2920 (Fam) (Roberts J, 27 June 2014, unreported)
L v M　　[2014] EWHC 2220 (Fam) (Mr B Blair QC, 1 July 2014, unreported)
Hopkins v Hopkins　　[2015] EWHC 812 (Fam) (Mr N Cusworth QC, 26 March 2015, unreported)
WW v HW (prenuptial agreement:
  needs: conduct)　　[2015] EWHC 1844 (Fam), [2016] 2 FLR 299
DB v PB (prenuptial agreement: jurisdiction)　　[2016] EWHC 3431 (Fam), [2017] 2 FLR 1540; sub nom DB v PB (financial
    provision) (prenuptial agreement: prorogation clause) [2017] 4 WLR 44

Appealing out of time

Barder v Barder (Caluori intervening)　　[1988] AC 20, [1987] 2 All ER 440, [1987] 2 WLR 1350, [1987] 2 FLR 480, HL
Cornick v Cornick　　[1994] 2 FLR 530

Leading Cases

Appealing out of time (Cont'd)
Benson v Benson (deceased)	[1996] 1 FLR 692
Harris (formerly Manahan) v Manahan	[1996] 4 All ER 454, [1997] 1 FLR 205
Kean v Kean	[2002] 2 FLR 28
S v S (ancillary relief: consent order)	[2002] EWHC 223 (Fam), [2003] Fam 1, [2002] 3 WLR 1372, [2002] 1 FLR 992
Rose v Rose (No 2)	[2003] EWHC 505 (Fam), [2003] 2 FLR 197
Reid v Reid	[2003] EWHC 2878 (Fam), [2004] 1 FLR 736
Williams v Lindley	[2005] EWCA Civ 103, [2005] 2 FLR 710
Den Heyer v Newby	[2005] EWCA Civ 1311, [2006] 1 FLR 1114
Dixon v Marchant	[2008] EWCA Civ 11, [2008] 1 FLR 655
Horne v Horne	[2009] EWCA Civ 487, [2009] 2 FLR 1031
Myerson v Myerson (No 2)	[2009] EWCA Civ 282, [2010] 1 WLR 114, [2009] 2 FLR 147
Walkden v Walkden	[2009] EWCA Civ 627, [2010] 1 FLR 174
S v S (No 2) (ancillary relief: application to set aside order)	[2009] EWHC 2377 (Fam), [2010] 1 FLR 993
Kingdon v Kingdon	[2010] EWCA Civ 1251, [2011] 1 FLR 1409
Richardson v Richardson	[2011] EWCA Civ 79, [2011] 2 FLR 244
CS v ACS (consent order: non-disclosure: correct procedure)	[2015] EWHC 1005 (Fam), [2016] 1 FLR 131; sub nom S v S [2015] 1 WLR 4592
Critchell v Critchell	[2015] EWCA Civ 436, [2016] 1 FLR 400

Appeals
Ladd v Marshall	[1954] 3 All ER 745, [1954] 1 WLR 1489, (1954) FLR Rep 422, CA
Piglowska v Piglowski	[1999] 3 All ER 632, [1999] 1 WLR 1360, [1999] 2 FLR 763, HL
Cordle v Cordle	[2001] EWCA Civ 1791, [2002] 1 WLR 1441, [2002] 1 FLR 207
Akintola v Akintola	[2001] EWCA Civ 1989, [2002] 1 FLR 701
B v B (Mesher order)	[2002] EWHC 3106 (Fam), [2003] 2 FLR 285
Vaughan v Vaughan	[2007] EWCA Civ 1085, [2008] 1 FLR 1108
Behzadi v Behzadi	[2008] EWCA Civ 1070, [2009] 2 FLR 649
Kaur v Matharu	[2010] EWCA Civ 930, [2011] 1 FLR 698
N v N (financial orders: appellate role)	[2011] EWCA Civ 940, [2012] 1 FLR 622
Alexander v Alexander	[2011] EWCA Civ 1019
HH v BLW (appeal: costs: proportionality)	[2012] EWHC 2199 (Fam), [2013] 1 FLR 420
TF v FF	[2013] EWHC 390 (Fam) (Peter Jackson J, 26 February 2013, unreported)
B v B	[2014] EWHC 4545 (Fam) (Roberts J, 28 November 2014, unreported)
P v P (variation of post-nuptial settlement)	[2015] EWCA Civ 447, [2016] 1 FLR 437

Arbitration
AI v MT (alternative dispute resolution)	[2013] EWHC 100 (Fam), [2013] 2 FLR 371
S v S (financial remedies: arbitral award)	[2014] EWHC 7 (Fam), [2014] All ER (D) 63 (Jan), [2014] 1 FLR 1257; sub nom S v S (arbitral award: approval) [2014] 1 WLR 2299
DB v DLJ (challenge to arbitral award)	[2016] EWHC 324 (Fam), [2016] 2 FLR 1308; sub nom J v B (family law arbitration: award) [2016] 1 WLR 3319

Arrears, enforcement/remission
Fowler v Fowler	(1981) FLR 141, CA
Russell v Russell	[1986] 1 FLR 465, CA
Bernstein v O'Neill	[1989] 2 FLR 1
B v C (enforcement: arrears)	[1995] 1 FLR 467
R v Bristol Justices, exp. Hodge	[1997] QB 974, [1997] 2 WLR 756, [1997] 1 FLR 88
C v S (maintenance order: enforcement)	[1997] 1 FLR 298
R v Slough Justices, exp. Lindsay	[1997] 1 FLR 695
R v Cardiff Magistrates' Court, exp. Czech	[1999] 1 FLR 95
Constantinides v Constantinides	[2013] EWHC 3688 (Fam), [2014] 1 WLR 1934, [2014] 2 FLR 736

Avoidance of dispositions
Green v Green	[1981] 1 All ER 97, [1981] 1 WLR 391
K v K	(1983) FLR 31, CA
Kemmis v Kemmis	[1988] 1 WLR 1307, [1988] 2 FLR 223, CA
Sherry v Sherry	[1991] 1 FLR 307, CA
Purba v Purba	[2000] 1 FLR 444, CA
Mubarak v Mubarik (No 6)	[2007] EWHC 220 (Fam), [2007] 2 FLR 364
Ansari v Ansari	[2008] EWCA Civ 1456, [2010] Fam 1, [2009] 3 WLR 1092, [2009] 1 FLR 1121
AC v DC (financial remedy: effect of s37 avoidance order)	[2012] EWHC 2032 (Fam), [2013] 2 FLR 1483
Joy v Joy-Morancho	[2014] EWHC 3769 (Fam) (Sir Peter Singer, 15 April 2014, unreported)
ABC v PM & Anor	[2015] EWFC 32, [2015] All ER (D) 122 (Apr)

Bankruptcy

For Leading Cases on Bankruptcy see @eGlance and previous editions of At A Glance.

Children: capital provision
Chamberlain v Chamberlain	[1974] 1 All ER 33, [1973] 1 WLR 1557, (1973) FLR Rep 125, CA
Lilford (Lord) v Glynn	[1979] 1 All ER 441, [1979] 1 WLR 78, (1978) FLR Rep 427, CA
Griffiths v Griffiths	[1984] Fam 70, [1984] 2 All ER 626, [1984] 3 WLR 165, [1984] FLR 662, CA
Kiely v Kiely	[1988] 1 FLR 248, CA
K v K	[1992] 2 All ER 727, [1992] 1 WLR 530, [1992] 2 FLR 220, CA
J v J (a minor: property transfer)	[1993] 2 FLR 56

Leading Cases

Children: capital provision (Cont'd)

A v A (minor: capital provision)	[1994] 1 FLR 657
T v S (financial provision for children)	[1994] 2 FLR 883
Phillips v Peace	[1996] 2 FLR 230
J v C (child: financial provision)	[1999] 1 FLR 152
V v V (child maintenance)	[2001] 2 FLR 799
P (child: financial provision), Re	[2003] EWCA Civ 837, [2003] 2 FLR 865
W v W (joinder of Trusts of Land and Children Act applications)	[2003] EWCA Civ 924, [2004] 2 FLR 321
F v G (child: financial provision)	[2004] EWHC 1848 (Fam), [2005] 1 FLR 261
Re S (child: financial provision)	[2004] EWCA Civ 1685, [2005] Fam 316, [2005] 2 WLR 895, [2005] 2 FLR 94
Phillips v Peace (No 2)	[2004] EWHC 3180 (Fam), [2005] 1 WLR 3246, [2005] 2 FLR 1212
Re S (unmarried parents: financial provision)	[2006] EWCA Civ 479, [2006] 2 FLR 950
M-T v T	[2006] EWHC 2494 (Fam), [2007] 2 FLR 925
Morgan v Hill	[2006] EWCA Civ 1602, [2007] 1 FLR 1480; sub nom Hill v Morgan [2007] 1 WLR 855
MT v OT (financial provision: costs)	[2007] EWHC 838 (Fam), [2008] 2 FLR 1311
Re N (payments for benefit of child)	[2009] EWHC 11 (Fam), [2009] 1 FLR 1442; sub nom In re N (a child) (financial provision: dependency) [2009] 1 WLR 1621
H v C	[2009] 2 FLR 1540
B v R	[2009] EWHC 2026 (Fam), [2010] 1 FLR 563
M v V (child maintenance: jurisdiction: Brussels I)	[2010] EWHC 1453 (Fam), [2011] 1 FLR 109
CF v KM (financial provision for child: costs of legal proceedings)	[2010] EWHC 1754 (Fam), [2011] 1 FLR 208
DE v AB (financial provision for child)	[2011] EWHC 3792 (Fam), [2012] 2 FLR 1396
R v F (Schedule 1: child maintenance: mother's costs of contact proceedings)	[2011] 2 FLR 991
O v P (jurisdiction under Children Act 1989 Sch 1)	[2011] EWHC 2425 (Fam), [2012] 1 FLR 329
G v A (financial remedy: enforcement) (No 3)	[2011] EWHC 2377 (Fam), [2012] 1 FLR 415
G v A (financial remedy: enforcement) (No 4)	[2011] EWHC 2377 (Fam), [2012] 1 FLR 427
PK v BC (financial remedies: Schedule 1)	[2012] EWHC 1382 (Fam), [2012] 2 FLR 1426
PG v TW (No 1) (child: financial provision: legal funding)	[2012] EWHC 1892 (Fam), [2014] 1 FLR 508
PG v TW (No 2) (child: financial provision)	[2014] 1 FLR 923
N v C	[2013] EWHC 399 (Fam) (HHJ Hayward Smith QC, 14 January 2013, unreported)
O v P (No 2) (Sch 1 application: stay: forum conveniens)	[2014] EWHC 2225 (Fam), [2015] 2 FLR 77
MG and JG v JF (child maintenance: costs allowance)	[2015] EWHC 564 (Fam), [2016] 1 FLR 424
Re A (a child: financial provision)	[2014] EWCA Civ 1577, [2015] 2 FLR 625; sub nom In re A (a child) (financial provision: wealthy parent) [2015] Fam 277, [2015] 3 WLR 48
BC v DE (legal costs funding)	[2016] EWHC 1806 (Fam), [2017] 1 FLR 1521; sub nom In re F (a child) (financial provision: legal costs funding) [2016] 1 WLR 4720
MG v FG (Schedule 1: application to strike out; estoppel; legal costs funding)	[2016] EWHC 1964 (Fam) (Cobb J, 28 July 2016, unreported)
DB v PB (prenuptial agreement: jurisdiction)	[2016] EWHC 3431 (Fam), [2017] 2 FLR 1540; sub nom DB v PB (financial provision) (prenuptial agreement: prorogation clause) [2017] 4 WLR 44
G v S (Children Act 1989: Schedule 1)	[2017] EWHC 365 (Fam), [2017] 2 FLR 1207

Children: income provision, marital

GW v RW (financial provision: departure from equality)	[2003] EWHC 611 (Fam), [2003] 2 FLR 108

Children: income provision, non-marital

Haroutunian v Jennings	(1980) FLR 62, Div Ct
Osborn v Sparks	(1982) FLR 90, Div Ct
C v F (disabled child: maintenance orders)	[1998] 2 FLR 1, CA
P (child: financial provision), Re	[2003] EWCA Civ 837, [2003] 2 FLR 865
F v G (child: financial provision)	[2004] EWHC 1848 (Fam), [2005] 1 FLR 261
S (child: financial provision), Re	[2004] EWCA Civ 1685, [2005] Fam 316, [2005] 2 WLR 895, [2005] 2 FLR 94
SW v RC	[2008] EWHC 73 (Fam), [2008] 1 FLR 1703
Cook v Plummer	[2008] EWCA Civ 484, [2008] 2 FLR 989
H v C	[2009] 2 FLR 1540
G v G (child maintenance: interim costs provision)	[2009] EWHC 2080 (Fam), [2010] 2 FLR 1264
B v R	[2009] EWHC 2026 (Fam), [2010] 1 FLR 563
M v V (child maintenance: jurisdiction: Brussels I)	[2010] EWHC 1453 (Fam), [2011] 1 FLR 109
CF v KM (financial provision for child: costs of legal proceedings)	[2010] EWHC 1754 (Fam), [2011] 1 FLR 208
DE v AB (financial provision for child)	[2011] EWHC 3792 (Fam), [2012] 2 FLR 1396
R v F (Schedule 1: child maintenance: mother's costs of contact proceedings)	[2011] 2 FLR 991

Leading Cases

Children: income provision, non-marital (Cont'd)

O v P (jurisdiction under Children Act 1989 Sch 1)	[2011] EWHC 2425 (Fam), [2012] 1 FLR 329
G v A (financial remedy: enforcement) (No 3)	[2011] EWHC 2377 (Fam), [2012] 1 FLR 415
PG v TW (No 1) (child: financial provision: legal funding)	[2012] EWHC 1892 (Fam), [2014] 1 FLR 508
PG v TW (No 2) (child: financial provision)	[2014] 1 FLR 923
Re A (a child: financial provision)	[2014] EWCA Civ 1577, [2015] 2 FLR 625; sub nom In re A (a child) (financial provision: wealthy parent) [2015] Fam 277, [2015] 3 WLR 48
MG and JG v JF (child maintenance: costs allowance)	[2015] EWHC 564 (Fam), [2016] 1 FLR 424
A v B (Case C-184/14)	[2016] 3 WLR 607, [2015] All ER (D) 15 (Aug), [2015] 2 FLR 637, CJEU
TW v TM (minors) (child maintenance: jurisdiction and departure from formula)	[2015] EWHC 3054 (Fam), [2015] All ER (D) 237 (Oct), [2016] 2 FLR 1386
GN v MA (child maintenance: Children Act Sch 1)	[2015] EWHC 3939 (Fam), [2017] 1 FLR 285
BC v DE (legal costs funding)	[2016] EWHC 1806 (Fam), [2017] 1 FLR 1521; sub nom In re F (a child) (financial provision: legal costs funding) [2016] 1 WLR 4720
MG v FG (Schedule 1: application to strike out; estoppel; legal costs funding)	[2016] EWHC 1964 (Fam) (Cobb J, 28 July 2016, unreported)
DB v PB (prenuptial agreement: jurisdiction)	[2016] EWHC 3431 (Fam), [2017] 2 FLR 1540; sub nom DB v PB (financial provision) (prenuptial agreement: prorogation clause) [2017] 4 WLR 44

Child Support Act

Crozier v Crozier	[1994] Fam 114, [1994] 2 All ER 362, [1994] 2 WLR 444, [1994] 1 FLR 126
B v M (child support: revocation of order)	[1994] 1 FLR 342
Mawson v Mawson	[1994] 2 FLR 985
Smith v McInerney	[1994] 2 FLR 1077
Dorney-Kingdom v Dorney-Kingdom	[2000] 2 FLR 855, CA
V v V (child maintenance)	[2001] 2 FLR 799
Smith v SSWP and another	[2006] UKHL 35, [2006] 3 All ER 907, [2007] 1 FLR 166
Chandler v SSWP and another	[2007] EWCA Civ 1211, [2008] 1 WLR 734, [2008] 1 FLR 638
Hakki v SSWP	[2014] EWCA Civ 530, [2015] 1 FLR 547
Dickson v Rennie	[2014] EWHC 4306 (Fam), [2015] 2 FLR 978

For other Leading Cases on Child Support see @eGlance and previous editions of At A Glance.

Clean break/termination

Hanlon v Hanlon	[1978] 2 All ER 889, [1978] 1 WLR 592, (1977) FLR Rep 297, CA
Pearce v Pearce	(1980) FLR 261, CA
Richardson v Richardson	[1993] 4 All ER 673, [1994] 1 WLR 186, [1994] 1 FLR 286
N v N (consent order: variation)	[1993] 2 FLR 868, CA
Richardson v Richardson (No. 2)	[1996] 2 FLR 617, CA
Flavell v Flavell	[1997] 1 FLR 353, CA
C v C (financial relief: short marriage)	[1997] 2 FLR 26, CA
Jones v Jones	[2001] Fam 96, [2000] 3 WLR 1505, [2000] 2 FLR 307, CA
F v F (clean break: balance of fairness)	[2003] 1 FLR 847
Fleming v Fleming	[2003] EWCA Civ 1841, [2004] 1 FLR 667
D v D (financial provision: periodical payments)	[2004] EWHC 445 (Fam), [2004] 1 FLR 988
S v S	[2008] EWHC 519 (Fam), [2008] 2 FLR 113
Vaughan v Vaughan	[2010] EWCA Civ 349, [2010] 3 WLR 1209, [2010] 2 FLR 242
L v L (financial remedies: deferred clean break)	[2011] EWHC 2207 (Fam), [2012] 1 FLR 1283
Matthews v Matthews	[2013] EWCA Civ 1874, [2014] 2 FLR 1259
H v H (periodical payments: variation: clean break)	[2014] EWHC 760 (Fam), [2014] 2 FLR 1338

Companies

Potter v Potter	[1982] 3 All ER 321, [1982] 1 WLR 1255, (1983) FLR 331, CA
Smith v Smith	(1983) FLR 154, CA
Re Bird Precision Bellows	[1984] Ch 419, [1984] 3 All ER 444, [1984] 2 WLR 869
Nicholas v Nicholas	[1984] FLR 285, CA
Buckingham v Francis	[1986] 2 All ER 738
Bullock v Bullock	[1986] 1 FLR 372, CA
B v B	[1989] 1 FLR 119
P v P	[1989] 2 FLR 241
Evans v Evans	[1990] 2 All ER 147, [1990] 1 FLR 319
Poon v Poon	[1994] 2 FLR 857
Mubarak v Mubarak (No 1)	[2001] 1 FLR 673
C v C (variation of post-nuptial settlement: company shares)	[2003] EWHC 1222 (Fam), [2003] 2 FLR 493
P v P (financial relief: illiquid assets)	[2004] EWHC 2277 (Fam), [2005] 1 FLR 548
R v R (financial relief: company valuation)	[2005] 2 FLR 365
A v A	[2004] EWHC 2818 (Fam), [2006] 2 FLR 115

Leading Cases

Companies (Cont'd)
Irvine v Irvine   [2006] EWHC 583 (Ch), [2006] 4 All ER 102
H v H (periodical payments: variation:
clean break)   [2014] EWHC 760 (Fam), [2014] 2 FLR 1338
Ben Hashem v Al Shayif   [2008] EWHC 2380 (Fam), [2009] 1 FLR 115
Prest v Petrodel Resources Ltd and others   [2013] UKSC 34, [2013] 2 AC 415, [2013] 3 WLR 1, [2013] 2 FLR 732

Compensation: compensatory element included
Miller v Miller; McFarlane v McFarlane   [2006] UKHL 24, [2006] 2 AC 618, [2006] 2 WLR 1283, [2006] 1 FLR 1186
Lauder   [2007] EWHC 1227 (Fam), [2007] 2 FLR 802
H v H (periodical payments: variation:
   clean break)   [2014] EWHC 760 (Fam), [2014] 2 FLR 1338

Compensation: compensatory element not included
RP v RP   [2006] EWHC 3409 (Fam), [2007] 1 FLR 2105
S v S (non-matrimonial property: conduct)   [2006] EWHC 2793 (Fam), [2007] 1 FLR 1496
H v H   [2007] EWHC 459 (Fam), [2007] 2 FLR 548
CR v CR   [2007] EWHC 3206 (Fam), [2008] 1 FLR 323
VB v JP   [2008] EWHC 112 (Fam), [2008] 1 FLR 742
McFarlane v McFarlane   [2009] EWHC 891 (Fam), [2009] 2 FLR 1322
SA v PA (pre-marital agreement: compensation)   [2014] EWHC 392 (Fam), [2014] 2 FLR 1028

Conduct: financial misconduct
Martin v Martin   [1976] Fam 335, [1976] 3 All ER 625, [1976] 3 WLR 580, (1976) FLR Rep 436, CA
Primavera v Primavera   [1992] 1 FLR 16, CA
Le Foe v Le Foe   [2001] 2 FLR 970
B v B (financial provision:
   welfare of child and conduct)   [2002] 1 FLR 555
F v F   [2008] Fam Law 183
MF v SF (financial remedy: financial conduct)   [2015] EWHC 1273 (Fam), [2016] 2 FLR 622
R v B and others   [2017] EWFC 33, [2017] 3 FCR 519

Conduct: misconduct of proceedings
B v B (real property: assessment of interests)   [1988] 2 FLR 490
T v T (interception of documents)   [1994] 2 FLR 1083
Tavoulareas v Tavoulareas   [1998] 2 FLR 418, CA
B v B (financial provision:
   welfare of child and conduct)   [2002] 1 FLR 555
Al-Khatib v Masry   [2002] EWHC 108 (Fam), [2002] 1 FLR 1053
R v B and others   [2017] EWFC 33, [2017] 3 FCR 519

Conduct: sexual
Brett v Brett   [1969] 1 All ER 1007, [1969] 1 WLR 487, (1968) FLR Rep 83, CA
Harnett v Harnett   [1973] Fam 156, [1973] 3 WLR 1; affd [1974] 1 WLR 219, (1973) FLR Rep 305,
                                                               CA
Cuzner v Underdown   [1974] 2 All ER 351, [1974] 1 WLR 641, (1973) FLR Rep 176, CA
Bailey v Tolliday   (1983) FLR 542

Conduct: violence, etc
Jones v Jones   [1976] Fam 8, [1975] 2 All ER 12, [1975] 2 WLR 606, CA
M v M (financial provision: conduct)   (1982) FLR 83
Kyte v Kyte   [1988] Fam 145, [1987] 3 All ER 1041, [1987] 3 WLR 1114, [1988] 1 FLR 469
Evans v Evans   [1989] 1 FLR 351, CA
H v H (financial provision: conduct)   [1994] 2 FLR 801
H v H (financial relief:
   attempted murder as conduct)   [2005] EWHC 2911 (Fam), [2006] 1 FLR 990

Conduct: other
Robinson v Robinson   (1981) FLR 1, CA
Robinson v Robinson   [1983] Fam 42, [1983] 1 All ER 391, [1983] 2 WLR 146, (1983) FLR 521, CA
Vasey v Vasey   [1985] FLR 596, CA
K v K (conduct)   [1990] 2 FLR 225
Whiston v Whiston   [1995] Fam 198, [1998] 1 All ER 423, [1995] 3 WLR 405, [1995] 2 FLR 268, CA
S-T (formerly J) v J (transsexual:
   ancillary relief)   [1998] Fam 103, [1998] 1 All ER 431, [1997] 3 WLR 1287, [1997] 1 FLR 402, CA
Clark v Clark   [1999] 2 FLR 498, CA
Rampal v Rampal (No 2)   [2001] EWCA Civ 989, [2002] Fam 85, [2001] 3 WLR 795, [2001] 2 FLR 1179
Al-Khatib v Masry   [2002] EWHC 108 (Fam), [2002] 1 FLR 1053
Miller v Miller; McFarlane v McFarlane   [2006] UKHL 24, [2006] 2 AC 618, [2006] 2 WLR 1283, [2006] 1 FLR 1186
S v S (non-matrimonial property: conduct)   [2006] EWHC 2793 (Fam), [2007] 1 FLR 1496

Contributions
White v White   [2001] 1 AC 596, [2001] 1 All ER 1, [2000] 3 WLR 1571, [2000] 2 FLR 981, HL
Cowan v Cowan   [2001] EWCA Civ 679, [2002] Fam 97, [2001] 3 WLR 684, [2001] 2 FLR 192
Lambert v Lambert   [2002] EWCA Civ 1685, [2003] Fam 103, [2003] 2 WLR 631, [2003] 1 FLR 139
Norris v Norris (No 1)   [2002] EWHC 2996 (Fam), [2003] 1 FLR 1142
GW v RW (financial provision:
   departure from equality)   [2003] EWHC 611 (Fam), [2003] 2 FLR 108
Foster v Foster   [2003] EWCA Civ 565, [2003] 2 FLR 299
Sorrell v Sorrell   [2005] EWHC 1717 (Fam), [2006] 1 FLR 497

Leading Cases

Contributions (Cont'd)
Miller v Miller; McFarlane v McFarlane | [2006] UKHL 24, [2006] 2 AC 618, [2006] 2 WLR 1283, [2006] 1 FLR 1186
Charman v Charman (No 2) | [2006] EWHC 1879 (Fam), [2007] 1 FLR 593
Charman v Charman (No 3) | [2007] EWCA Civ 503; sub nom Charman v Charman (No 4), [2007] 1 FLR 1246
Cooper-Hohn v Hohn | [2014] EWHC 4122 (Fam), [2015] 1 FLR 745
Robertson v Robertson | [2016] EWHC 613 (Fam), [2017] 1 FLR 1174
Work v Gray | [2017] EWCA Civ 270, [2017] 3 WLR 535, [2017] 2 FLR 1297

Costs: inter partes
Calderbank v Calderbank | [1976] Fam 93, [1975] 3 All ER 333, [1975] 3 WLR 586, (1975) FLR Rep 113
Leadbeater v Leadbeater | [1985] FLR 789
Leary v Leary | [1987] 1 All ER 261, [1987] 1 WLR 72, [1987] 1 FLR 384, CA
Gojkovic v Gojkovic (No. 2) | [1992] Fam 40, [1992] 1 All ER 267, [1991] 3 WLR 621, [1991] 2 FLR 233, CA
Sears Tooth (a firm) v
  Payne Hicks Beach (a firm) and others | [1997] 2 FLR 116
RH v RH | [2008] EWHC 347 (Fam), [2008] 2 FLR 2142
KSO v MJO and JMO (PSO intervening) | [2008] EWHC 3031 (Fam), [2009] 1 FLR 1036
Judge v Judge | [2008] EWCA Civ 1458, [2009] 1 FLR 1287
Ben Hashem v Ali Shayif and Radfan Ltd | [2009] EWHC 864 (Fam), [2009] 2 FLR 896
M v M | [2009] EWHC 1941 (Fam), [2010] 1 FLR 256
Baker v Rowe | [2009] EWCA Civ 1162, [2010] 1 FLR 761
GS v L (No 2) (financial remedies: costs) | [2011] EWHC 2116 (Fam), [2013] 1 FLR 407
LS v JS (appeal: costs) | [2012] EWHC 2960 (Fam) (Mostyn J, 25 January 2012, unreported)
R v R (financial remedies: needs
  and practicalities) | [2011] EWHC 3093 (Fam), [2013] 1 FLR 120
Ezair v Ezair | [2012] EWCA Civ 893, [2013] 1 FLR 281
HH v BLW (appeal: costs: proportionality) | [2012] EWHC 2199 (Fam), [2013] 1 FLR 420
T v T | [2013] EWHC B3 (Fam) (Parker J, 28 January 2013, unreported)
TF v FF | [2013] EWHC 390 (Fam) (Peter Jackson J, 26 February 2013, unreported)
KS v ND (Schedule 1: appeal: costs) | [2013] 464 (Fam), [2013] All ER(D) 169 (Mar), [2013] 2 FLR 698
Evans v Evans | [2013] EWHC 506 (Fam), [2013] All ER (D) 243 (Mar), [2013] 2 FLR 999
M v M and others (costs) | [2013] EWHC 3372 (Fam), [2014] 1 FLR 499
Maughan v Wilmot | [2014] EWHC 1288 (Fam), [2015] 1 FLR 567
US v SR (No 3) | [2014] EWFC 24 (Roberts J, 24 July 2014, unreported)
H v W (cap on wife's share of
  bonus payments) (No 2) | [2014] EWHC 2846 (Fam), [2015] 2 FLR 161
J v J | [2014] EWHC 3654 (Fam) (Mostyn J, 6 November 2014, unreported)
Thiry v Thiry | [2014] EWHC 4046 (Fam), [2015] 2 FLR 743
MF v SF (financial remedy: financial conduct) | [2015] EWHC 1273 (Fam), [2016] 2 FLR 622
WD v HD | [2015] EWHC 1547 (Fam), [2017] 1 FLR 160
Joy v Joy-Morancho & Others (No 3) | [2015] EWHC 2507 (Fam), [2016] 1 FLR 815
Veluppillai v Veluppillai | [2015] EWHC 3095 (Fam), [2016] 2 FLR 681
K v K (appeal: excessive costs) | [2016] EWHC 2002 (Fam), [2016] 4 WLR 143
AB v CD | [2016] EWHC 2482 (Fam) (Roberts J, 11 October 2016, unreported)

*For the current **Costs** provisions and **Editors' Note** see page 79 ante.*
*For more Leading Cases on the previous costs regime see **@eGlance** and earlier editions of **At A Glance**.*

Costs: orders against lawyers and others
Chrulew v Borm-Reid & Co | [1992] 1 All ER 953, [1992] 1 WLR 176
Ridehalgh v Horsefield | [1994] Ch 205, [1994] 3 All ER 848, [1994] 3 WLR 462, [1994] 2 FLR 194, CA
C v C (wasted costs order) | [1994] 2 FLR 34
Sarra v Sarra | [1994] 2 FLR 880, sub nom S v S [1995] 1 FCR 185
O (costs: liability of Legal Aid Board), Re | [1997] 1 FLR 465, CA
G (minors) (care proceedings:
  wasted costs), Re | [2000] Fam 104, [1999] 4 All ER 371, [2000] 2 WLR 1007, [2000] 1 FLR 52
CH (family proceedings: court bundles), Re | [2000] 2 FCR 193
Phillips v Symes | [2004] EWHC 2330 (Ch), [2005] 4 All ER 519
D v H (costs) | [2008] EWHC 559 (Fam), [2008] 2 FLR 824
Re X and Y (bundles) | [2008] EWHC 2058 (Fam), [2008] 2 FLR 2053
Fisher Meredith v JH and PH (financial
  remedy: appeal: wasted costs) | [2012] EWHC 408 (Fam), [2012] 2 FLR 536
Re Capita Translation and Interpreting Ltd | [2015] EWFC 5, [2015] 3 All ER 123, [2015] 2 FLR 1269

Delay
Hill v Hill | [1998] 1 FLR 198, CA
Rossi v Rossi & Rossi | [2006] EWHC 1482 (Fam), [2007] 1 FLR 790
S v S (ancillary relief after lengthy separation) | [2006] EWHC 2339 (Fam), [2007] 1 FLR 2120
Gordon (formerly Stefanou) v Stefanou | [2010] EWCA Civ 1601, [2011] 1 FLR 1582
Wyatt v Vince | [2015] UKSC 14, [2015] 2 All ER 755, [2015] 1 WLR 1228, [2015] 1 FLR 972
Briers v Briers | [2017] EWCA Civ 15, [2017] 1 FCR 309

Duxbury income capitalisation
Duxbury v Duxbury | [1992] Fam 62n, [1990] 2 All ER 77, [1991] 3 WLR 639, [1987] 1 FLR 7, CA
B v B (financial provision) | [1990] 1 FLR 20
Gojkovic v Gojkovic | [1992] Fam 40, [1990] 2 All ER 84, [1991] 3 WLR 621, [1990] 1 FLR 140, CA
F v F (ancillary relief: substantial assets) | [1995] 2 FLR 45
F v F (Duxbury calculation: rate of return) | [1996] 1 FLR 833

Leading Cases

Duxbury income capitalisation (Cont'd)
A v A (financial provision)	[1998] 2 FLR 180
Fournier v Fournier	[1998] 2 FLR 990, CA
A v A (elderly applicant: lump sum)	[1999] 2 FLR 969
White v White	[2001] 1 AC 596, [2001] 1 All ER 1, [2000] 3 WLR 1571, [2000] 2 FLR 981, HL
GW v RW (financial provision: departure from equality)	[2003] EWHC 611 (Fam), [2003] 2 FLR 108
Pearce v Pearce	[2003] EWCA Civ 1054, [2004] 1 WLR 68, [2003] 2 FLR 1144
W v W (financial provision: Form E)	[2003] EWHC 2254 (Fam), [2004] 1 FLR 494
McCartney v Mills-McCartney	[2008] EWHC 401 (Fam), [2008] 1 FLR 1508
Simon v Helmot	[2012] UKPC 5, [2012] All ER (D) 215 (Mar)
H v H	[2014] EWCA Civ 1523, [2015] 2 FLR 447
JL v SL (No 3) (post-judgment amplification)	[2015] EWHC 555 (Fam), [2015] 2 FLR 1220

Enforcement

*For Leading Cases on Enforcement see **@eGlance** and previous editions of **At A Glance**.*

Equality of division: departure from
(see also **Resources**, below)
White v White	[2001] 1 AC 596, [2001] 1 All ER 1, [2000] 3 WLR 1571, [2000] 2 FLR 981, HL
Cowan v Cowan	[2001] EWCA Civ 679, [2002] Fam 97, [2001] 3 WLR 684, [2001] 2 FLR 192
Lambert v Lambert	[2002] EWCA Civ 1685, [2003] Fam 103, [2003] 2 WLR 631, [2003] 1 FLR 139
McFarlane v McFarlane; Parlour v Parlour	[2004] EWCA Civ 872, [2005] Fam 171, [2004] 3 WLR 1480, [2004] 2 FLR 893
Sorrell v Sorrell	[2005] EWHC 1717 (Fam), [2006] 1 FLR 497
Miller v Miller	[2005] EWCA Civ 984, [2006] 1 FLR 151
Miller v Miller; McFarlane v McFarlane	[2006] UKHL 24, [2006] 2 AC 618, [2006] 2 WLR 1283, [2006] 1 FLR 1186
Rossi v Rossi & Rossi	[2006] EWHC 1482 (Fam), [2007] 1 FLR 790
Charman v Charman (No 2)	[2006] EWHC 1879 (Fam), [2007] 1 FLR 593
Charman v Charman (No 3)	[2007] EWCA Civ 503; sub nom Charman v Charman (No 4), [2007] 1 FLR 1246
McCartney v Mills-McCartney	[2008] EWHC 401 (Fam), [2008] 1 FLR 1508
B v B (ancillary relief: distribution of assets)	[2008] EWCA Civ 284, [2008] 1 WLR 2362, [2008] 1 FLR 1627
Behzadi v Behzadi	[2008] EWCA Civ 1070, [2009] 2 FLR 649
SK v WL (ancillary relief: post-separation accrual)	[2010] EWHC 457 (Fam), [2011] 1 FLR 1471
N v N (ancillary relief)	[2010] EWHC 717 (Fam), [2010] 2 FLR 1093
FZ v SZ (ancillary relief: conduct: valuations)	[2010] EWHC 1630 (Fam), [2011] 1 FLR 64
Robson v Robson	[2010] EWCA Civ 1171, [2011] 1 FLR 751
Jones v Jones	[2011] EWCA Civ 41, [2012] Fam 1, [2011] 3 WLR 582, [2011] 1 FLR 1723
N v F (financial orders: pre-acquired wealth)	[2011] EWHC 586 (Fam), [2011] 2 FLR 533
J v J (financial orders: wife's long term needs)	[2011] EWHC 1010 (Fam), [2011] 2 FLR 1280
K v L	[2011] EWCA Civ 550, [2011] 3 All ER 733, [2012] 1 WLR 306; sub nom K v L (non-matrimonial property: special contribution) [2011] 2 FLR 980
Mansfield v Mansfield	[2011] EWCA Civ 1056, [2012] 1 FLR 117
AR v AR (treatment of inherited wealth)	[2011] EWHC 2717 (Fam), [2012] 2 FLR 1
S v AG (financial remedy: lottery prize)	[2011] EWHC 2637 (Fam), [2012] 1 FLR 651
A v L (departure from equality: needs)	[2011] EWHC 3150 (Fam), [2012] 1 FLR 985
Lawrence v Gallagher	[2012] EWCA Civ 394, [2012] 2 FLR 643
Y v Y (financial orders: inherited wealth)	[2012] EWHC 2063 (Fam), [2013] 2 FLR 924
R v R (financial remedies: needs and practicalities)	[2011] EWHC 3093 (Fam), [2013] 1 FLR 120
JL v SL (No 2) (appeal: non-matrimonial property)	[2014] EWHC 360 (Fam), [2015] 2 FLR 1202
Robertson v Robertson	[2016] EWHC 613 (Fam), [2017] 1 FLR 1174
BD v FD (financial remedies: needs)	[2016] EWHC 594 (Fam), [2017] 1 FLR 1420
X v X (financial remedies: share valuation discount: date for computation of assets)	[2016] EWHC 1995 (Fam), [2017] 2 FLR 840
Chai v Peng and others (financial remedies: resulting trusts)	[2017] EWHC 792 (Fam), [2018] 1 FLR 248
WM v HM (financial remedies: sharing principle: special contribution)	[2017] EWFC 25, [2018] 1 FLR 313
Sharp v Sharp	[2017] EWCA Civ 408, [2017] 2 FLR 1095
Hart v Hart	[2017] EWCA Civ 1306, [2018] 2 WLR 509

Equality of division: principle applied
White v White	[2001] 1 AC 596, [2001] 1 All ER 1, [2000] 3 WLR 1571, [2000] 2 FLR 981, HL
H-J v H-J (financial provision: equality)	[2002] 1 FLR 415
G v G (financial provision: equal division)	[2002] EWHC 1339 (Fam), [2002] 2 FLR 1143
Lambert v Lambert	[2002] EWCA Civ 1685, [2003] Fam 103, [2003] 2 WLR 631, [2003] 1 FLR 139
Norris v Norris (No 1)	[2002] EWHC 2996 (Fam), [2003] 1 FLR 1142
Parra v Parra	[2002] EWCA Civ 1886, [2003] 1 FLR 942
C v C (variation of post-nuptial settlement: company shares)	[2003] EWHC 1222 (Fam), [2003] 2 FLR 493
P v P (financial relief: illiquid assets)	[2004] EWHC 2277 (Fam), [2005] 1 FLR 548
R v R (financial relief: company valuation)	[2005] 2 FLR 365
Miller v Miller; McFarlane v McFarlane	[2006] UKHL 24, [2006] 2 AC 618, [2006] 2 WLR 1283, [2006] 1 FLR 1186

Leading Cases

Equality of division: principle applied (Cont'd)
E v E (shared residence: financial relief: yardstick of equality)	[2006] EWCA Civ 843), [2006] 2 FLR 1228
S v S (ancillary relief: importance of FDR)	[2007] EWHC 1975 (Fam), [2008] 1 FLR 944
CR v CR	[2007] EWHC 3206 (Fam), [2008] 1 FLR 323
SK v TK	[2013] EWHC 834 (Fam) (Moor J, 11 April 2013, unreported)
MCJ v MAJ (financial provision: treatment of non-matrimonial property)	[2016] EWHC 1672 (Fam) (Roberts J, 6 July 2016, as yet unreported)

Experts
Daniels v Walker	[2000] 1 WLR 1382, CA
Cooper-Hohn v Hohn	[2014] EWCA Civ 896 (18 June 2014, unreported)
Buehrlen v Buehrlen	[2017] EWHC 3643 (Fam) (Moor J, 24 November 2017, unreported)

For more Leading Cases on Experts see @eGlance and previous editions of At A Glance.

Farms
P v P	[1978] 3 All ER 70, [1978] 1 WLR 483, (1977) FLR Rep 546, CA
S v S	(1980) 10 Fam Law 240
White v White	[2001] 1 AC 596, [2001] 1 All ER 1, [2000] 3 WLR 1571, [2000] 2 FLR 981, HL
R v R (lump sum repayments)	[2003] EWHC 3197 (Fam), [2004] 1 FLR 928
P v P (inherited property)	[2004] EWHC 1364 (Fam), [2005] 1 FLR 576

Financial relief after overseas divorce
Jordan v Jordan	[2000] 1 WLR 210, [1999] 2 FLR 1069, CA
Agbaje v Agbaje	[2010] UKSC 13, [2010] AC 628, [2010] 2 WLR 709, [2010] 1 FLR 1813
M v M	[2011] EWHC 3574 (Fam) and [2010] EWHC 2817 (Fam), [2011] 1 FLR 1773
Schofield v Schofield	[2011] EWCA Civ 174, [2011] 1 FLR 2129
Traversa v Freddi	[2011] EWCA Civ 81, [2011] 2 FLR 272
Golubovich v Golubovich	[2011] EWCA Civ 479, [2011] 2 FLR 1193
Z v A (financial remedy after overseas divorce)	[2012] EWHC 1434 (Fam), [2014] 2 FLR 109
M v W (application after New Zealand financial agreement)	[2014] EWHC 925 (Fam), [2015] 1 FLR 465
Barnett v Barnett	[2014] EWHC 2678 (Fam) (Holman J, 24 July 2014, unreported)
AA v BB (application to set aside leave: s.13, MFPA 1984)	[2014] EWHC 4210 (Fam), [2015] 2 FLR 1251
MA v SK; S Investments v MA (financial relief after Saudi divorce)	[2015] EWHC 887 (Fam), [2016] 1 FLR 310
De Renee v Galbraith-Marten	[2016] EWCA Civ 537 (13 April 2016, unreported)
Johnson v Takieddine & Anor	[2016] EWHC 1895 (Fam) (Moylan J, 2 June 2016, unreported)
Juffali v Juffali	[2016] EWHC 1684 (Fam), [2016] 4 WLR 119, [2017] 1 FLR 729
Al-Baker v Al-Baker	[2016] EWHC 2510 (Fam) (Mr N Cusworth QC, 12 October 2016, unreported)
Zimina v Zimin	[2017] EWCA Civ 1429, [2018] 1 FCR 164

Forum conveniens
Spiliada Maritime Corpn v Cansulex Ltd, The Spiliada	[1987] AC 460, [1986] 3 All ER 843, [1986] 3 WLR 972, HL
de Dampierre v de Dampierre	[1988] AC 92, [1987] 2 All ER 1, [1987] 2 FLR 300, HL
W v W (financial relief: appropriate forum)	[1997] 1 FLR 257
S v S (divorce: staying proceedings)	[1997] 1 WLR 1200, [1997] 2 FLR 100
Butler v Butler (Nos 1 and 2)	[1997] 2 All ER 822, [1998] 1 WLR 1208, [1997] 2 FLR 311, CA
Connelly v RTZ Corporation plc	[1998] AC 854, [1997] 4 All ER 335, [1997] 3 WLR 373, HL
D v P (forum conveniens)	[1998] 2 FLR 25, CA
Krenge v Krenge	[1999] 1 FLR 969
Otobo v Otobo	[2002] EWCA Civ 949, [2003] 1 FLR 192
Armstrong v Armstrong	[2003] EWHC 777 (Fam), [2003] 2 FLR 375
Owusu v Jackson (Case C-281/02)	[2005] QB 801, [2005] 2 All ER (Comm) 577, [2005] 2 WLR 942, ECJ
Cook v Plummer	[2008] EWCA Civ 484, [2008] 2 FLR 989
JKN v JCN (divorce: forum)	[2010] EWHC 843 (Fam), [2011] 1 FLR 826
T v P (jurisdiction: Lugano Convention and forum conveniens)	[2012] EWHC 1627 (Fam), [2013] 1 FLR 478
Mittal v Mittal	[2013] EWCA Civ 1255, [2014] Fam 102, [2013] All ER (D) 200 (Oct), [2014] 2 WLR 1033, [2014] 1 FLR 1514
O v P (No 2) (Sch 1 application: stay: forum conveniens)	[2014] EWHC 2225 (Fam), [2015] 2 FLR 77
Chai v Peng	[2014] EWHC 3518 & 3519 (Fam), [2015] 2 FLR 424 & 412
Peng v Chai	[2015] EWCA Civ 1312, [2017] 1 FLR 318
J v U; U v J (No 2) (domicile)	[2017] EWHC 449 (Fam), [2017] 1 FCR 545

Inheritance (Provision for Family and Dependants) Act 1975
Ilott v The Blue Cross and others	[2017] UKSC 17, [2017] 4 All ER 545, [2017] 2 WLR 979, [2017] 1 FLR 1717

For more Leading Cases on the IPFDA 1975 see @eGlance and previous editions of At A Glance.

Injunctions in support of financial remedies: section 37 injunctions
Jordan v Jordan	(1965) Sol Jo 353
Smith v Smith	(1974) 4 Fam Law 80
Jackson v Jackson	(1979) 9 Fam Law 56, CA
Hamlin v Hamlin	[1986] Fam 11, [1985] 2 All ER 1037, [1985] 3 WLR 629, [1986] 1 FLR 61, CA

Leading Cases

Injunctions in support of financial remedies: section 37 injunctions (Cont'd)
Crittenden v Crittenden	[1990] 2 FLR 361, CA
Shipman v Shipman	[1991] 1 FLR 250
Bater v Bater	[1999] 4 All ER 944, [1999] 2 FLR 993, CA
Khreino v Khreino (No 2)	
(court's power to grant injunctions)	[2000] 1 FCR 80, CA
ND v KP (freezing order: ex parte	
application)	[2011] EWHC 457 (Fam), [2011] 2 FLR 662
UL v BK (freezing orders: safeguards:	
standard examples)	[2013] EWHC 1735 (Fam), [2013] All ER (D) 277 (Jun), [2014] 2 WLR 914; sub nom L v K (freezing orders: principles and safeguards) [2014] Fam 35
C v C and anor	[2015] EWHC 2795 (Fam) (Roberts J, 30 September 2015, unreported)
Tobias v Tobias	[2017] EWFC 46, [2017] 4 WLR 146, [2018] 1 FLR 616

Injunctions in support of financial remedies: freezing and mandatory injunctions
Mareva Cia Naviera SA v	
International Bulkcarriers SA	[1980] 1 All ER 213, CA
Shipman v Shipman	[1991] 1 FLR 250
Ghoth v Ghoth	[1992] 2 All ER 920, [1992] 2 FLR 300, CA
Crédit Suisse Fides Trust SA v Cuoghi	[1997] 3 All ER 724, [1997] 3 WLR 871, CA
Khreino v Khreino (No 2)	
(court's power to grant injunctions)	[2000] 1 FCR 80, CA
W v H (Family Division:	
without notice orders)	[2001] 1 All ER 300, [2000] 2 FLR 927
S (a child) (Family Division:	
without notice orders), Re	[2001] 1 All ER 362, [2001] 1 WLR 211, [2001] 1 FLR 308
Rhode v Rhode and Pembroke Square Ltd	[2007] EWHC 496 (Fam), [2007] 2 FLR 971
N v R (injunction)	[2008] EWHC 1347 (Fam), [2009] 2 FLR 342
ND v KP (freezing order: ex parte	
application)	[2011] EWHC 457 (Fam), [2011] 2 FLR 662
KY v DD (injunctions)	[2011] EWHC 1277 (Fam), [2012] 2 FLR 200
JSC BTA Bank v Solodchenko & Ors	[2011] EWHC 2163 (Ch), [2012] 1 All ER 735
UL v BK (freezing orders: safeguards:	
standard examples)	[2013] EWHC 1735 (Fam), [2013] All ER (D) 277 (Jun), [2014] 2 WLR 914; sub nom L v K (freezing orders: principles and safeguards) [2014] Fam 35
DN v HN	[2014] EWHC 3435 (Fam), [2016] 1 FLR 1171
C v C and anor	[2015] EWHC 2795 (Fam) (Roberts J, 30 September 2015, unreported)
Goyal v Goyal	[2016] EWCA Civ 792, [2016] 4 WLR 140, [2017] 2 FLR 223
Goyal v Goyal (No 3)	[2017] EWFC 1, [2017] 4 WLR 31, [2017] 2 FCR 159
Tobias v Tobias	[2017] EWFC 46, [2017] 4 WLR 146, [2018] 1 FLR 616

Injunctions in support of financial remedies: search (Anton Piller) orders
Anton Piller KG v	
Manufacturing Processes Ltd	[1976] Ch 55, [1976] 1 All ER 779, CA
Burgess v Burgess	[1996] 2 FLR 34, CA
Araghchinchi v Araghchinchi	[1997] 2 FLR 142, CA

Injunctions in support of financial remedies: writ ne exeat regno, etc
B v B (injunction:	
restraint on leaving jurisdiction)	[1997] 3 All ER 258, [1998] 1 WLR 329, [1997] 2 FLR 148
Young v Young	[2012] EWHC 138 (Fam), [2012] Fam 198, [2012] 3 WLR 266, [2012] 2 FLR 470

Injunctions in support of financial remedies: anti-suit / Hemain injunctions
Société Nationale Industrielle	
Aérospatiale v Lee Kui Jak	[1987] AC 871, [1987] 3 All ER 510, [1987] 3 WLR 59, PC
Hemain v Hemain	[1988] 2 FLR 388, CA
Bloch v Bloch	[2002] EWHC 1711 (Fam), [2003] 1 FLR 1
R v R (divorce: Hemain injunction)	[2003] EWHC 2113 (Fam), [2005] 1 FLR 386
Turner v Grovit (Case C-159/02)	[2005] 1 AC 101, [2004] 3 WLR 1193, ECJ
S v S (Hemain injunction)	[2009] EWHC 3224 (Fam), [2010] 2 FLR 502
Golubovich v Golubovich	[2010] EWCA Civ 810, [2011] Fam 88, [2010] 3 WLR 1607, [2010] 2 FLR 1614

For other Leading Cases on injunctions in support of financial remedies see @eGlance and previous editions of At A Glance.

Interim capital orders/orders for sale
Wicks v Wicks	[1998] 1 All ER 977, [1998] 3 WLR 277, [1998] 1 FLR 470, CA
Miller-Smith v Miller-Smith	[2009] EWCA Civ 1297, [2010] 1 FLR 1402
BR v VT (financial remedies: interim)	[2015] EWHC 2727 (Fam), [2016] 2 FLR 519
WS v HS	[2018] EWFC 11 (Cobb J, 28 February 2018, unreported)

Jurisdiction: EU Regulations
de Cavel v de Cavel (Case 143/78)	[1979] ECR 1055, ECJ
de Cavel v de Cavel (No 2) (Case 120/79)	[1980] ECR 731, [1980] 3 CMLR 1, ECJ
K v B (Brussels Convention)	[1994] 1 FLR 267
Van den Boogaard v Laumen	[1997] QB 759, [1997] 3 WLR 284, [1997] 2 FLR 399, ECJ
Farrell v Long	[1997] QB 842, [1997] All ER (EC) 449, [1998] 1 FLR 559, ECJ
D v P (forum conveniens)	[1998] 2 FLR 25, CA
Canada Trust Co v Stolzenberg (No 2)	[2000] 4 All ER 481, [2000] 3 WLR 1376, HL
Wermuth v Wermuth (No 1)	[2002] EWHC 3049 (Fam), [2003] 1 FLR 1022

Leading Cases

Jurisdiction: EU Regulations (Cont'd)

Wermuth v Wermuth (No 2)	[2002] EWCA Civ 50, [2003] 1 WLR 942, [2003] 1 FLR 1029
Rogers-Headicar v Headicar	[2004] EWCA Civ 1867, [2005] 2 FCR 1
Chorley v Chorley	[2005] EWCA Civ 68, [2005] 1 WLR 1469, [2005] 2 FLR 38
L-K v K (Brussels II revised: maintenance pending suit)	[2006] EWHC (Fam) 153, [2006] 2 FLR 1114
Prazic v Prazic	[2006] EWCA Civ 497, [2006] 2 FLR 1128
Bentinck v Bentinck	[2007] EWCA Civ 175, [2007] 2 FLR 1
Moore v Moore	[2007] EWCA Civ 361, [2007] 2 FLR 339
L-K v K (No 2)	[2006] EWHC 3280 (Fam), [2007] 2 FLR 729
L-K v K (No 3)	[2006] EWHC 3281 (Fam), [2007] 2 FLR 741
Re N (jurisdiction)	[2007] EWHC 1274 (Fam), [2007] 2 FLR 1196
Leman-Klammers v Klammers	[2007] EWCA Civ 919, [2008] 1 FLR 692
Marinos v Marinos	[2007] EWHC 2047 (Fam), [2007] 2 FLR 1018
Sundelind Lopez v Lopez Lizazo (Case C-68/07)	[2008] Fam 21, [2008] 3 WLR 338, [2008] 1 FLR 582, ECJ
Munro v Munro	[2007] EWHC 3315 (Fam), [2008] 1 FLR 1613
Olafisoye v Olafisoye	[2010] EWHC 3539 (Fam), [2011] 2 FLR 553
C v S (divorce: jurisdiction)	[2010] EWHC 2676 (Fam), [2011] 2 FLR 19
V v V (divorce: jurisdiction)	[2011] EWHC 1190 (Fam), [2011] 2 FLR 778
N v N (stay of maintenance proceedings)	[2012] EWHC 4282 (Fam), [2014] 1 FLR 1399
EA v AP	[2013] EWHC 2344 (Fam), [2013] All ER (D) 209 (Sep)
Jefferson v O'Connor	[2014] EWCA Civ 38, [2014] All ER (D) 197 (Jan), [2014] 2 FLR 759
Baldwin v Baldwin	[2014] EWHC 4857 (Fam), [2015] All ER (D) 261 (Nov)
Tan v Choy	[2014] EWCA Civ 251, [2015] 1 FLR 492
S v S (Brussels II revised: Articles 19(1) and (3): reference to CJEU)	[2014] EWHC 3613 (Fam), [2015] 2 FLR 364
AA v BB (application to set aside leave: s.13, MFPA 1984)	[2014] EWHC 4210 (Fam), [2015] 2 FLR 1251
Ville de Bauge v China	[2014] EWHC 3975 (Fam), [2015] 2 FLR 873
AB v JJB (EU Maintenance Regulation: modification application procedure)	[2015] EWHC 192 (Fam), [2015] 2 FLR 1143
Sanders v Verhaegen; Huber v Huber (Cases C-400/13 & C-408/13)	[2015] 2 FLR 1229, CJEU
G v G	[2015] EWHC 2101 (Fam), [2016] 4 WLR 22
A v B (Case C-184/14)	[2015] All ER (D) 15 (Aug), [2015] 2 FLR 637, CJEU
A v B (Case C-489/14)	[2016] Fam 345, [2016] 3 WLR 607, [2016] 1 FLR 31, CJEU
Ramadani v Ramadani	[2015] EWCA Civ 1138, [2016] 2 FLR 1233
E v E (BIIA: arts 16 and 19)	[2015] EWHC 3742 (Fam), [2017] 1 FLR 658
Komu and others v Komu and another (Case C-605/14)	[2016] 4 WLR 26, CJEU
Re V (European Maintenance Regulation)	[2016] EWHC 668 (Fam), [2017] 1 FLR 1083
Thum v Thum	[2016] EWHC 2634 (Fam), [2016] 4 WLR 171
Magiera v Magiera	[2016] EWCA Civ 1292, [2017] Fam 327, [2017] 3 WLR 41
DB v PB (prenuptial agreement: jurisdiction)	[2016] EWHC 3431 (Fam), [2017] 2 FLR 1540; sub nom DB v PB (financial provision) (prenuptial agreement: prorogation clause) [2017] 4 WLR 44
MS v PS (Case C-283/16)	[2017] 4 WLR 72, [2017] 1 FLR 1163, CJEU
W, V v X (Case C-499/15)	[2017] 2 FLR 828, CJEU
B v B (Maintenance Regulation: stay)	[2017] EWHC 1029 (Fam), [2017] WLR(D) 326, [2017] 3 FCR 240

Jurisdiction: domicile

Irvin v Irvin	[2001] 1 FLR 178
Mark v Mark	[2005] UKHL 42, [2006] 1 AC, [2005] 3 WLR 111, [2005] 2 FLR 1193
R v R (divorce jurisdiction: domicile)	[2006] 1 FLR 389
Cyganik v Agulian	[2006] EWCA Civ 129, [2006] 1 FCR 406
Munro v Munro	[2007] EWHC 3315 (Fam), [2008] 1 FLR 1613
Henwood v Barlow Clowes International Ltd (in liquidation) and others	[2008] EWCA Civ 577, [2008] All ER (D) 330 (May)
F v F (divorce: jurisdiction)	[2009] EWHC 1448 (Fam), [2009] 2 FLR 1496
M v M (divorce: domicile)	[2010] EWHC 982 (Fam), [2011] 1 FLR 919
Holliday v Musa	[2010] EWCA Civ 335, [2010] 2 FLR 702
Olafisoye v Olafisoye	[2010] EWHC 3539 (Fam), [2011] 2 FLR 553
Divall v Divall	[2014] EWHC 95 (Fam), [2014] 2 FLR 1104
Ray v Sekhri	[2014] EWCA Civ 119, [2014] 2 FLR 1168
J v U; U v J (No 2) (domicile)	[2017] EWHC 449 (Fam), [2017] 1 FCR 545

Jurisdiction: habitual residence

Mark v Mark	[2005] UKHL 42, [2006] 1 AC, [2005] 3 WLR 111, [2005] 2 FLR 1193
L-K v K (No 2)	[2006] EWHC 3280 (Fam), [2007] 2 FLR 729
Marinos v Marinos	[2007] EWHC 2047 (Fam), [2007] 2 FLR 1018
Munro v Munro	[2007] EWHC 3315 (Fam), [2008] 1 FLR 1613
Z v Z (divorce: jurisdiction)	[2009] EWHC 2626 (Fam), [2010] 1 FLR 694
Olafisoye v Olafisoye	[2010] EWHC 3539 (Fam), [2011] 2 FLR 553
C v S (divorce: jurisdiction)	[2010] EWHC 2676 (Fam), [2011] 2 FLR 19
V v V (divorce: jurisdiction)	[2011] EWHC 1190 (Fam), [2011] 2 FLR 778
Tan v Choy	[2014] EWCA Civ 251, [2015] 1 FLR 492
Chai v Peng	[2014] EWHC 3518 & 3519 (Fam), [2015] 2 FLR 424 & 412

Leading Cases

Jurisdiction: habitual residence (Cont'd)
Peng v Chai   [2015] EWCA Civ 1312, [2017] 1 FLR 318

Legal Aid

For Leading Cases on Legal Aid and its sub-categories see @eGlance and previous editions of At A Glance.

Length of marriage: cohabitation before
GW v RW (financial provision:
   departure from equality)   [2003] EWHC 611 (Fam), [2003] 2 FLR 108
CO v CO (ancillary relief:
   pre-marriage cohabitation)   [2004] EWHC 287 (Fam), [2004] 1 FLR 1095

Length of marriage: short
Miller v Miller   [2005] EWCA Civ 984, [2006] 1 FLR 151
Miller v Miller; McFarlane v McFarlane   [2006] UKHL 24, [2006] 2 AC 618, [2006] 2 WLR 1283, [2006] 1 FLR 1186
McCartney v Mills-McCartney   [2008] EWHC 401 (Fam), [2008] 1 FLR 1508
MD v D   [2008] EWHC 1929 (Fam), [2009] 1 FLR 810
AB v FC (financial provision) (short
   marriage: needs)   [2016] EWHC 3285 (Fam), [2017] 4 WLR 35
Sharp v Sharp   [2017] EWCA Civ 408, [2017] 2 FLR 1095

Lump sums
Tilley v Tilley   (1980) 10 Fam Law 89, CA
L v L (lump sum: interest)   [1994] 2 FLR 324
Penrose v Penrose   [1994] 2 FLR 621, CA
Masefield v Alexander (lump sum:
   extension of time)   [1995] 1 FLR 100, CA
M v B (ancillary proceedings: lump sum)   [1998] 1 FLR 53, CA
R v R (lump sum repayments)   [2003] EWHC 3197 (Fam), [2004] 1 FLR 928
Hamilton v Hamilton   [2013] EWCA Civ 13, [2013] 1 Fam 292, [2013] 2 WLR 1440, [2014] 1 FLR 55
Thiry v Thiry   [2014] EWHC 4046 (Fam), [2015] 2 FLR 743

Maintenance pending suit/LSPO
F v F (maintenance pending suit)   (1983) FLR 382
F v F (ancillary relief: substantial assets)   [1995] 2 FLR 45
A v A (maintenance pending suit:
   payment of legal fees)   [2001] 1 WLR 605, [2001] 1 FLR 377
G v G (maintenance pending suit: legal costs) [2002] EWHC 306 (Fam), [2003] 2 FLR 71
M v M (maintenance pending suit)   [2002] EWHC 317 (Fam), [2002] 2 FLR 123
Moses-Taiga v Taiga   [2005] EWCA Civ 1013, [2006] 1 FLR 1074
TL v ML and others (ancillary relief:
   claim against assets of extended family)   [2005] EWHC 2860 (Fam), [2006] 1 FLR 1263
Currey v Currey (No 2)   [2006] EWCA Civ 1338, [2006] All ER (D) 218 (Oct), [2007] 1 FLR 946
Moore v Moore   [2010] EWCA Civ 1427, [2010] 1 FLR 1413
Rubin v Rubin   [2014] EWHC 611 (Fam), [2014] 1 WLR 3289, [2014] 2 FLR 1018
BD v FD   [2014] EWHC 4443 (Fam), [2016] 1 FLR 390

Media access, etc
Clibbery v Allen   [2001] 2 FLR 819
Clibbery v Allen (No 2)   [2002] EWCA Civ 45, [2002] Fam 261, [2002] 2 WLR 1511, [2002] 1 FLR 565
Re S (a child) (identification:
   restriction on publication)   [2004] UKHL 47, [2005] 1 AC 593, [2004] 3 WLR 1129, [2005] 1 FLR 591
D v D (divorce: media presence)   [2009] EWHC 946 (Fam), [2009] 2 FLR 324
Spencer v Spencer   [2009] EWHC 1529 (Fam), [2009] 2 FLR 1416
Re X (a child) (residence and
   contact: rights of media attendance)   [2009] EWHC 1728 (Fam), [2009] 2 FLR 1467
Lykiardopulo v Lykiardopulo   [2010] EWCA Civ 1315, [2011] 1 FLR 1427
W v M (TOLATA proceedings: anonymity)   [2012] EWHC 1679 (Fam), [2013] 1 FLR 1513
Rapisarda v Colladon   [2014] EWFC 1406, [2015] 3 All ER 974, [2015] 1 FLR 584
Cooper-Hohn v Hohn   [2014] EWHC 2314 (Fam), [2014] All ER (D) 252 (Jul), [2015] 1 FLR 19
DL v SL (financial remedy proceedings:
   privacy)   [2015] EWHC 2621 (Fam), [2016] 2 FLR 552; sub nom L v L (ancillary relief
               proceedings: anonymity) [2016] 1 WLR 1259
Appleton v Gallagher & Ors   [2015] EWHC 2689 (Fam), [2016] 2 FLR 1
Veluppillai v Veluppillai   [2015] EWHC 3095 (Fam), [2016] 2 FLR 681
X v X (anonymisation)   [2016] EWHC 3512 (Fam) (Bodey J, 16 December 2016, unreported)
Norman v Norman   [2017] EWCA Civ 49, [2018] 1 All ER 769, [2017] 1 WLR 2523,
               [2018] 1 FLR 426

Money: small
Barnes v Barnes   [1972] 3 All ER 872, [1972] 1 WLR 1381
Peacock v Peacock   [1984] 1 All ER 1069, [1984] 1 WLR 532, [1984] FLR 263
Freeman v Swatridge   [1984] FLR 762, CA
Ashley v Blackman   [1988] Fam 85, [1988] 3 WLR 222, [1988] 2 FLR 278
Delaney v Delaney   [1990] 2 FLR 457, CA
SRJ v DWJ (financial provision)   [1999] 2 FLR 176, CA

Negligence (by lawyers and others)

For Leading Cases on Negligence (by lawyers and others) see @eGlance and previous editions of At A Glance.

Leading Cases

Non-disclosure/discovery
J v J | [1955] P 215, [1955] 2 All ER 617, [1955] 3 WLR 72, (1955) FLR Rep 402, CA
Livesey v Jenkins | [1985] AC 424, [1985] 1 All ER 106, [1985] 2 WLR 47, [1985] FLR 813, HL
Baker v Baker | [1995] 2 FLR 829, CA
Al-Khatib v Masry | [2002] EWHC 108 (Fam), [2002] 1 FLR 1053
W v W (financial provision: Form E) | [2003] EWHC 2254 (Fam), [2004] 1 FLR 494
OS v DS (oral disclosure: preliminary
  hearing) | [2004] EWHC 2376 (Fam), [2005] 1 FLR 675
Minwalla v Minwalla & others | [2004] EWHC 2823 (Fam), [2005] 1 FLR 771
Imerman v Tchenguiz | [2010] EWCA Civ 908, [2011] Fam 116, [2011] 2 WLR 592, [2010] 2 FLR 814
NG v SG (appeal: non-disclosure) | [2011] EWHC 3270 (Fam), [2012] 1 FLR 1211
Kremen v Agrest (financial remedy:
  non-disclosure: post-nuptial agreement) | [2012] EWHC 45 (Fam), [2012] 2 FLR 414
N v N (periodical payments: non-disclosure) | [2014] EWCA Civ 314, [2015] 1 FLR 241
Sharland v Sharland | [2015] UKSC 60, [2016] AC 871, [2016] 1 All ER 671, [2015] 3 WLR 1070,
    [2015] 2 FLR 1367
Gohil v Gohil | [2015] UKSC 61, [2016] AC 849, [2016] 1 All ER 685, [2015] 2 FLR 1289; sub
    nom Gohil v Gohil (No 2), [2015] 3 WLR 1085
AB v CD (financial remedy consent order:
  non-disclosure) | [2016] EWHC 10 (Fam), [2016] 4 WLR 36, [2017] 1 FLR 13
Roocroft v Ball | [2016] EWCA Civ 1009, [2017] 1 WLR 1137, [2017] 2 FLR 810
Goddard-Watts v Goddard-Watts | [2016] EWHC 3000 (Fam), [2017] 4 WLR 13, [2017] 2 FLR 114

Non-parties, disclosure by
Morgan v Morgan | [1977] Fam 122, [1977] 2 All ER 515, [1977] 2 WLR 712, (1976) FLR Rep 473
Wynne v Wynne & Jeffers | [1980] 3 All ER 659, [1981] 1 WLR 69, (1980) 10 Fam Law 241, CA
W v W (disclosure by third party) | (1981) FLR 291
H v H (disclosure by third party) | (1981) FLR 303
Re T (divorce: interim maintenance:
  discovery) | [1990] 1 FLR 1
Frary v Frary | [1993] 2 FLR 696, CA
B v B (production appointment:
  procedure) | [1995] 1 FLR 913
D v D (production appointment) | [1995] 2 FLR 497
Charman v Charman | [2005] EWCA Civ 1606, [2006] 2 FLR 422

Orders over property
Mesher v Mesher & Hall | [1980] 1 All ER 126n, CA
Martin v Martin | [1978] Fam 12, [1977] 3 All ER 762, [1977] 3 WLR 101, (1977) FLR Rep 444, CA
Dunford v Dunford | [1980] 1 All ER 122, [1980] 1 WLR 5, (1980) FLR 22, CA
Harvey v Harvey | [1982] Fam 83, [1982] 1 All ER 693, [1982] 2 WLR 283, (1982) FLR 141, CA
Thompson v Thompson | [1986] Fam 38, [1985] 2 All ER 243, [1985] 3 WLR 17, [1985] FLR 863, CA
Mortimer v Mortimer-Griffin | [1986] 2 FLR 315, CA
Clutton v Clutton | [1991] 1 All ER 340, [1991] 1 WLR 359, [1991] 1 FLR 242, CA
Popat v Popat | [1991] 2 FLR 163, CA
N v N (valuation: charge-back order) | [1996] 1 FLR 361
Omielan v Omielan | [1996] 2 FLR 306, CA
Jones v Jones | [1997] Fam 59, [1997] 2 WLR 373, [1997] 1 FLR 27, CA
B v B (Mesher order) | [2002] EWHC 3106 (Fam), [2003] 2 FLR 285
TL v ML and others (ancillary relief:
  claim against assets of extended family) | [2005] EWHC 2860 (Fam), [2006] 1 FLR 1264
Rossi v Rossi & Rossi | [2006] EWHC 1482 (Fam), [2007] 1 FLR 790
Fisher-Aziz v Aziz | [2010] EWCA Civ 673, [2010] 2 FLR 1053
CH v WH (power to order indemnity) | [2017] EWHC 2379 (Fam), [2017] 4 WLR 178, [2018] 1 FLR 495

Pensions: military
Walker v Walker | [1983] Fam 68, [1983] 2 All ER 909, [1983] 3 WLR 421, (1983) FLR 779, CA
Ranson v Ranson | [1988] 1 WLR 183, [1988] 1 FLR 292, CA
Legrove v Legrove | [1994] 2 FLR 119, CA
R (Smith) v SSD & SSWP | [2004] EWHC 1797 (Admin), [2005] 1 FLR 97

Pensions: other
Cowan v Cowan | [2001] EWCA Civ 679, [2002] Fam 97, [2001] 3 WLR 684, [2001] 2 FLR 192
Rye v Rye | [2002] EWHC 956 (Fam), [2002] 2 FLR 981
Maskell v Maskell | [2002] EWCA Civ 858, [2003] 1 FLR 1138
Norris v Norris (No 1) | [2002] EWHC 2996 (Fam), [2003] 1 FLR 1142
Martin-Dye v Martin-Dye | [2006] EWCA Civ 681, [2006] 4 All ER 779, [2006] 2 FLR 901
H v H | [2009] EWHC 3739 (Fam), [2010] 2 FLR 173
Blight and others v Brewster | [2012] EWHC 165 (Ch), [2012] All ER (D) 190 (Feb), [2012] 1 WLR 2841
JS v RS | [2015] EWHC 2921 (Fam), [2016] 2 FLR 839
WS v WS | [2015] EWHC 3941 (Fam) (HHJ Lord Meston QC, 11 December 2015, unrptd)
Goyal v Goyal | [2016] EWCA Civ 792, [2016] 4 WLR 140, [2017] 2 FLR 223
Goyal v Goyal (No 2) | [2016] EWFC 50, [2016] 4 WLR 170, [2017] 2 FLR 236
Goyal v Goyal (No 3) | [2017] EWFC 1, [2017] 4 WLR 31, [2017] 2 FCR 159

For more Leading Cases on Pensions: other see @eGlance and previous editions of At A Glance.

Periodical payments: capitalisation of
Boylan v Boylan | [1988] 1 FLR 282

Leading Cases

Periodical payments: capitalisation of (Cont'd)

Harris v Harris	[2001] 1 FCR 68, CA
Cornick v Cornick (No 3)	[2001] 2 FLR 1240
Pearce v Pearce	[2003] EWCA Civ 1054, [2004] 1 WLR 68, [2003] 2 FLR 1144
W v W (financial provision: Form E)	[2003] EWHC 2254 (Fam), [2004] 1 FLR 494
CO v CO (ancillary relief: pre-marriage cohabitation)	[2004] EWHC 287 (Fam), [2004] 1 FLR 1095
Lauder v Lauder	[2007] EWHC 1227 (Fam), [2007] 2 FLR 802
Dixon v Marchant	[2008] EWCA Civ 11, [2008] 1 FLR 655
Vaughan v Vaughan	[2010] EWCA Civ 349, [2011] Fam 46, [2010] 3 WLR 1209, [2010] 2 FLR 242

Periodical payments: principles of award

V v V (financial relief)	[2005] 2 FLR 697
Miller v Miller; McFarlane v McFarlane	[2006] UKHL 24, [2006] 2 AC 618, [2006] 2 WLR 1283, [2006] 1 FLR 1186
Q v Q (ancillary relief: periodical payments)	[2005] EWHC 402 (Fam), [2005] 2 FLR 640
RP v RP	[2006] EWHC 3409 (Fam), [2007] 1 FLR 2105
Lauder v Lauder	[2007] EWHC 1227 (Fam), [2007] 2 FLR 802
CR v CR	[2007] EWHC 3206 (Fam), [2008] 1 FLR 323
VB v JP	[2008] EWHC 112 (Fam), [2008] 1 FLR 742
H v H	[2008] EWHC 935 (Fam), [2008] 1 FLR 2092
B v S (financial remedy: marital property regime)	[2012] EWHC 265 (Fam), [2012] 2 FLR 502
H v W (cap on wife's share of bonus payments)	[2013] EWHC 4105 (Fam), [2015] 1 FLR 75
SA v PA (pre-marital agreement: compensation)	[2014] EWHC 392 (Fam), [2014] 2 FLR 1028
H v H (periodical payments: variation: clean break)	[2014] EWHC 760 (Fam), [2014] 2 FLR 1338
SS v NS (spousal maintenance)	[2014] EWHC 4183 (Fam), [2015] 2 FLR 1124
Aburn v Aburn	[2016] EWCA Civ 72, [2017] 1 FLR 72
AB v CD (jurisdiction: global maintenance orders)	[2017] EWHC 3164 (Fam), [2018] 1 FCR 199

Periodical payments: variation of

Primavera v Primavera	[1992] 1 FLR 16, CA
Jones v Jones	[2001] Fam 96, [2000] 3 WLR 1505, [2000] 2 FLR 307, CA
Harris v Harris	[2001] 1 FCR 68, CA
Mubarak v Mubarik (No 4)	[2004] EWHC 1158 (Fam), [2004] 2 FLR 932
Laing v Laing	[2005] EWHC 3152 (Fam), [2007] 2 FLR 199
North v North	[2007] EWCA Civ 760, [2007] All ER (D) 386 (Jul), [2008] 2 FLR 158
VB v JP	[2008] EWHC 112 (Fam), [2008] 1 FLR 742
McFarlane v McFarlane	[2009] EWHC 891 (Fam), [2009] 2 FLR 1322
Hvorostovsky v Hvorostovsky	[2009] EWCA Civ 791, [2009] 2 FLR 1574
H v W (cap on wife's share of bonus payments)	[2013] EWHC 4105 (Fam), [2015] 1 FLR 75
H v H (periodical payments: variation: clean break)	[2014] EWHC 760 (Fam), [2014] 2 FLR 1338
Morris v Morris	[2016] EWCA Civ 812, [2017] 1 WLR 554
Joy v Joy-Morancho (dismissal of variation application	[2017] EWHC 2086 (Fam), [2018] 1 FCR 346

Practice and procedure

W v W (ancillary relief: practice)	[2000] Fam Law 473
Rose v Rose (No 1)	[2002] EWCA Civ 208, [2002] 1 FLR 978
OS v DS (oral disclosure: preliminary hearing)	[2004] EWHC 2376 (Fam), [2005] 1 FLR 675
Re X and Y (bundles)	[2008] EWHC 2058 (Fam), [2008] 2 FLR 2053
P v P (financial relief: procedure)	[2008] EWHC 2953 (Fam), [2009] 1 FLR 696
Myerson v Myerson	[2008] EWCA Civ 1376, [2009] 1 FLR 826
P v P	[2010] 1 FLR 1126
Imerman v Tchenguiz	[2010] EWCA Civ 908, [2011] Fam 116, [2011] 2 WLR 592, [2010] 2 FLR 814
Fisher Meredith v JH and PH (financial remedy: appeal: wasted costs)	[2012] EWHC 408 (Fam), [2012] 2 FLR 536
X v X (financial remedies: preparation and presentation)	[2012] EWHC 538 (Fam), [2012] 2 FLR 590
HMRC v Charman and Charman	[2012] EWHC 1448 (Fam), [2012] 2 FLR 1119
Tchenguiz-Imerman v Imerman	[2012] EWHC 4277 (Fam), [2014] 1 FLR 865
Arif v Zar & Anor	[2012] EWCA Civ 986, [2012] All ER (D) 243 (Jul), [2012] WLR(D) 239
UL v BK (freezing orders: safeguards: standard examples)	[2013] EWHC 1735 (Fam), [2013] All ER (D) 277 (Jun), [2014] 2 WLR 914; sub nom L v K (freezing orders: principles and safeguards) [2014] Fam 35
Young v Young	[2013] EWHC 3637 (Fam), [2013] All ER (D) 313 (Nov), [2014] 2 FLR 786
Durrant v Chief Constable of Avon & Somerset Constabulary	[2013] EWCA Civ 1624, [2014] 2 All ER 757, [2014] 1 WLR 4313
Luckwell v Limata	[2014] EWHC 536 (Fam), [2015] 1 FLR 1252
JP v NP (financial remedies: costs)	[2014] EWHC 1101 (Fam), [2014] WLR (D) 172, [2015] 1 FLR 659; sub nom P v P (divorce: financial remedy order) [2014] 1 WLR 4607
Chai v Peng (No 2)	[2014] EWHC 1519 (Fam), [2015] 1 FLR 637
J v J	[2014] EWHC 3654 (Fam) (Mostyn J, 6 November 2014, unreported)

Leading Cases

Practice and procedure (Cont'd)

Seagrove v Sullivan	[2014] EWHC 4110 (Fam), [2015] 2 FLR 602
Wyatt v Vince	[2015] UKSC 14, [2015] 2 All ER 755, [2015] 1 WLR 1228, [2015] 1 FLR 972
Dellal v Dellal and others	[2015] EWHC 907 (Fam) (Mostyn J, 1 April 2015, unreported)
Re B (litigants in person: timely service of documents)	[2016] EWHC 2365 (Fam) (Peter Jackson J, 30 September 2016, unreported)
Roocroft v Ball	[2016] EWCA Civ 1009, [2017] 1 WLR 1137, [2017] 2 FLR 810
Assoun v Assoun (No 1)	[2017] EWCA Civ 21, [2017] 2 FLR 1137
Norman v Norman (No 2)	[2017] EWCA Civ 120, [2017] 1 WLR 2554
Quan v Bray and others	[2017] EWCA Civ 405, [2017] 3 FCR 648
Wilmot v Vaughan	[2017] EWCA Civ 1668, [2017] All ER (D) 12 (Nov), [2017] WLR(D) 756
Barton v Wright Hassall LLP	[2018] UKSC 12, [2018] All ER (D) 109 (Feb), [2018] 1 WLR 1119

Proceeds of Crime Act

Bowman v Fels	[2005] EWCA (Civ) 226, [2005] 2 FLR 247

Property, beneficial interest in

For Leading Cases on Property, beneficial interest in, see the extensive TOLATA section in @eGlance. It contains 23 subject categories and over 90 Leading Cases covering all aspects of TOLATA claims, together with a procedural Table.

Remarriage and cohabitation: prospects

Wachtel v Wachtel	[1973] Fam 72, [1973] 1 All ER 829, [1973] 2 WLR 366, CA
Smith v Smith	[1976] Fam 18n, [1975] 2 WLR 615n, sub nom S v S (1973) FLR Rep 649n
Livesey v Jenkins	[1985] AC 424, [1985] 1 All ER 106, [1985] 2 WLR 47, [1985] FLR 813, HL

Remarriage and cohabitation: actual remarriage

H v H	[1975] Fam 9, [1975] 1 All ER 367, [1975] 2 WLR 124
Stockford v Stockford	(1982) FLR 58, CA
Slater v Slater	(1982) FLR 364, CA
Prow (formerly Brown) v Brown	(1983) FLR 352, CA
Camm v Camm	(1983) FLR 577, CA

Remarriage and cohabitation: cohabitation

Suter v Suter and Jones	[1987] Fam 111, [1987] 2 All ER 336, [1987] 3 WLR 9, [1987] 2 FLR 232, CA
Atkinson v Atkinson	[1988] Fam 93, [1987] 3 All ER 849, [1988] 2 WLR 204, [1988] 2 FLR 353, CA
R v R	[1988] 1 FLR 89, CA
Hepburn v Hepburn	[1989] 1 FLR 373, CA
Duxbury v Duxbury	[1992] Fam 62n, [1990] 2 All ER 77, [1991] 3 WLR 639, [1987] 1 FLR 7, CA
Atkinson v Atkinson	[1995] 2 FLR 356
Atkinson v Atkinson (No 2)	[1996] 1 FLR 51, CA
Hill v Hill	[1998] 1 FLR 198, CA
Fleming v Fleming	[2003] EWCA Civ 1841, [2004] 1 FLR 667
Grey v Grey	[2009] EWCA Civ 1424, [2010] 1 FLR 1764
Grey v Grey (No 3)	[2010] EWHC 1055 (Fam), [2010] 2 FLR 1848
AB v CB (financial remedy: variation of trust)	[2014] EWHC 2998 (Fam), [2015] 2 FLR 25

Resources: computation and extent of

Thomas v Thomas	[1995] 2 FLR 668, CA
White v White	[2001] 1 AC 596, [2001] 1 All ER 1, [2000] 3 WLR 1571, [2000] 2 FLR 981, HL
Norris v Norris (No 1)	[2002] EWHC 2996 (Fam), [2003] 1 FLR 1142
TL v ML and others (ancillary relief: claim against assets of extended family)	[2005] EWHC 2860 (Fam), [2006] 1 FLR 1264
G v G (matrimonial property: rights of extended family)	[2005] EWHC 1560 (Fam), [2006] 1 FLR 62
Miller v Miller; McFarlane v McFarlane	[2006] UKHL 24, [2006] 2 AC 618, [2006] 2 WLR 1283, [2006] 1 FLR 1186
A v A	[2007] EWHC 99 (Fam), [2007] 2 FLR 467
Vaughan v Vaughan	[2007] EWCA Civ 1085, [2008] 1 FLR 1108
McCartney v Mills-McCartney	[2008] EWHC 401 (Fam), [2008] 1 FLR 1508
SR v CR (ancillary relief: family trusts)	[2008] EWHC 2329 (Fam), [2009] 2 FLR 1083
Behzadi v Behzadi	[2008] EWCA Civ 1070, [2009] 2 FLR 649, CA
B v B (ancillary relief)	[2009] EWHC 3422 (Fam), [2010] 2 FLR 887
Marano v Marano	[2010] EWCA Civ 119, [2010] 1 FLR 1903
M v W (ancillary relief)	[2010] EWHC 1155 (Fam), [2010] 2 FLR 1484
Whaley v Whaley	[2011] EWCA Civ 617, [2012] 1 FLR 735
BJ v MJ (financial remedy: overseas trusts)	[2011] EWHC 2708 (Fam), [2012] 1 FLR 667
RK v RK (financial resources: trust assets)	[2011] EWHC 3910 (Fam), [2013] 1 FLR 329
Prest v Petrodel Resources Ltd and others	[2013] UKSC 34, [2013] 2 AC 415, [2013] 3 WLR 1, [2013] 2 FLR 732
US v SR (No 3)	[2014] EWFC 24 (Roberts J, 24 July 2014, unreported)
MAP v MFP (financial remedies: add-back)	[2015] EWHC 627 (Fam), [2016] 1 FLR 70
BD v FD (financial remedies: needs)	[2016] EWHC 594 (Fam), [2017] 1 FLR 1420
Alireza v Radwan & Ors	[2017] EWCA Civ 1545, [2017] 4 WLR 206, [2018] 1 FCR 289

Resources: (il)liquidity of

Newton v Newton	[1990] 1 FLR 33, CA
Wells v Wells	[2002] EWCA Civ 476, [2002] 2 FLR 97
N v N (financial provision: sale of company)	[2001] 2 FLR 69
G v G (financial provision: equal division)	[2002] EWHC 1339 (Fam), [2002] 2 FLR 1143
F v F (clean break: balance of fairness)	[2003] 1 FLR 847

Leading Cases

Resources: (il)liquidity of (Cont'd)
GW v RW (financial provision:
   departure from equality) [2003] EWHC 611 (Fam), [2003] 2 FLR 108
C v C (variation of post-nuptial
   settlement: company shares) [2003] EWHC 1222 (Fam), [2003] 2 FLR 493
R v R (lump sum repayments) [2003] EWHC 3197 (Fam), [2004] 1 FLR 928
P v P (inherited property) [2004] EWHC 1364 (Fam), [2005] 1 FLR 576
P v P (financial relief: illiquid assets) [2004] EWHC 2277 (Fam), [2005] 1 FLR 548
R v R (financial relief: company valuation) [2005] 2 FLR 365
V v V (financial relief) [2005] 2 FLR 697
Miller v Miller; McFarlane v McFarlane [2006] UKHL 24, [2006] 2 AC 618, [2006] 2 WLR 1283, [2006] 1 FLR 1186
Re C (divorce: financial relief) [2007] EWHC 1911 (Fam), [2008] 1 FLR 625

Resources, non-matrimonial: pre-marital
White v White [2001] 1 AC 596, [2001] 1 All ER 1, [2000] 3 WLR 1571, [2000] 2 FLR 981, HL
Miller v Miller; McFarlane v McFarlane [2006] UKHL 24, [2006] 2 AC 618, [2006] 2 WLR 1283, [2006] 1 FLR 1186
McCartney v Mills-McCartney [2008] EWHC 401 (Fam), [2008] 1 FLR 1508
L v L (ancillary relief) [2008] EWHC 882 (Fam), [2008] 1 FLR 142
B v B (ancillary relief: distribution of assets) [2008] EWCA Civ 284, [2008] 1 WLR 2362, [2008] 1 FLR 1627
N v N (ancillary relief) [2010] EWHC 717 (Fam), [2010] 2 FLR 1093
FZ v SZ (ancillary relief: conduct: valuations) [2010] EWHC 1630 (Fam), [2011] 1 FLR 64
Robson v Robson [2010] EWCA Civ 1171, [2011] 1 FLR 751
Jones v Jones [2011] EWCA Civ 41, [2012] Fam 1, [2011] 3 WLR 582, [2011] 1 FLR 1723
N v F (financial orders: pre-acquired wealth) [2011] EWHC 586 (Fam), [2011] 2 FLR 533
J v J (financial orders: wife's long term needs) [2011] EWHC 1010 (Fam), [2011] 2 FLR 1280
K v L [2011] EWCA Civ 550, [2011] 3 All ER 733, [2012] 1 WLR 306; sub nom K v L
   (non-matrimonial property: special contribution) [2011] 2 FLR 980
Mansfield v Mansfield [2011] EWCA Civ 1056, [2012] 1 FLR 117
AR v AR (treatment of inherited wealth) [2011] EWHC 2717 (Fam), [2012] 2 FLR 1
V v V (prenuptial agreement) [2011] EWHC 3230 (Fam), [2012] 1 FLR 1315
B v B (assessment of assets:
   pre-marital property) [2012] EWHC 314 (Fam), [2012] 2 FLR 22
Y v Y (financial orders: inherited wealth) [2012] EWHC 2063 (Fam), [2013] 2 FLR 924
Robertson v Robertson [2016] EWHC 613 (Fam), [2017] 1 FLR 1174
BD v FD (financial remedies: needs) [2016] EWHC 594 (Fam), [2017] 1 FLR 1420
MCJ v MAJ (financial provision: treatment
   of non-matrimonial property) [2016] EWHC 1672 (Fam) (Roberts J, 6 July 2016)
Scatliffe v Scatliffe (BVI) [2016] UKPC 36, [2017] AC 93, [2017] 2 WLR 106, [2017] 2 FLR 933
WM v HM (financial remedies:
   sharing principle: special contribution) [2017] EWFC 25, [2018] 1 FLR 313
Hart v Hart [2017] EWCA Civ 1306, [2018] 2 WLR 509

Resources, non-matrimonial: acquired during marriage
Daubney v Daubney [1976] Fam 267, [1976] 2 All ER 453, [1976] 2 WLR 959, (1976) FLR Rep 214, CA
Wagstaff v Wagstaff [1992] 1 All ER 275, [1992] 1 WLR 320, [1992] 1 FLR 333, CA
C v C (financial provision: personal damages) [1995] 2 FLR 171
White v White [2001] 1 AC 596, [2001] 1 All ER 1, [2000] 3 WLR 1571, [2000] 2 FLR 981, HL
Norris v Norris (No 1) [2002] EWHC 2996 (Fam), [2003] 1 FLR 1142
Miller v Miller; McFarlane v McFarlane [2006] UKHL 24, [2006] 2 AC 618, [2006] 2 WLR 1283, [2006] 1 FLR 1186
S v AG (financial remedy: lottery prize) [2011] EWHC 2637 (Fam), [2012] 1 FLR 651

Resources, non-matrimonial: acquired post-separation
Lombardi v Lombardi [1973] 3 All ER 625, [1973] 1 WLR 1276, CA
Pearce v Pearce (1980) FLR 261, CA
Schuller v Schuller [1990] 2 FLR 193, CA
White v White [2001] 1 AC 596, [2001] 1 All ER 1, [2000] 3 WLR 1571, [2000] 2 FLR 981, HL
A v B (financial relief: agreements) [2005] EWHC 314 (Fam), [2005] 2 FLR 730
Miller v Miller; McFarlane v McFarlane [2006] UKHL 24, [2006] 2 AC 618, [2006] 2 WLR 1283, [2006] 1 FLR 1186
Rossi v Rossi & Rossi [2006] EWHC 1482 (Fam), [2007] 1 FLR 790
S v S (ancillary relief after lengthy separation) [2006] EWHC 2339 (Fam), [2007] 1 FLR 2120
H v H [2007] EWHC 459 (Fam), [2007] 2 FLR 548
CR v CR [2007] EWHC 3206 (Fam), [2008] 1 FLR 323
P v P (post separation accruals
   and earning capacity) [2007] EWHC 2877 (Fam), [2008] 2 FLR 1135
H v H (financial provision) [2009] EWHC 494 (Fam), [2009] 2 FLR 795
B v B (ancillary relief: post separation
   income) [2010] EWHC 193 (Fam), [2010] 2 FLR 1214
SK v WL (ancillary relief: post-
   separation accrual) [2010] EWHC 457 (Fam), [2011] 1 FLR 1471
Gordon (formerly Stefanou) v Stefanou [2010] EWCA Civ 1601, [2011] 1 FLR 1582
Cooper-Hohn v Hohn [2014] EWHC 4122 (Fam), [2015] 1 FLR 745
JL v SL (No 2) (appeal: non-matrimonial
   property) [2014] EWHC 360 (Fam), [2015] 2 FLR 1202
JB v MB [2015] EWHC 1846 (Fam) (Mr N Cusworth QC, 10 June 2015, unreported)
Alireza v Radwan & Ors [2017] EWCA Civ 1545, [2017] 4 WLR 206, [2018] 1 FCR 289

Third parties, claims by/against
Tebbutt v Haynes [1981] 2 All ER 238, CA

Leading Cases

Third parties, claims by/against (Cont'd)
Harwood v Harwood	[1991] 2 FLR 274, CA
T v T (joinder of third parties)	[1996] 2 FLR 357
Laird v Laird	[1999] 1 FLR 791, CA
TL v ML and others (ancillary relief: claim against assets of extended family)	[2005] EWHC 2860 (Fam), [2006] 1 FLR 1264
Rossi v Rossi & Rossi	[2006] EWHC 1482 (Fam), [2007] 1 FLR 790
A v A (No 2) (ancillary relief: costs)	[2007] EWHC 1810 (Fam), [2008] 1 FLR 1428
Ben Hashem v Al Shayif	[2008] EWHC 2380 (Fam), [2009] 1 FLR 115
Gourisaria v Gourisaria	[2010] EWCA Civ 1019, [2011] 1 FLR 262
Goldstone v Goldstone	[2011] EWCA Civ 39, [2011] 1 FLR 1926
Edgerton v Edgerton and Zaffirili Shaikh	[2012] EWCA Civ 181, [2012] 2 FLR 273
Fisher Meredith v JH and PH (financial remedy: appeal: wasted costs)	[2012] EWHC 408 (Fam), [2012] 2 FLR 536

Trusts
Howard v Howard	[1945] P 1, [1945] 1 All ER 91, (1944) FLR Rep 337, CA
Londonderry's Settlement, Re	[1965] Ch 918, [1964] 3 All ER 855, [1965] 2 WLR 229, CA
B v B	(1982) FLR 298, CA
Browne v Browne	[1989] 1 FLR 291, CA
E v E	[1990] 2 FLR 233
T v T (joinder of third parties)	[1996] 2 FLR 357
Murphy's Settlements, Re	[1999] 1 WLR 282, [1998] 3 All ER 1
Fuller v Evans	[2000] 1 All ER 636, [2000] 2 FLR 13
Schmidt v Rosewood Trust Ltd	[2003] UKPC 26, [2003] 3 All ER 76
Charalambous v Charalambous	[2004] EWCA Civ 1030, [2004] 2 FLR 1093, CA; sub nom C v C (ancillary relief: nuptial settlement) [2005] Fam 250, [2005] 2 WLR 241
Minwalla v Minwalla & others	[2004] EWHC 2823 (Fam), [2005] 1 FLR 771
A v A	[2007] EWHC 99 (Fam), [2007] 2 FLR 467
Charman v Charman (No 3)	[2007] EWCA Civ 503; sub nom Charman v Charman (No 4), [2007] 1 FLR 1246
K v K (ancillary relief: deed of appointment)	[2007] EWHC 3485 (Fam), [2009] 2 FLR 936
Breakspear v Ackland	[2008] EWHC 220 (Ch), [2009] Ch 32, [2008] 3 WLR 698
Mubarak v Mubarik	[2008] JRC 136, [2009] 1 FLR 664, Royal Court of Jersey
B v B (ancillary relief)	[2009] EWHC 3422 (Fam), [2010] 2 FLR 887
C v C (ancillary relief: trust fund)	[2009] EWHC 1491 (Fam), [2010] 1 FLR 337
D v D and others and the I Trust	[2009] EWHC 3062 (Fam), [2011] 2 FLR 29
M v W (ancillary relief)	[2010] EWHC 1155 (Fam), [2010] 2 FLR 148
Whaley v Whaley	[2011] EWCA Civ 617, [2012] 1 FLR 735
BJ v MJ (financial remedy: overseas trusts)	[2011] EWHC 2708 (Fam), [2012] 1 FLR 667
RK v RK (financial resources: trust assets)	[2011] EWHC 3910 (Fam), [2013] 1 FLR 329
G v G (financial remedies: short marriage: trust assets)	[2012] EWHC 167 (Fam), [2012] 2 FLR 48
Hope v Krejci and others	[2012] EWHC 1780 (Fam), [2013] 1 FLR 182
DR v GR and ors (financial remedy: variation of overseas trust)	[2013] EWHC 1196 (Fam), [2013] All ER (D) 230 (May), [2013] 2 FLR 1534
AB v CB (financial remedy: variation of trust)	[2014] EWHC 2998 (Fam), [2015] 2 FLR 25
P v P (variation of post-nuptial settlement)	[2015] EWCA Civ 447, [2016] 1 FLR 437
Joy v Joy-Morancho & Others (No 3)	[2015] EWHC 2507 (Fam), [2016] 1 FLR 815
NR v AB (financial remedies)	[2016] EWHC 277 (Fam), [2017] 1 FLR 1030
Quan v Bray and others	[2017] EWCA Civ 405, [2017] 3 FCR 648

Variation of final orders
Tilley v Tilley	(1980) 10 Fam Law 89, CA
Carson v Carson	[1983] 1 All ER 478, [1983] 1 WLR 285, (1981) FLR 352, CA
Sandford v Sandford	[1986] 1 FLR 412, CA
Thompson v Thompson	[1986] Fam 38, [1985] 2 All ER 243, [1985] 3 WLR 17, [1985] FLR 863, CA
Dinch v Dinch	[1987] 1 All ER 818, [1987] 1 WLR 252, [1987] 2 FLR 162, HL
Peacock v Peacock	[1991] 1 FLR 324
Popat v Popat	[1991] 2 FLR 163, CA
Omielan v Omielan	[1996] 2 FLR 306, CA
Mubarak v Mubarik (No 6)	[2007] EWHC 220 (Fam), [2007] 2 FLR 364
Birch v Birch	[2017] UKSC 53, [2018] 1 All ER 108, [2017] 1 WLR 2959, [2017] 2 FLR 1031
A v A	[2018] EWHC 340 (Fam) (Cohen J, 28 February 2018, unreported)

Brussels II Revised and
FPR 7.27: Extracts

Council Regulation (EC) No 2201/2003 of 27 November 2003 concerning jurisdiction and the recognition and enforcement of judgments in matrimonial matters and the matters of parental responsibility, repealing Regulation (EC) No 1347/2000 *(extract)*

Article 3

General jurisdiction

1. In matters relating to divorce, legal separation or marriage annulment, jurisdiction shall lie with the courts of the Member State
   (a) in whose territory:
       – the spouses are habitually resident, or
       – the spouses were last habitually resident, insofar as one of them still resides there, or
       – the respondent is habitually resident, or
       – in the event of a joint application, either of the spouses is habitually resident, or
       – the applicant is habitually resident if he or she resided there for at least a year immediately before the application was made, or
       – the applicant is habitually resident if he or she resided there for at least six months immediately before the application was made and is either a national of the Member State in question or, in the case of the United Kingdom and Ireland, has his or her 'domicile' there;
   (b) of the nationality of both spouses or, in the case of the United Kingdom and Ireland, of the 'domicile' of both spouses.
2. For the purpose of this Regulation, 'domicile' shall have the same meaning as it has under the legal systems of the United Kingdom and Ireland.

*　　*　　*　　*　　*

Article 6
Exclusive nature of jurisdiction under Articles 3, 4 and 5
A spouse who:
   (a) is habitually resident in the territory of a Member State; or
   (b) is a national of a Member State, or, in the case of the United Kingdom and Ireland, has his or her 'domicile' in the territory of one of the latter Member States,
may be sued in another Member State only in accordance with Articles 3, 4 and 5.

Article 7
Residual jurisdiction

1. Where no court of a Member State has jurisdiction pursuant to Articles 3, 4 and 5, jurisdiction shall be determined, in each Member State, by the laws of that State.
2. As against a respondent who is not habitually resident and is not either a national of a Member State or, in the case of the United Kingdom and Ireland, does not have his 'domicile' within the territory of one of the latter Member States, any national of a Member State who is habitually resident within the territory of another Member State may, like the nationals of that State, avail himself of the rules of jurisdiction applicable in that State.

*　　*　　*　　*　　*

Article 16
Seising of a Court

1. A court shall be deemed to be seised:
   (a) at the time when the document instituting the proceedings or an equivalent document is lodged with the court, provided that the applicant has not subsequently failed to take the steps he was required to take to have service effected on the respondent; or
   (b) if the document has to be served before being lodged with the court, at the time when it is received by the authority responsible for service, provided that the applicant has not subsequently failed to take the steps he was required to take to have the document lodged with the court.

Article 17
Examination as to jurisdiction
Where a court of a Member State is seised of a case over which it has no jurisdiction under this Regulation and over which a court of another Member State has jurisdiction by virtue of this Regulation, it shall declare of its own motion that it has no jurisdiction.

Brussels II Revised and FPR 7.27: Extracts

Article 18
Examination as to admissibility

1. Where a respondent habitually resident in a State other than the Member State where the action was brought does not enter an appearance, the court with jurisdiction shall stay the proceedings so long as it is not shown that the respondent has been able to receive the document instituting the proceedings or an equivalent document in sufficient time to enable him to arrange for his defence, or that all necessary steps have been taken to this end.

2. Article 19 of Regulation (EC) No 1348/2000 shall apply instead of the provisions of paragraph 1 of this Article if the document instituting the proceedings or an equivalent document had to be transmitted from one Member State to another pursuant to that Regulation.

3. Where the provisions of Regulation (EC) No 1348/2000 are not applicable, Article 15 of the Hague Convention of 15 November 1965 on the service abroad of judicial and extrajudicial documents in civil or commercial matters shall apply if the document instituting the proceedings or an equivalent document had to be transmitted abroad pursuant to that Convention.

Article 19
Lis pendens and dependent actions

1. Where proceedings relating to divorce, legal separation or marriage annulment between the same parties are brought before courts of different Member States, the court second seised shall of its own motion stay its proceedings until such time as the jurisdiction of the court first seised is established.

2. Where proceedings relating to parental responsibility relating to the same child and involving the same cause of action are brought before courts of different Member States, the court second seised shall of its own motion stay its proceedings until such time as the jurisdiction of the court first seised is established.

3. Where the jurisdiction of the court first seised is established, the court second seised shall decline jurisdiction in favour of that court.

In that case, the party who brought the relevant action before the court second seised may bring that action before the court first seised.

Article 20
Provisional, including protective, measures

1. In urgent cases, the provisions of this Regulation shall not prevent the courts of a Member State from taking such provisional, including protective, measures in respect of persons or assets in that State as may be available under the law of that Member State, even if, under this Regulation, the court of another Member State has jurisdiction as to the substance of the matter.

2. The measures referred to in paragraph 1 shall cease to apply when the court of the Member State having jurisdiction under this Regulation as to the substance of the matter has taken the measures it considers appropriate.

*   *   *   *   *

Family Procedure Rules 2010 (part)

Note: FPR 2010 rule 7.27(2) provides for stay of the main suit if required (or if it may be) for want of jurisdiction by virtue of Arts 16 to 19 of the Council Regulation (*above*). This may have the effect of staying any pending financial remedy proceedings.

7.27- Stay of proceedings

... (2) Where at any time after the making of an application under this Part it appears to the court in matrimonial proceedings that, under Articles 16 to 19 of the Council Regulation, the court does not have jurisdiction to hear the application and is or may be required to stay the proceedings, the court will -

(a) stay the proceedings; and

(b) fix a date for a hearing to determine the questions of jurisdiction and whether there should be a further stay or other order.

(3) The court must give reasons for its decision under Articles 16 to 19 of the Council Regulation and, where it makes a finding of fact, state such finding of fact.

... (5) The court may, if all parties agree, deal with any question about the jurisdiction of the court without a hearing.

The full text of the Regulation and of the Rules is easily accessed in *@eGlance.*

Note on the EU Maintenance Regulation

The Regulation is highly complex, detailed and in some instances unclear, and this Note is no substitute for specialised and case-specific legal advice.

Since 18 June 2011 Council Regulation (EC) No 4/2009 of 18 December 2008 on jurisdiction, applicable law, recognition and enforcement of decisions and co-operation in matters relating to maintenance obligations ('the Regulation') has replaced the Brussels I Regulation so far as maintenance matters are concerned. It also limits the scope of the European Enforcement Order Regulation ((EC) No 805/2004) to EEOs issued in the UK for enforcement in other Member States apart from Denmark (art 68(2)). **Transitional provisions** apply (art 75).

This note deals solely with the Regulation's key provisions concerning ambit, jurisdiction, *lis pendens* and the recognition and enforcement of judgments.

The UK, Denmark and Ireland did not initially opt in to the Regulation owing to their objection to 'applicable law' provisions now contained in art 15 and the Hague Protocol of 23 November 2007 on the Law Applicable to Maintenance Obligations (Council Decision 2009/941/EC). The Regulation was subsequently applied to the UK and Denmark by, respectively, Commission Decision 2009/451/EC and the Agreement at (2009) OJ L149/80 (activating the potential opt-in to which recitals 47 and 48 of the Regulation refer). The UK and Denmark are not bound by the Hague Protocol (recitals 11 and 12). Thus, English and Danish courts continue to apply their national law. All other Member States including Ireland have opted in to the Hague Protocol so that their courts will as a general rule apply the law of the country of the maintenance creditor's habitual residence (Regulation, art 15; Hague Protocol, art 3(1)).

'Maintenance creditor' includes applicants for a maintenance order, as well as for enforcement of an existing order: *Farrell v Long* (Case No 2-295/95) [1997] QB 842; *M v M* [2014] EWHC 925 (Fam).

As the Regulation has **direct effect in national law**, no implementing legislation as such is needed. However, substantial amendment of both primary and secondary legislation has been required to ensure consistency with the Regulation, principally by means of the Civil Jurisdiction and Judgments (Maintenance) Regulations 2011 ('CJJMR'). Thus, *inter alia*, MCA 1973, ss 27, 35 and 52; DPMCA 1978, s 30; MFPA 1984, ss 15 and 16; CA 1989, Sch 1, paras 10 and 14; the corresponding provisions of CPA 2004; and CSA 1991, s 44 have all been amended to give priority to the Regulation's rules on jurisdiction. References to the CJJMR are to those rules as amended to accommodate the Family Court.

As with Brussels I and the EEO Regulations, the Regulation does not define **maintenance**. But for the purpose of EU maintenance legislation that term has its own autonomous meaning developed by ECJ case law (*de Cavel v de Cavel (No 1)* [1979] ECR 1055; *de Cavel v de Cavel (No 2)* [1980] ECR 731; *van den Boogaard v Laumen* [1997] ECR I-1147, [1997] 2 FLR 399).

The principles were summarised in *Moore v Moore* [2007] 2 FLR 339, CA at [80]: the 'label' given to the claim in national law is not decisive. Whether a claim is for 'maintenance' depends on its purpose, and in particular whether it is designed to enable one spouse to provide for himself or herself, or if the needs and resources of each of the spouses are taken into consideration in the determination of its amount, or where the capital sum is designed to ensure a predetermined level of income. Particular care must be taken where the relief sought or the order is 'hybrid', with both maintenance and non-maintenance provisions: see *Traversa v Freddi* [2011] 2 FLR 272, CA, at [35–36] and [59–64] and the article at [2010] Fam Law 385.

As to whether another EU court's maintenance order precludes such an order (or a maintenance-based pension sharing order) under Part III of MFPA 1984 see [2012] Fam Law 191 and Family Law Week, 25 January 2016.

The main grounds of **jurisdiction** under the Regulation are set out in art 3 (but see also arts 4 to 7) which provides that jurisdiction lies with the court:

(a) for the place where the defendant is habitually resident; or

(b) for the place where the creditor is habitually resident; or

(c) which, according to its own law, has jurisdiction to entertain proceedings concerning the status of a person if the matter relating to maintenance is ancillary to those proceedings, unless that jurisdiction is based solely on the nationality (but in the case of the UK and Ireland, the domicile: art 2(3)) of one of the parties; or

(d) which, according to its own law, has jurisdiction to entertain proceedings concerning parental responsibility if the matter relating to maintenance is ancillary to those proceedings, unless that jurisdiction is based solely on the nationality (or, in the case of the UK and Ireland, domicile) of one of the parties.

Art 3(d) takes precedence over art 3(c) where there is dual jurisdiction: *A v B (Case C-184/14)* [2015] 2 FLR 637; *EA v AP* [2013] EWHC 234 (Fam) is the related English case.

The combined effect of recital 15 and art 3(c) appears to be that the divorce court has no jurisdiction in respect of maintenance where the divorce jurisdiction is based on the domicile of one spouse alone, even in those cases where no other EU State has jurisdiction in respect of maintenance. This seems to be so unless the defendant enters an appearance other than to contest jurisdiction (art 5), or where jurisdiction is based on choice (art 4 – see *below*) or *forum necessitatis* (art 7) (as to which see

Note on the EU Maintenance Regulation

Baldwin v Baldwin [2014] EWHC 4857 (Fam)). A 'subsidiary jurisdiction' based on the spouses' *common* domicile is available where none of the grounds of jurisdiction in arts 3 to 5 is made out and where no non-EU Lugano State has jurisdiction under that Convention (art 6). CJJMR, Sch 6 governs jurisdiction as between the constituent parts of the UK; and see *Re V (European Maintenance Regulation)* [2016] EWHC 668 (Fam), [2017] 1 FLR 1083.

Competing claims to jurisdiction are resolved by 'first seised' rules familiar from the Brussels I and IIR Regulations: art 12 (*lis pendens*, mandatory stay) and art 13 ('related actions', discretionary stay). Article 12 applies to enforcement proceedings: *B v B* [2017] EWHC 1029 (Fam). See also *N v N* [2014] 1 FLR 1399; *Ramadani v Ramadani* [2015] EWCA Civ 1138, [2016] 2 FLR 1233; and FPR 9.26A. It remains an open question whether discretionary stays under the *forum conveniens* doctrine survive the Regulation where the other forum is a non-EU State.

Subject to certain criteria being met, art 4 gives the parties **the right to choose forum**: but not in relation to child maintenance (art 4(3)). This may have important implications where a pre-nuptial agreement records agreement as to jurisdiction: see *DB v PB* [2016] EWHC 3431 (Fam), [2017] 4 WLR 44, the discussion at [2011] Fam Law 389 and *Baldwin v Baldwin, above*.

As to **variation applications** (art 8), the basic rule (subject to exceptions) is that the maintenance debtor must apply in the country of the maintenance creditor's habitual residence, if that is where the original order was made and the creditor still habitually resides. The creditor's right to apply to vary is not so restricted. See the discussion at Family Law Week, 17 March 2015.

So far as **recognition and enforcement** are concerned, the aim of the Regulation is to permit maintenance decisions (as to the meaning of which see *Ramadani, above*), court settlements and authenticated instruments made in one Member State to be recognised and enforced in another without further formality (recital 9). However, as a result of Denmark and the UK's decision not to opt in to the Hague Protocol, the Regulation creates two distinct regimes. Seen from the UK perspective:

- Outgoing orders etc. to all States require a declaration of enforceability (exequatur) to be obtained in the state of enforcement (Chapter IV, Sections 2 and 3 of the Regulation; FPR 34.39 and 34.40 (as amended by the Family Procedure (Amendment No. 3) Rules 2013)).
- Incoming orders etc. from 2007 Hague Protocol States (i.e. all States save Denmark) are enforceable directly, without the need for a declaration of enforceability (i.e registration) (Chapter IV, Sections 1 and 3 of the Regulation; CJJMR, reg 3 and Sch 1, Part 2; FPR 34.36C; PD 34E, paras 7.1 to 7.3).
- Incoming orders etc. from Denmark require registration in the UK (Chapter IV, Sections 2 and 3 of the Regulation; FPR 34.28A to 34.36A; CJJMR, reg 3 and Sch 1, Part 3; PD 34E, paras 4.1 to 4.5).

Enforcement proceedings may be stayed under art 12: *B v B* [2017] EWHC 1029 (Fam). Subject to the transitional provisions, it is no longer possible to enforce maintenance orders within the EU under the Reciprocal Enforcement (Maintenance Orders) Act 1972, Pt I (CJJMR, Sch 7, paras 25 to 28). The Regulation takes precedence over Pt II of the 1972 Act (art 69(2)). For discussion of the recognition and enforcement provisions see [2012] Fam Law 39 and [2011] IFL 187.

A **Central Authority** ('CA') is established for the purpose, *inter alia*, of transmitting applications for maintenance and enforcement under the Regulation. The CA for England and Wales is the Lord Chancellor (CJJMR, reg 3 and Sch 1, para 2(1)(a)), who acts via the REMO Unit of the Office of the Official Solicitor and Public Trustee. The procedure followed on receipt by REMO of an application from another Member State for a maintenance order or a variation order is set out in Part 5 of Sch 1 to the CJJMR. Since 22 April 2014 such applications have been dealt with in the Family Court and are allocated initially to lay justices (Family Court (Composition and Distribution of Business) Rules 2014, r15(1) and Sch 1). An applicant for enforcement may either use the CA process or apply direct to the enforcing court (*MS v PS* (Case C-283/16), [2017] 1 FLR 1163, CJEU, a reference from the English High Court (*MS v PS* [2016] EWHC 88 (Fam)). By contrast, in *AB v JJB (EU Maintenance Regulation: modification application procedure)* [2015] EWHC 192 (Fam), [2015] 2 FLR 1143 it was held that an application for modification (i.e. variation) must be made through the CA, using the Annex VII form: *sed quaere* in light of *MS v PS*. See also [2015] IFL 252 and 258. (For the current versions of the Annex VII forms (downloadable in *@eGlance*) see Commission Implementing Regulation (EU) 2015/228.)

FPR Part 34 has been significantly amended to ensure procedural conformity with the Regulation, and to reflect the fact that enforcement applications are now made to the Family Court. PD 34C (Applications for Recognition and Enforcement To or From European Union Member States) clarifies the relationship between the Regulation and other international instruments, summarises the rules governing recognition and enforcement and provides useful clarification of the transitional provisions in art 75. PD 34E (Reciprocal Enforcement of Maintenance Orders – Designated Family Judge Areas) makes further provision concerning enforcement procedure in the Family Court.

CMEC (functions now transferred to the SSWP) is a 'court' for the purpose of art 2.2 (Commission Implementing Regulation (EU) No 1142/2011).

Useful Websites

@eGlance Update Service	www.classlegal.com/software/eglance
Australasian Legal Information Institute	www.austlii.edu.au
Automobile Association	www.theAA.com
Bar Council	www.barcouncil.org.uk
Benefits (general information)	www.gov.uk/browse/benefits
British and Irish Legal Information Institute	www.bailii.org
Chartered Institute of Arbitrators	www.ciarb.org
Child Support Agency/Child Maintenance Service	www.gov.uk/child-maintenance
Child Support Commissioners' Decisions	www.judiciary.gov.uk/media/tribunal-decisions/osccs-decisions
Civil Procedure Rules	www.justice.gov.uk/courts/procedure-rules/civil
Class Legal	www.classlegal.com
Companies House	www.companies-house.gov.uk
Countries of the world	http://news.bbc.co.uk/1/hi/country_profiles/default.stm
Currency rates worldwide	www.xe.com
Economist Intelligence Unit (EIU)	www.eiu.com
European Court of Human Rights	www.echr.coe.int
European Court of Justice	https://curia.europa.eu/jcms/jcms/j_6/
European e-Justice Portal	https://e-justice.europa.eu/content_european_judicial_atlas_in_civil_matters-321-en.do
European Judicial Network	http://ec.europa.eu/civiljustice/index_en.htm
European legislation	http://eur-lex.europa.eu/en/index.htm
Family arbitration information resource	www.familyarbitrator.com
Family Law/Jordans	www.familylaw.co.uk
Family Law news	www.familylaw.co.uk/news_and_comment
FLR (full text)	www.familylaw.co.uk/online-services
Family Law Bar Association	www.flba.co.uk
Family Law Week	www.familylawweek.co.uk
Family Lore	http://news.familylorefocus.com
Financial Times	www.ft.com
Government Actuary's Department	www.gad.gov.uk
Government Information Service	www.gov.uk
Hague Conference on Private International Law	www.hcch.net
Hague Maintenance Convention 2007	www.hcch.net/en/instruments/conventions/specialised-sections/child-support
1 Hare Court	www.1hc.com
HM Courts and Tribunals Service	www.justice.gov.uk/about/hmcts
Daily Court Lists, Family Division	www.justice.gov.uk/courts/court-lists/list-family
HM Revenue and Customs	www.hmrc.gov.uk/home.htm
House Price Indices (Nationwide)	www.nationwide.co.uk/about/house-price-index/headlines
ICLR Case Search	www.iclr.co.uk
Independent Schools Council	www.isc.co.uk
Information for Lawyers	www.infolaw.co.uk
Institute of Family Law Arbitrators	www.ifla.org.uk
International Academy of Family Lawyers	www.iafl.com
Land Registry	www.landregistry.gov.uk
Law Society	www.lawsociety.org.uk
Legal Aid	www.justice.gov.uk/legal-aid
Lexis Nexis	www.lexisnexis.co.uk
Life assurance quotes	www.lifeassureonline.co.uk
Ministry of Justice	www.gov.uk/government/organisations/ministry-of-justice
National Savings and Investments	www.nsandi.com
Office for National Statistics	www.ons.gov.uk
Official Solicitor	www.justice.gov.uk/about/ospt
Pension annuity quotes	www.pensionsorter.co.uk/annuities
QEB Chambers	www.qeb.co.uk
Resolution	www.resolution.org.uk
RPI (full table)	www.ons.gov.uk/economy/inflationandpriceindices/timeseries/chaw/mm23
Share prices	www.iii.co.uk
Statutes	www.legislation.gov.uk/ukpga
Statutory Instruments	www.legislation.gov.uk/uksi
Supreme Court (decided cases)	www.supremecourt.uk/decided-cases/
Sweet & Maxwell	www.sweetandmaxwell.co.uk
UK Parliament	www.parliament.uk
Hansard: Parliamentary Debates	https://hansard.parliament.uk
House of Lords Judgments	www.publications.parliament.uk/pa/ld/ldjudgmt.htm
Zoopla (regional data)	www.zoopla.co.uk